Edinburgh Textbooks in Applied Linguistics
Series Editors: Alan Davies and Keith Mitchell

An Introduction to Applied Linguistics

From Practice to Theory

Alan Davies

Edinburgh University Press

© Alan Davies, 1999

Edinburgh University Press Ltd
22 George Square, Edinburgh

Typeset in Garamond
by Norman Tilley Graphics, Northampton,
and printed and bound in Great Britain
by The University Press, Cambridge

A CIP record for this book is available from
the British Library

ISBN 0 7486 1257 2 (hardback)
ISBN 0 7486 1258 0 (paperback)

The right of Alan Davies
to be identified as author of this work
has been asserted in accordance with
the Copyright, Designs and Patents Act 1988.

An Introduction to Applied Linguistics

''Tis of great use to the sailor to know the length of his line, though he cannot with it fathom all the depths of the ocean. 'Tis well he knows that it is long enough to reach the bottom, at such places as are necessary to direct his voyage, and caution him against running upon shoals that may ruin him. Our business here is not to know all things, but those which concern our conduct. If we can find out those measures whereby a rational creature, put in that state which man is in the world, may and ought to govern his opinions and actions depending thereon, we need not be troubled that some other things escape our knowledge.'

(John Locke, *An Essay Concerning Human Understanding*, 1695.)

Contents

Series Editors' Preface

This new series of single-author volumes published by Edinburgh University Press takes a contemporary view of applied linguistics. The intention is to make provision for the wide range of interests in contemporary applied linguistics which are provided for at the Master's level.

The expansion of Master's postgraduate courses in recent years has had two effects:

1. What began almost half a century ago as a wholly cross-disciplinary subject has found a measure of coherence so that now most training courses in Applied Linguistics have similar core content.
2. At the same time the range of specialisms has grown, as in any developing discipline. Training courses (and professional needs) vary in the extent to which these specialisms are included and taught.

Some volumes in the series will address the first development noted above, while the others will explore the second. It is hoped that the series as a whole will provide students beginning postgraduate courses in Applied Linguistics, as well as language teachers and other professionals wishing to become acquainted with the subject, with a sufficient introduction for them to develop their own thinking in applied linguistics and to build further into specialist areas of their own choosing.

The view taken of applied linguistics in the Edinburgh Textbooks in Applied Linguistics Series is that of a theorising approach to practical experience in the language professions, notably, but not exclusively, those concerned with language learning and teaching. It is concerned with the problems, the processes, the mechanisms and the purposes of language in use.

Like any other applied discipline, applied linguistics draws on theories from related disciplines with which it explores the professional experience of its practitioners and which in turn are themselves illuminated by that experience. This two-way relationship between theory and practice is what we mean by a theorising discipline.

The volumes in the series are all premised on this view of Applied Linguistics as a theorising discipline which is developing its own coherence. At the same time, in order to present as complete a contemporary view of applied linguistics as possible other approaches will occasionally be expressed.

Each volume presents its author's own view of the state of the art in his or her topic. Volumes will be similar in length and in format, and, as is usual in a textbook series, each will contain exercise material for use in class or in private study.

Alan Davies
W. Keith Mitchell

Preface

The argument of this book and the ground-bass to the whole Edinburgh Textbooks in Applied Linguistics series is that applied linguistics is best understood by doing it rather than by studying or reading about it. It is, as I explain in Chapter 1, an experiential activity, an activity of experience. That being so, there is a paradox inherent in writing an Introduction to Applied Linguistics if the book is intended for beginners whose lack of experience in the field denies them the background needed to understand the book. But the paradox is more apparent than real since, as is also explained in Chapter 1, beginners in formal, academic applied linguistics will normally have considerable experience of informal applied linguistics, through language teaching and other forms of working professionally with language. It is for these 'beginners' – and of course for others interested in reviewing arguments about the relationship between linguistics and applied linguistics – that the book is intended.

There is a further paradox. This book, as the first in the new Edinburgh Textbooks in Applied Linguistics Series, introduces both the series and applied linguistics. It attempts to do both by surveying the field of applied linguistics as practised today. In so doing, reference is made to those areas of the field to be taken up in subsequent volumes. The paradox here lies in the apparent claim to introduce applied linguistics in general when in fact what is discussed here is largely restricted to what is done in English and in the United Kingdom. The hope of course is that the concepts and issues raised in the book will have a wider resonance. The book is also a very personal account and, as disclaimers often say, must not be taken to represent the view of colleagues, of other contributors to the series or indeed of anyone other than the author.

Acknowledgements

AUTHOR'S ACKNOWLEDGEMENTS

I am grateful to those colleagues and students with whom I have worked in the Department of Applied Linguistics at the University of Edinburgh since the early 1960s. For much of that period Applied Linguistics and Linguistics were together in one department, allowing me to reflect on the relationship between the two disciplines, an issue central to the argument of this volume. Towards the end of my career in Edinburgh I worked for some years in the University of Melbourne, as Director of the National Language and Literacy Institute of Australia Language Testing Research Centre. In Melbourne I found again the excitement of the early years in Edinburgh and I want to thank all those with whom I shared that experience.

At a recent Film Academy awards ceremony, the actor Kim Bassinger accepted her Oscar award with a very short speech of thanks. All she said was that she wanted to thank everyone she had ever met in her whole life. After nearly 40 years in applied linguistics, I think I know what she meant. But I do want to express my particular gratitude to several colleagues whose views on applied linguistics have influenced me: Pit Corder, Ron Asher, Henry Widdowson, Chris Brumfit, John Maher, Terry Quinn and Cathie Elder. But the views expressed in this volume are of course my own and for them I take full responsibility. I am grateful to my co-editor of this Series, Keith Mitchell, for a critical read of my manuscript and I want to thank Jackie Jones of Edinburgh University Press for her encouragement and support.

PUBLISHER'S ACKNOWLEDGEMENTS

We are grateful to the following publishers and authors for permission to publish copyright material:

Addison Wesley Longman Ltd (extracts from Pennycook 1994a, Fairclough 1989, Aijmer and Altenberg 1991)
American Anthropological Association (extract from Haugen 1966)
Australian Language Matters (extract from Garner 1998)
Cambridge University Press (extracts from Crystal 1995)
CILT (extract from Trim 1988)

Manchester University Press (extract from Ilson 1986)

Newbury House (extract from R. B. Kaplan 1981)

Oxford University Press (extracts from Malony and Lovekin 1985, Harris 1978)

Pergamon Press Ltd (extract from Asher 1994)

Routledge (extracts from Kerr 1993, Culler 1981, Peim 1993, Ball 1993, Hickey 1990)

The Scotsman (extract from O'Henley and Gray 1999, 9 March)

University of Chicago Press (extract from A. Kaplan 1993)

University of New South Wales Press (extract from Gibbons 1995)

We have been unable to trace the copyright holder of the poem 'The Lost Preposition' by Morris Bishop and would appreciate any information which would enable us to do so.

Abbreviations

AAAL	American Association of Applied Linguistics
AILA	Association de Linguistique Appliquée (International Association of Applied Linguistics)
ALAA	Applied Linguistics Association of Australia
BAAL	British Association of Applied Linguistics
CIEFL	Central Institute for English and Foreign Languages
CLA	Child Language Acquisition
EFL	English as a Foreign Language
ELTS	English Language Testing System
ESL	English as a Second Language
ESP	English for Specific Purposes
IATEFL	International Association for the Teaching of English as a Foreign Language
IELTS	International English Language Testing Service
LOTE	Language Other Than English
LSP	Languages for Specific Purposes
SLA(R)	Second Language Acquisition (Research)
TESOL	Teachers of English to Speakers of Other Languages
TOEFL	Test of English as a Foreign Language
UCH	Unitary Competence Hypothesis

Dedication

For Cathie

Chapter 1

History and 'definitions'

'In Anna Karenina and Onegin not a single problem is solved but they satisfy you completely just because all the problems are correctly presented.'
(Anton Chekov, letter to Alexei Suvorin, 27 October 1888, in L. Hellman (ed.), *Selected Letters of Anton Chekov*, 1955, translated by S. Lederer.)

1 AVOIDING DEFINING

In St Paul's Cathedral in London there is no monument to its architect, Sir Christopher Wren. Instead, an inscription in the cathedral reads:

Si monumentum requiris, circumspice.
(If you seek a monument, gaze around.)

The inscription is attributed to Wren's son. Whoever the author, its message is clear: the cathedral is itself a monument to its great creator. Christopher Wren needs nothing more than his own work to memorialise his achievement.

One definition of applied linguistics is of this kind. It takes what we shall call the 'function' view of applied linguistics. According to this view, applied linguistics must be defined through demonstration, that is by giving examples of its work. One reason for this is that providing a definition of applied linguistics is difficult. Its purpose, the amelioration of language 'problems' (see Chapter 6) is not disputed. What is at issue is what sort of applied linguistics content leads to the skills and knowledge that will provide that amelioration. Even medicine, so obvious in its target, the amelioration of health 'problems', is hard put to make clear its theoretical position and to establish agreement on what the right content of medical education is that helps to provide a coherent framework for medicine and is not just opportunist visitations from different disciplines, anatomy, biochemistry, psychology and so on.

Like medicine there is little disagreement about the purpose of applied linguistics, which is to solve or at least ameliorate social problems involving language. The problems applied linguistics concerns itself with are likely to be: How can we teach languages better? How can we diagnose speech pathologies better? How can we improve the training of translators and interpreters? How can we write a valid language examination? How can we evaluate a school bilingual programme? How can we determine the literacy levels of a whole population? How can we helpfully discuss the language of a text? What advice can we offer the Ministry of Education on a proposal to introduce a new medium of instruction? How can we compare the acquisition of a European and an Asian language? What advice should we give a defence lawyer on the authenticity of a police transcript of an interview with a suspect?

These 'problems' of applied linguistics are not normally about more general social issues, such as unemployment, except very marginally. However what has come to be called 'critical applied linguistics' does make that link. It takes up the kinds of applied linguistics 'problems' we have listed and then places them within a broader political framework. I refer to critical applied linguistics in Chapter 2 and return to it more fully in Chapter 7.

So far I have used the term 'applied linguistics' as if it were one word. But it is of course two words, like applied science, applied mathematics. The *Shorter Oxford English Dictionary* defines 'applied' as: 'put to practical use; practical as opposed to abstract or theoretical'. That seems straightforward enough. Let me turn to the second word, 'linguistics'.

2 WHAT IS LINGUISTICS?

According to Widdowson: 'Linguistics is the name given to the discipline which studies human language' (1996: 3). He maintains that its purpose is to identify some relatively stable linguistic knowledge which underlies language behaviour. Access to that linguistic knowledge is achieved by a process of idealization. Widdowson offers two reasons for idealising in this way. The first is feasibility: 'the actuality of language behaviour is too elusive to capture by any significant generalization'. The second reason is validity: 'the data of actual behaviour are disregarded ... because they are of little theoretical interest' (ibid: 70).

In the late 1950s generative linguistics, with its increasing interest in universal grammar, became dominant in the field of linguistics and moved it away from its traditional concerns with language in all its manifestations, into a non-accountable, never applied, laboratory of cognition and the mind. This core linguistic view of language focuses on language forms, ignoring the context in which those forms are used. Widdowson comments that within linguistics itself both reasons he mentions (feasibility and validity), used to support this essentially formalist view of language, are now being challenged. The advent of corpus linguistics has made the appeal to elusiveness less convincing. And there is a growing recognition that excessive idealisation is self-defeating: complete idealisation is never possible and the more the language is idealised, the less of real language value is left for study. Hence the increasing focus within linguistics on units of language larger than the sentence and on context.

Linguistics indeed has a long tradition of concern with social problems (for example the need for education in the local vernacular) and this has triggered much of the work in descriptive linguistics (for example writing dictionaries and grammars of unrecorded languages). The ambiguity of the term 'educational linguistics' highlights the distinct purposes and points of departure for linguistics and applied linguistics. For linguistics, educational linguistics is about the teaching of linguistics in education, ranging from courses in language awareness to university introductory courses in linguistics given in the final school year. The latter may well include materials on correctness and on myths about language. The applied linguistics version of educational linguistics is very different. Here educational linguistics is applied linguistics for education (and in some uses synonymous with applied linguistics) and as such works on the problems presented by language in its educational settings. That being so, applied linguistics is more likely to respond to expressed needs than to offer the knowledge and skills it possesses because they are believed to be of value in education which is the linguistics position. The applied linguist is unlikely to offer his or her knowledge and skills in the absence of the stakeholders (such as school teachers) reporting a problem.

Applied linguistics established itself in part as a response to the narrowing of interest in linguistics and has always maintained a socially accountable role, demonstrated by its central interest in language problems. Meanwhile, in moving away from its narrowly formalist concern back to a more socially accountable role, linguistics has since the 1980s begun to share some of the interests of applied linguistics.

3 WHAT IS APPLIED LINGUISTICS?

Two questions frequently put to applied linguists, as much about professional demarcation as about epistemology of knowledge, are (1) who does applied linguistics and (2) what distinguishes applied linguistics from linguistics? I shall discuss these questions in order.

3.1 Who does applied linguistics?

Traditionally, reference has been made to 'applications of linguistics' as often as to 'applied linguistics'. The crucial ambiguity of 'applied linguistics' (is it a unity 'applied linguistics', or a disjunction 'applied' + 'linguistics' ?) is thus avoided since 'applications of linguistics' makes it clear that the activity is a spin-off of linguistics. Those linguists who have remained apart from the recently dominating paradigm of the independence of language from context and speaker have continued to maintain this position. This is very much the case with those influenced by functional views of language, notably Roman Jakobson and the Prague School and those influenced by anthropological views of language, such as Dell Hymes in the USA, M. A. K. Halliday in the UK and Australia, and Roy Harris in the UK.

Linguists in these functional traditions celebrate the seamlessness of the relationship between linguistics and applied linguistics. This view, which we have called traditional in linguistics, can be restated thus: applied linguistics is a component of linguistics; it is linguistics outside the library or study (just as general medicine is applied medical research). All linguists can participate. And, just as important (and the medical analogy holds), only linguists can participate.

This traditional view, which has been held by linguists as diverse as the American Leonard Bloomfield and the British Henry Sweet, the real-life inspiration for Shaw's phonetic expert, Henry Higgins, sees applied linguistics as an activity of linguistics, sheltering under its umbrella and drawing on it for inspiration and status.

There are divergent views. One is that linguistics has no role in applied linguistics: we will return to this. There is an even more aberrant view, one that has not received the discussion it deserves. This is the view that the argument needs to be stood on its head: not that applied linguistics is part of linguistics but rather that linguistics is part of applied linguistics. In other words, all knowledge-based activity is predicated on attaining a practical outcome, on solving a (social) problem. That being so, all such activity is applied. Some part of it is reflective, seeking to model theoretical constructs on the basis of empirical observation. (This is the 'research-then-theory' position advocated by Ellis 1990.) But all such theoretical work contributes towards the overarching applied goal. Hence linguistics is a component of applied linguistics, which extends from theoretical studies of language to practical concerns with language in the classroom and elsewhere.

This extreme view (Widdowson 1980) suggests that applied linguistics does not belong with any exclusivity to linguists. The practitioners of applied linguistics, according to this view, are drawn from a wider pool (Rampton 1997). This of course takes us back to what we have called the 'crucial ambiguity' of applied linguistics: is it a unity or a disjunction? For if its practitioners are drawn more widely, does this mean that anyone can 'do' applied linguistics? As we shall see, this question, whether there is a discrete profession of applied linguists, and, if so, how are they trained and certified, is central to the whole discussion of what is applied linguistics (see Chapter 6 below).

There is a compromise position. Here, applied linguists are really still linguists who happen to be involved in applications, which they may label as applied linguistics. However, their knowledge and skill are insufficient for those applications. They need the cooperation of other professionals in relevant fields, professionals such as educationists, psychologists, statisticians, sociologists, speech therapists, translators, literary critics, computer scientists, anthropologists and so on.

It has been suggested that all those involved in applications of linguistics in this broader sense are 'doing applied linguistics'. Indeed this broad interpretation must necessarily incorporate language teachers who, after all, spend their professional lives working with language. Just as anyone who plays tennis is a tennis-player, so, the argument goes, anyone who does applied linguistics is an applied linguist.

Such a generously catholic view is commendable against the exclusivity mentioned above. But it raises problems of who can legitimately be called applied linguists. Since we accept that those involved in language work are all equally stakeholders, it becomes difficult to exclude any one group from the equation.

And so the answer to our first question: 'Who does applied linguistics?' must be incomplete. The reason for the uncertainty is the central ambiguity which we have mentioned. It is, as we shall see, an ambiguity which remains unresolved. It is as though there is some agreement on what applied linguistics is but less agreement on who is authorised to do it. It is, of course, not accidental that the name the professional associations use in their title is the professional activity rather than the name of the profession (what you do rather than what you are: this relates to the point made at the beginning about defining by function). Thus: American, Australian, British (and so on) Association for Applied Linguistics (not Linguists); Association Internationale de Linguistique Appliquée, not Linguistes.

3.2 What distinguishes applied linguistics from linguistics?

The second question is what distinguishes applied linguistics from linguistics? When you are doing applied linguistics are you doing (1) linguistics only, (2) linguistics plus something else, or (3) only something else?

To simplify to the heart of the question: does applied linguistics need any linguistics? (which after all is another version of the question in 3.1: who does applied linguistics?) First, we should note that there are different areas assembled under the general heading 'linguistics'. The list includes theoretical linguistics, descriptive linguistics, historical linguistics, comparative linguistics, cognitive linguistics, computational linguistics, structural linguistics, text linguistics, systemic linguistics, synchronic linguistics, diachronic linguistics; the differently named semiotics, phonology and phonetics; the linguistics of particular languages and language families (English, German, Dravidian and so on); the compounds psycho-linguistics, sociolinguistics, anthropological linguistics; the eponymous Saussurean linguistics, Chomskyan linguistics; plus the parallel philology, which to some is synonymous with linguistics and to others is primarily concerned with diachronic studies.

So wide a compass may explain the assumption among many linguists (professing one or other of these sub-disciplines) that applied linguistics is just another area, part of linguistics, just as text linguistics is. The reality is that these apparently equal sub-disciplines have very different theoretical status. Theoretical linguistics, for example, is a highly abstract study which attempts to develop a formal grammatical model applicable to all languages and at all stages of language development, including child language acquisition. Descriptive linguistics uses some of these theoretical insights to propose grammars of distinct languages. Text linguistics, still further from theory, examines actual written and spoken texts in search of patterns so as to propose that text performance is rule governed.

What links these sub-disciplines together is that they all start from theoretical linguistics, some closer and some further away but all recognising the guiding ideas of linguistic theory and accepting that they all share a common purpose, which is to further that theory.

This is not the case with applied linguistics which therefore seems not to fit into the list of the linguistic sub-disciplines. The purpose of applied linguistics is, as has been suggested, to explain and solve institutional problems involving language, not to further a linguistic theory. (Of course, it is possible that applied linguistics research will indirectly do just that.)

Pit Corder, an important innovator in the field, took the view that there could be no theory of applied linguistics and that the applied linguist was a 'consumer of theories' from elsewhere. For him, applied linguistics mediated between linguistics and language teaching. He took the disjunctive view, regarding applied linguistics as the application of linguistics: 'I am enough of a purist to believe that "applied linguistics" presupposes "linguistics"; that one cannot apply what one does not possess' (Corder 1973: 7).

Given this insistence, it is somewhat ironical that Corder was largely responsible for the development in the UK of specialised courses in applied linguistics. These courses produced in time a cadre of 'applied linguists' who were distinct from both linguists and language teachers. To linguists they were not linguistic enough; to language teachers they were too linguistic!

In the 1990s Corder's 'mediating' model, with applied linguistics acting as interpreter between (theoretical) linguistics and (practical) language teaching, is still relevant. Still too, while applied linguists are expected to know something of linguistics, there is no reciprocal requirement for linguists.

The journal *Language Learning: A Journal of Applied Linguistics*, published from the University of Michigan, is an important chronicle of the development of applied linguistics over the past fifty years (Catford 1998). In a 1993 editorial the journal gave late recognition to the range of coverage beyond linguistics which applied linguistics embraced. Such recognition is significant. Coming out of the tradition of Charles Fries and Robert Lado at the University of Michigan, *Language Learning*, founded in 1948, was 'the first journal in the world to carry the term "applied linguistics" in its title' (*Language Learning* 1967: 1). But by 'applied linguistics' what was meant was the 'linguistics-applied' version.

In the 1990s the journal seems to have finally accepted the broader church that represents an 'applied-linguistics' (as distinct from a 'linguistics-applied') approach to language problems. We acknowledge, the 1993 editors' remark: 'the wide range of foundation theories and research methodologies now used to study language issues' (Cumming 1993). And they state that they intend to:

> encourage the submission of more manuscripts from (a) diverse disciplines, in-cluding applications of methods and theories from linguistics, psycholinguistics, cognitive science, ethnography, ethnomethodology sociolinguistics, sociology, semiotics, educational inquiry, and cultural or historical studies, to address: (b) fundamental issues in language learning, such as bilingualism, language acquisition, second and foreign language education, literacy, culture, cognition, pragmatics, and intergroup relations.

However, the official recognition of the 'wide range of foundation theories and research methodologies now used to study language issues' comes at a price. That price is the abandoning of the term 'applied linguistics' as a sub-heading in the journal's title. The explanation for this removal is that its replacement title: *Language Learning: A Journal of Research in Language Studies* is now seen to be wider.

We have then a paradox: what seemed like recognition from a founding institution in the field (the University of Michigan) of the broadening of applied linguistics must now be seen as a refusal to equate this broadening with what is actually done in the name of 'applied linguistics'. It appears that while the journal *Language Learning* has in practice moved beyond its early 'linguistics-applied' orientation, its institutional base at the University of Michigan may have not. For that university, 'applied linguistics' still must be interpreted as 'linguistics applied'. Some irony here! A hugely successful journal, purveying what the world increasingly has come to recognise as the broader interpretation of applied linguistics, is unable to continue to use the subtitle because to do so might be to give institutional blessing to this wide-ranging view.

The official *Language Learning* view of 'applied linguistics' has therefore not changed since its inception in 1948, reported on in a 1967 editorial: 'the majority of articles in *Language Learning* have, indeed, dealt with applications of linguistic theory in the teaching and learning of languages' (*Language Learning* 1967: 1).

It is a strangely literal view that 'applied linguistics' must mean 'applications of linguistic theory' and nothing more. After all the Chair of English Literature at the University of Edinburgh retains its somewhat quaint title 'Rhetoric and English Literature', while the Chair of Physics at the same university is still called by its medieval name 'Natural Philosophy'. Nobody suggests that the names should be changed. How odd that linguists, whose profession makes them so conscious of word magic, should be so easily seduced by its lures!

It appears then that the editor of the 1993 new-look journal has acted cleverly in removing the term 'applied linguistics' from the title of *Language Learning* and replacing it with *Language Learning: A Journal of Research in Language Studies*. In so doing, he is declaring his interpretation of what applied linguistics is, knowing full well that the readers of the journal will understand 'a journal of research in language studies' as a functional interpretation of 'applied linguistics'. The fact that the University of Michigan authorities still understand applied linguistics to mean the narrower 'linguistics applied' is unimportant since what the editor has really done is to provide a Wren-like monument to applied linguistics. If you want to know what applied linguistics is, he is saying, look at what the journal contains.

Getting rid altogether of the label 'applied linguistics' has been widely canvassed, on the grounds that it was the wrong term in the first place, introduced only to give academic respectability to degrees, courses and departments. Such was the view taken in the 1960s by the authors of a key text (Halliday et al. 1964). They recognised the oddity of the label 'applied linguistics' but seemed prepared to live with it. The label was, they opined, misleading. It was misleading because (at the time of writing) it excluded many activities of linguistics (e.g. machine translation, sociolinguistics) as well as activities which had a bearing on language teaching (e.g. psychology, educational theory).

The aim of courses in applied linguistics, such as are now available, for example at Edinburgh, Leeds and London, is not to produce specialists in linguistics and phonetics ... but to give a solid grounding in those aspects of these and other subjects which lie behind the language class.

(ibid: 169)

In consequence, the label 'applied linguistics' was not used in the title of their book: *The Linguistic Sciences and Language Teaching* (1964). Shades of the *Language Learning* unease about the term?

There have always been other voices, willing to take a non-literal view of labels. Peter Strevens, for example, one of the authors of the *Linguistic Sciences and Language Teaching*, was, ten years later and in his own authorial voice, pragmatic: 'applied linguistics ... whereby linguistics, psychology, educational research, educational technology and other potential sources of illumination are brought together' (1975: 154).

Or Van Els and his colleagues, who take exception to what they regard as Corder's narrowness: 'Our objection to the way Corder sets out the area of applied linguistics ... is that the contribution of other disciplines to foreign language teaching does not receive enough attention, or is not sufficiently integrated' (Van Els et al. 1977: 10).

Some scholars go further, maintaining that there is indeed a principled basis to applied linguistics. The Australian, David Ingram, takes the view that:

[A]pplied linguistics is that science which seeks insights from linguistics and other language-informative sciences, insights which produce principles on which is developed a methodology to solve specific language-related problems.

(1980: 54)

Ingram and *Language Learning* are not in any disagreement about what contributes to applied linguistics studies but, unlike *Language Learning*, Ingram can accept a non-literal name. And he takes this easy accommodation even further. He points out that applied linguistics (like, of course, all disciplines) is likely to change over time, as new ideas and information become available. But for him this is not a reason to change its name.

Brumfit writes: 'both linguistics and applied linguistics combine empirical and theoretical activity, but linguistics reifies "language". What does applied linguistics reify? More than just language – "language practices"' (1997b: 90).

Of course, broadening one's concept of a discipline contains the danger that the discipline ceases to have any boundaries and then becomes a kind of study of everything. Christophersen seems to feel that he avoids that fate by his use of 'systematic' but the knowledge base he claims is still wide, perhaps too much so:

This book is something of an exercise in applied linguistics – in the widest senses of that term in that it comprises all systematic knowledge about language in all its aspects.

(1973: 88)

As we shall see in Chapter 6, it may be possible to avoid the Catch 22 situation: applied linguistics is only linguistics (too narrow and manifestly untrue) or applied linguistics is the science of everything we know about language (too wide), by starting from the other end, that of function, and defining applied linguistics according to our Sir Christopher Wren model, by what it does. This is an approach favoured by Widdowson, who sees 'applied linguistics' as working in the opposite way to 'linguistics applied'. Instead of using linguistics in an explanatory manner, according to this interpretation what applied linguistics does is to illuminate its language encounters by reference to linguistic theories. Widdowson has gone further and speculated on how an appropriate theory of applied linguistics would be consumer based.

For his part, Robert Kaplan has pioneered the search for a theory of applied linguistics in North America. He takes issue with Corder's dismissive attitude and emphasises the urgency of the need for a theory of applied linguistics. In a 1980 paper he was optimistic that a theory (he used the more general term 'construct') was not far away (1980: b: viii).

The issue is of course epistemological. For a Corder or an Ingram or a Strevens there is either no need for a theory or the theories are elsewhere and drawn on as necessary. This may be called the 'subject' view of applied linguistics. For a Kaplan or a Widdowson this is not good enough. They take the 'discipline view', which requires a theorised body of knowledge within applied linguistics. Stubbs aligns himself with the theoretical camp: 'I find myself largely in agreement with Widdowson's view that applied linguistics should develop its own theory' (1986: 249).

For Brumfit the theoretical status of applied linguistics is no longer in doubt:

[A] working definition of applied linguistics will then be: the theoretical and empirical investigation of real-world problems in which language is a central issue.

(1997b: 93)

4 THE ROLE OF APPLIED LINGUISTICS

So far I have discussed the questions: (1) who does applied linguistics and (2) what distinguishes applied linguistics from linguistics? I want now to move closer to the question of what is thought to be the role of applied linguistics.

Dictionary definitions vary. Here is the Richards et al. (1985: 19) definition:

applied linguistics:
1. the study of second and foreign language learning and teaching;
2. the study of language and linguistics in relation to practical problems. Applied linguistics uses information from sociology, psychology, anthropology, and information theory as well as from linguistics in order to develop its own theoretical models of language and language use, and then uses this information and theory in practical areas such as syllabus design, speech therapy, language planning, stylistics etc.

This seems to belong on the Stubbs–Kaplan–Widdowson–Brumfit side.

Here is the Carter (1993: 3–4) definition: 'the application of linguistic theories, descriptions and methods to the solution of language problems which have arisen in a range of human, cultural and social contexts'. This fits on the Corder–Strevens–Ingram side.

Halliday et al. (1964: 138) were less idealistic about applications but still determined to keep a demarcation between linguistics and its applications: 'Applied linguistics starts when a description is specifically made, or an existing description used, for a further purpose which lies outside the linguistic sciences.'

Critics of applied linguistics tend to attack it for its lack of relevance to language problems, and, through its support for languages of wider communication, its support for colonial and successor regimes (Phillipson 1992; but see Davies 1996). Some observers query its right to exist. Bugarski (1987) for example is dismissive, although it is not clear whether the dismissal is because applied linguistics is not really 'linguistics applied' or because it does not take proper account of language-teaching methodology (1987: 13).

A particularly swingeing attack on applied linguistics was made by Sampson (1980). It is notable that Sampson is not merely objecting to the name (arguing that applied linguistics is not just the application of linguistics). He is also and very deliberately denying that linguistics has any application at all: 'what is relevant ... is not a special applied version of linguistics, but straightforward descriptive linguistics' (Sampson 1980: 10–11). Such a view, robbed of its arrogance, is not so very different from the views that applied linguistics is properly a form of linguistics applied.

For the most part, those who write about applied linguistics regard its activity as worthwhile. And again for the most part they accept that the label 'applied linguistics' refers to language teaching (in its widest interpretation, therefore including speech therapy, translation and interpreting studies, language planning and so on). Applied linguistics in this tradition is not new, whether from the more practical perspective: 'Throughout the history of formal language teaching there has always been some sort of applied linguistics, as it is known today' (Mackey 1965: 253) or whether we consider its role in the academy:

> Applied linguistics is not the recent development that is sometimes supposed, but derives from the involvement of linguists in America, particularly Leonard Bloomfield and Charles C. Fries, in specialized language-teaching programmes during and immediately after the Second World War.
>
> (Howatt 1984: 265)

Within that tradition, applied linguistics has an honourable role: 'if there is one single source which has been responsible for stimulating innovation and activity' (in language teaching), 'it is (in one or other of its various guises) applied linguistics. It has not performed miracles, but as a focus of enquiry, critical self-examination, and new ideas, it has enriched the profession at least as much as it has irritated it' (ibid: 226).

Corder (1973) was well aware that in limiting the coverage of applied linguistics to language teaching he was open to criticism. To some extent his defence was the mirror-image of the *Language Learning* change of name, to which we have already referred. There the rationale was that the input was too undefined and therefore it was sensible to remove the label of applied linguistics. Corder argues that it is the output that is without shape and therefore it makes sense to limit the area of concern to one main object, that of language teaching.

Spolsky (1978) has proposed a different solution, that is to limit the name of the output to Corder's area of concern and to call it 'educational linguistics'. Spolsky does not suggest limiting the input disciplines to linguistics alone. But his proposal for the name 'educational linguistics' has not been taken up. Stubbs (1986) uses it, but it is unclear if the source is Spolsky.

Of course there are voices insisting that applied linguistics should fulfil a role wider than language teaching (e.g. Kaplan 1980a). There is a seductive appeal in such a view, an appeal which slips all too easily into a position parallel to the claim of linguistics itself, that the whole world is its oyster, that the area of concern is every-where, the science of everything position, destabilising the applied linguist, who is left both site-less and sightless.

M. Bloomfield appears to beckon to this (M. Bloomfield 1975: xviii):

> This volume then concentrates on the human problems of language and tries to identify some of them and to indicate what is being done about them. The rise of ethnic consciousness and militancy as well as a general dissatisfaction with the 'way things are' have led to a new stress on what may be called applied linguistics and the social dialect problems … Problems of literacy, translation, bilingualism, language teaching, language and nationalism, the role of dialects and so forth have become urgent and some of our best minds have begun to turn towards these matters.

What is disturbing about sentiments of this kind is partly their patronising extension of the legitimate interest of applied linguistics, and partly their promise of a solution to 'the way things are'. This position is surely overreaching, surely aiming towards nemesis. Perhaps Pit Corder's modest restriction of the scope of applied linguistics to language teaching had something to commend it after all.

The extent to which applied linguists see themselves as agents of change is controversial. As current concerns with the ethics of the human sciences remind us, there is a tension for social scientists between their role as objective students of society and as agents of change. Such an opposition was noted in the 1960s in the area of applied cultural anthropology. Commenting on the field, Margaret Mead wrote:

> There is some difference at present between (a) those who would regard applied anthropology as a profession for which anthropologists, in addition to a theor-etical education in some branch of anthropology, must be specially trained and within which professional standards should prevail; and (b) those who identify applied anthropology with a form of anthropological research which either con-

tinuously or at some point becomes part of, and affects, the process of change which it studies. It must be stressed that either view involves a search for values, rooted in the discipline of anthropology, which can guide the applied anthropologist in any use of his knowledge at any level of interaction in human affairs.

(1964: 33)

The more involved with 'human affairs' the scholar becomes, the more difficult it is, so Mead argues, to resist the second alternative, which means that scientific objectivity is no longer possible (Skutnabb-Kangas and Phillipson 1994; Searle 1995). Like applied cultural anthropology, applied linguistics has also felt the tug of the particular and the urge to identify locally. We take up this dilemma in Chapter 2 and again in Chapter 7, where we discuss the contribution of critical discourse analysis and critical applied linguistics to this discussion.

The issue to which we keep returning is that of the distinction between two fundamental views of applied linguistics, that of 'linguistics applied' and that of 'applied linguistics'. The first starts with theory, the second with practice. It is to this basic division that I now turn.

5 LINGUISTICS APPLIED AND APPLIED LINGUSTICS

The 'linguistics-applied' view seems to derive from the coming together of two traditions:

1. The European philological tradition which was exported to the USA through scholars such as Roman Jakobson. We see different manifestations of this tradition in Henry Sweet's interest in language learning, the work of Bloomfield and Fries in intensive language training for the military during the Second World War, and the Prague Circle's interest in functionalism. This European tradition made no distinction between kinds of language study: analysing the grammar of the native speaker, teaching grammar to the second-language learner and translating a literary work are all connected, all grist to the linguist's mill (Jakobson 1987).

2. The North-American tradition of linguistic-anthropological field-work required the intensive use of non-literate informants and the linguistic description of indigenous languages for the purposes of cultural analysis. This tradition of doing anthropology among American Indians (North and South) is also seen in work on aboriginal languages in Australia. The use of linguistics for language descriptions was thought a very obvious application of linguistics (what Sampson refers to as 'descriptive linguistics'). Philosophically, language was regarded as a kind of cultural artefact rather than as a means of communication with the indigenes. As such it was not strictly necessary for the anthropologist to be able to speak the language of description/study. In the British tradition of anthropology, on the other hand, practised most notably in Africa and the Indian sub-continent, the anthropologist's view of language was much more as a means of communication. It was therefore normal for the

field-worker to learn to speak the local language; at the same time, anthropologists working in the British tradition were less interested in the linguistics of the languages they encountered during field-work (Gellner 1983).

The social value of applications of linguistics was widely canvassed. Bloomfield hoped that: 'The methods and results of linguistics … [and] the study of language may help us toward the understanding and control of human affairs' (1933: 509).

In the 1970s R. H. Robins, representing the European tradition, was eager to encourage the use of linguistic ideas and methods: 'The teacher who understands and can make use of the methods of scientific linguistics will find the task of presenting a language to his pupils very much lightened and facilitated' (1971: 308).

Fifty years after Bloomfield, Douglas Brown was still making a similar claim: 'Applied linguistics has been considered a subset of linguistics for several decades, and it has been interpreted to mean the applications of linguistics principles to certain more or less practical matters' (Brown 1987: 147).

This tradition represents the 'expert' view of knowledge and scholarship. It takes for granted that the methods and findings of linguistics are of value to others to solve their problems. But the applications must be carried out either by linguists themselves or by those who have understood and can make use of the methods of scientific linguistics. There is no place here for Corder's applied linguist as a consumer of theories, in which linguistics is one among a number of different source disciplines, let alone for the extreme proposal made by Widdowson that linguistics is itself part of applied linguistics. Critiques and counter-critiques in the journals suggest that the opposing traditions have become more entrenched. Gregg (1990) argues the case for a unitary position on second-language acquisition research, while Ellis (1990) and Tarone (1990) declare themselves in favour of the variationist position. Ellis contrasts two models of research, the research-then-theory position, which is essentially inductive, as against the theory-then-research, the mainstream classic tradition, which is essentially deductive. We may surmise that the theory-then-research approach is that of linguistics while the research-then-theory is that of applied linguistics. For Gregg, the research-then-theory approach is not serious because it is not based on theory.

So much for the 'linguistics-applied' tradition. What of the 'applied-linguistics' tradition? As has already been suggested, the two traditions overlap in the work of Henry Sweet. Howatt claims that: 'Sweet's work established an applied tradition in language teaching which has continued uninterruptedly to the present day' (1984: 189). Howatt also refers to the influence of J. R. Firth, holder of the first Chair of General Linguistics in the UK, who had first-hand experience of language learning and teaching in India, and who with the anthropologist Bronislaw Malinowski and their pupil Michael Halliday promoted the notion of the context of situation. No doubt because of Firth's lead, the identity of the context of situation school is still that of 'linguistics applied' in spite of its strong social orientation. John Trim records his view of the origin of the British Association of Applied Linguistics in an address which represents the view of the linguist looking at society's problems: 'Members of

Departments of Linguistics were present [at the inaugural meeting] because of their wish to see the findings of the science brought to bear on the social problems of the day' (Trim 1988: 9).

What some of these social problems were had been publicised for forty years by the journal *Language Learning*, which was, as we have seen, established in 1948 with a broad brief to: 'include studies in first language acquisition, in bilingualism, in translation (human and machine), in linguistic statistics, in sociolinguistics, in psycholinguistics, in the development of writing systems for unwritten languages, in the development of 'new' national languages' (*Language Learning* 1967: 2–3).

The real push to a coherent conception of the activity, an 'applied-linguistics' view, came from Corder, who, while insisting on the centrality of linguistics, accepted the need for other inputs. It came even more strongly from Peter Strevens, who was unashamedly eclectic in what he saw as a growing discipline. His account of the founding of the British Association for Applied Linguistics (BAAL) emphasises the sociological and institutional reasons for forming a new professional group:

> The fundamental question ... facing applied linguists in Britain in 1965 was whether they were sufficiently like linguists (i.e. theoretical linguists) to remain within the linguists' organisation, or whether they were sufficiently like teachers of foreign languages, including English, to remain within their organisations, or whether they were sufficiently different from both to merit an organisation of their own.
>
> (Strevens 1980: 31)

What made those inaugural members interested in founding the new British Association of Applied Linguistics (BAAL) was that they had first-hand experience of the social problems that linguistic applications were addressing. What they looked to 'applied linguistics' for was a framework for conceptualising and contemplating those problems.

Before a new association was formed (in Britain and elsewhere) a small number of postgraduate courses offering training in Applied Linguistics were already in existence. The establishment of these association(s) gave authority to such courses and encouraged the setting up of others.

6 TRAINING COURSES IN APPLIED LINGUISTICS

Training courses, especially vocational training courses, such as the MA in Applied Linguistics, are ways of defining the subject. In all cultures, the training of the young provides a *rite de passage*, a ritualised entry into senior status by the provision of the necessary keys to that culture. This is as true of a profession as of a society (see below, Chapter 6).

There seem to be two origins for a new teaching course. The first is when there is a new skill or area of knowledge, idea or dogma which arouses interest. Gender Studies might be an example. Others might be post-colonialism or feminism. The second is where there is a new vocational need (off-shore petroleum engineering, business administration, peace-keeping, social work or computer science). Applied linguistics belongs to the second category.

In both cases what happens first is that a new course (certificate, diploma or degree) is set up to which there is input from a number of impacting areas. Thus Gender Studies might draw on history, literature, genetics, sociology and linguistics. Applied linguistics has in the past drawn on linguistics, psychology, curriculum studies, anthropology, phonetics, psychometrics and statistics and literary theory. But in due course the graduates of these mosaic-like courses spread out to establish courses of their own. They are not themselves trained solely (or even mainly) in one of the feeder disciplines; they are trained in the mosaic. So they have a dual question to address: first, what do they call themselves, and, second, who should be the teachers on their own newly established courses?

Their answer to the first of these questions is easier for the vocational group than for the interest group ('applied linguists' seems to work better than 'post-colonialists'). But though salient (and amusing) this first question is less serious than the second: who teaches on their new courses? Is it their graduates and their peers? Or do they bring in 'specialists' from the feeder disciplines they were introduced to? This is both a practical and at the same time a deeply theoretical question about the nature of the applied linguistics. I shall return to this question in Chapter 6.

7 CONCLUSION

In this chapter we have defined 'applied linguistics' by comparing it with linguistics and with that use of linguistics, sometimes known as applications of linguistics and referred to by us as 'linguistics-applied'. We have distinguished between this linguistics-driven applied linguistics (linguistics applied) and the applied linguistics which is the subject of this book and indeed of the series. In order to clarify the difference, in Chapter 2 we illustrate the variety of language problems which applied linguistics confronts and the role of reflective experience in that confrontation. Then in Chapter 3 we explore further the relations between linguistics and applied linguistics, comparing their approaches in three areas of shared interest.

Chapter 2

Doing being applied linguists: the importance of experience

'I wanted to live deep and suck out all the marrow of life … to drive life into a corner and reduce it to its lowest terms, and, if it proved to be mean, why then to get the whole and genuine meanness of it, and publish its meanness to the world; or if it were sublime, to know it by experience.'

(H. D. Thoreau (1854), 'Where I lived and what I lived for', in *Walden*, published in *Writings* (1906), vol. 2, p. 101.)

1 INTRODUCTION

Chapter 2 begins with a brief discussion of the importance of individual experience in applied linguistics and on its drawbacks. I then illustrate the variety of language problems addressed by applied linguists by reference to five case studies. Finally, four pairs of study areas are described in order to illustrate the range of research and development work in applied linguistics.

2 INDIVIDUAL EXPERIENCE

We began Chapter 1 with the Wren inscription and commented that just as he is known best by the work he did, so applied linguistics is most usefully defined functionally, by observing what its practitioners do. In Chapter 2 we examine some of their work in order to gain an understanding of the problem-based need for applied linguistics, its purpose and the skills it draws on. I want to suggest that the skills that applied linguists bring to their work include their own reflection on their own experience of language problems. This of course is true of all professionals but is likely to be a stronger influence in a discipline which reifies language practices rather than, as linguistics does, language.

The importance of personal experience of institutional language problems becomes very clear in teaching applied linguistics. Those who have taught applied linguistics at both postgraduate and undergraduate levels will be aware how hard it is to give an undergraduate class the language-teaching (or other language professional) experience which they normally lack; as a result we may wonder whether applied linguistics is teachable at the undergraduate level. We often find that post-experience graduates meet us half way. They bring their own experience, their intuition about language problems and are ready for the courses we offer; they want to find their experience illuminated. Undergraduates do, of course, have experience of their own language learning, but they are unlikely to have reflected on that learning, to understand what it is that needs illuminating, they have not recognised the problems for which we may discuss explanations. No doubt the pragmatic answer to this pedagogic difficulty is to teach a very different applied linguistics at postgraduate and undergraduate levels, but the danger always is of providing examples and exercises (for example error analysis, comprehension questions and Labov-type markers) that are as unreal and idealised as any workbook in descriptive linguistics.

The link between reflective personal experience and instruction from others is the message of George Fox's account of his own spiritual quest. Fox, the founder of Quakerism, wrote in his journal:

> Now after I had received that opening from the Lord that to be bred at Oxford or Cambridge was not sufficient to fit a man to be a Minister of Christ, I regarded the priests less and looked more after the dissenting people ... I saw there was none among them all that could speak to my condition ... I heard a voice which said, 'There is one, even Christ Jesus, that can speak to thy condition', and when I heard it my heart did leap for joy ... Thus, when God doth work, who shall let it? And this I knew experimentally.
>
> (Nickells 1975: 11)

The *Oxford English Dictionary* still allows 'experientially' (in the light of experience) as one of the meanings of 'experimentally'. Fox's point is that he is rejecting scholastic theology (or as we might say theory) in favour of personal experience. It is not statements about God, however systematic they may be, that matter but personal experience.

However, relying wholly on experience brings its own problems. First, personal inspiration can be dangerous: the purpose of the religious intermediary such as a priest is to provide a necessary check on enthusiasm and a correction to delusion and at the same time to offer a framework within which individual experience can be understood. This framework was provided in Fox's case by ensuring that there was always a group judgement to provide an interpretation of individual experience.

Second, even this community re-interpretation was eventually found wanting, in part no doubt because it could not cope with the inevitable tendencies towards populism and anomie. Some kind of theology was found to be necessary to explain and connect individual and community experiences.

Applied linguistics may seem a long way from Quakerism but the insistence on the necessity to begin with experience is the link. As we shall see, again like Quakerism, applied linguistics has found its own need for theorising. The insistence on function, the appeal to looking at what applied linguists do, at their actual experience rather than what they say they do, these are also close parallels. What do applied linguists do? That is the central theme of this chapter.

But first I want to consider the question in the light of my own experience. In

1962 I came back to the UK after a four-year period as an English teacher in a Kenyan secondary school, where English was the medium of instruction. I had gone there after some years teaching English in England and had had no training whatsoever in teaching English as a Foreign/Second Language. My four years were disturbing and informing. They made me aware of language teaching and language learning and conscious of my own inadequacy. In particular, I observed that the African students I was teaching were weak in advanced reading techniques (as I later came to call them); they could not summarise, they could not understand moderately difficult texts; they could not write coherently; and above all they lacked awareness of the cultural background on which much of their reading depended.

Contrariwise, it seemed to me that the demands made on the students, their examinations, were unrealistic, though against the background I had come from and in the institutional context in which they studied, those demands were understandable. In essence, they were no different from those of the native speaker. The native speaker! That useful myth whose abilities we take for granted, ignoring the gap between our idealised model and the real-life variation that surrounds us (Davies 1991a). The examinations my students presented for were, I thought, unfair. (Later I would call them invalid.) It seemed that others thought the same since, during my stay in Kenya, Makerere University College (at the time the only university-level institution in East Africa) decided it would no longer require a pass in English language for entrance, on the observable grounds that many able students (passing well in science subjects, for example, all in the medium of English) were failing in the English language examination.

I came back to the UK looking for informed advice. At the time I might have said I wanted a solution to the problems I had met: problems of inadequacy in myself, in my students and in the system. I looked first in a university English department but soon found that they could not understand the problem I found it hard to articulate. A university education department was more helpful in putting me in the way of a partial solution by setting me the task of (and giving me the facilities for) constructing an English language test for one level of proficiency in English as a Second Language.

What I needed, I came to think, and still think, was not a solution to the problems of second-language teaching, but an explanation or (perhaps we should not avoid the word) a theory. Explanation is a torch-like term, we tend not to question it, though in real life we are aware of how infinitely regressive explanation can be. What I was looking for was some coherent view (or even views) on language and language development.

Shortly afterwards, I was appointed to the staff of the Department of Applied Linguistics in the University of Edinburgh. And no, I did not find solutions. Nor did I find *the* explanation, but I did find an atmosphere in which language was discussed in ways that I have found helpful. And I am not alone in this. My experience is not unlike that of many of the graduate students who come to Applied Linguistics courses every year with 'problems' to which they want solutions. What they find is that no solutions are provided but explanations are. What they also find among their teachers and fellow-students is a community they can identify with, which shares a common language in which they can makes sense of their individual experience and which provides a discourse framework.

What all kinds of useful explanation have in common is that they demand generalisation, that is that they must be applicable to similar events and causes. What those students have found is that language learning in Japan is not so different from language learning in Germany or in Manchester. This is both releasing personally and effective academically because it permits objectivity. And in its turn objectivity clears the way for the kind of theorising which illuminates experience and is changed by it.

3 INSTITUTIONAL APPLIED LINGUISTICS

Instead of trying to define applied linguistics, it is instructive to look at what is actually going on institutionally. Applied Linguistics defines itself by actions rather than by definitions. The International Association of Applied Linguistics (commonly referred to as AILA, the acronym of its French name, Association Internationale de Linguistique Appliquée), for example, constantly runs into this definition problem and equally constantly avoids it by refusing to be tied down. So what does AILA do? Here is a list of its 'scientific commissions' as of November 1997:

Adult Language Learning
Child Language
Contrastive Linguistics and Error Analysis
Discourse Analysis
Educational Technology and Language Learning
Foreign Language Teaching Methodology and Teacher Education
Interpreting and Translating
Language and Education in Multilingual Settings
Language and Gender
Language for Special Purposes
Language Planning
Language Testing and Evaluation
Lexicography and Lexicology
Mother Tongue Education
Psycholinguistics
Rhetoric and Stylistics
Second-Language Acquisition
Sociolinguistics
Literacy
Language and Ecology
Language and Media
Communication in the Professions
Learner Autonomy in Language Learning

Of course not all these commissions are active, and of course a good deal is omitted. But this open-ended list is a better definition than any sentential definition. Its danger is that it leads to an anything linguistics, in which any kind of activity remotely connected with language can be brought under the applied-linguistics umbrella. That is both otiose and unscholarly.

Some steady view then is necessary and this must surely now mean an appeal to theory. New academic disciplines, like new religions, may manage without a theoretical base: just as Fox and his early followers found their own experience adequate so did the founding applied-linguists. But later applied linguists like later Quakers, removed from the original inspiration, need to theorise about their own experience.

4 FIVE CASE STUDIES

I turn now to five case studies so as to provide an illustration of the range of activities that applied linguists are involved in. They will serve as an indication of the extent to which we think of applied linguistics as a coherent discipline rather than as a collection of unconnected language projects. The examples I have chosen are:

1. language-programme evaluation;
2. literacy acquisition;
3. pedagogical grammar;
4. workplace communication; and
5. critical pedagogy.

What these examples illustrate is that projects in applied linguistics typically present as 'problems' for which explanations are desired, explanations which allow the researcher and teacher to make sense. (This of course takes us very close to our earlier discussion about the eventual need for theory: theory in macrocosm becomes explanation in microcosm.)

The fifth case study, 'critical pedagogy', offers a problem of a different kind in that it represents an alternative applied linguistics, known as critical applied linguistics (CAL). It does this in two ways, first by offering a critique of traditional applied linguistics (as represented, for example, in the first four case studies in this chapter); and second, by exemplifying one way of doing CAL, namely critical pedagogy. I shall suggest in Chapter 6 that CAL may represent an ethical response to traditional applied linguistics; then in Chapter 7 I look more closely at the origins of CAL and the claims it makes.

4.1 Language-programme evaluation

Accountability has traditionally been left to professionals to determine for themselves. It has been manifested through such stakeholder satisfaction criteria as client numbers, student successes on examinations and in employment, earnings and reputation. Such amorphous criteria are no longer acceptable. For the sake of the stakeholders and to make the participants better informed, as well as to improve the activity if repeated, language-programme evaluation is now widely practised. What it does is to determine to what extent the project/programme is meeting the original blue-print, to examine the changes brought about by the project/programme, and to question the extent to which this type of project is generalisable and should be generalisable. Was it worthwhile? Can we generalise to other situations?

In 1990 Jacob Tharu, of Hyderabad CIEFL, and I carried out an evaluation study of four projects in South India (Davies 1991b). The evaluation was concerned with externally funded English-language teaching (ELT) projects in tertiary institutions. The funding source was the British Government, through its Overseas Development Administration (ODA) and the British Council (BC) under the Key English Language Teaching (KELT) scheme. All four projects were (untypically for KELT) short term and made use of a two-way relationship between the (British) consultant's home institution and the Indian receiving institution, following a pattern of two-way visits over three to four years. The purpose of the evaluation was to determine what success such a project using short-term consultancies had had and to consider whether or not such a model could be applied in other developmental situations.

These four projects, institutionally separate from one another, were all concerned with curriculum change. Our terms of reference were as follows:

1. the overall design of the projects and their relevance to the Indian situation;
2. the effectiveness of the UK consultancies and of local input/support;
3. the appropriateness of materials produced and their usefulness to the target audience;
4. the extendibility of the ELT materials to other situations in India;
5. the changes that were brought about as a result of the project; and
6. the extent to which local expertise could take over and sustain the work of the project.

The four projects were based in:

Anna University, Madras (English Department)
Kerala University, Trivandrum (Institute of English)
Indian Institute of Science, Bangalore (Foreign Languages Section)
Osmania University, Hyderabad (English Department and ELT Centre)

The range of undergraduate/postgraduate, compulsory/special, full-time/part-time, general/specific, large/small departments against an underlying policy of curriculum change compelled us to consider urgently the need to generalise beyond the context of any one setting.

What became clear early on was the difficulty of determining any single criterion of project success, thereby supporting views widely expressed in the literature (e.g. Brumfit 1983; Kennedy 1989; Weir and Roberts 1994; Baldauf and Kaplan 1998). Success in a project may be achieved in a variety of ways and depends on a combination of factors, such as context and personal interactions, not all of which are manipulable. For that reason we were less concerned with analysis of past achievement and more concerned with diagnosis of project experience so as to inform future policy.

We decided on four criteria for determining success of a project: product, teacher development, sustainability and extendibility. By product we meant some public expression of a project outcome. At its most informal such a public expression could be a circulated syllabus document; at its most formal a published textbook. What we looked for was some product indicative of project completion; we did not attempt to estimate the professional quality of the product.

Teacher development, the second criterion, is essential to the continuation of an institution. And while the language-teaching profession may be more concerned with research output, administrators are probably more well disposed to the professionalism of their institution's teaching staff. We determined on a number of indicators to show professional development, such as recognition of the necessary link between materials and methodology, appointment as consultants to other institutions, stated intention to update their materials.

Sustainability has to do with the ability and willingness to continue without the support of the consultant. We decided on indicators such as: being responsive to the need to change aims while the project was still ongoing, team cohesion shown by a strong sense of professional interaction and a sense of ownership of the project.

Extendibility concerns the relevance of a project to other contexts and therefore is determined by indicators such as an understanding at a theoretical level among the project team members of why they did what they did in the project, an awareness by professionals in other institutions of the seriousness of the project, and a capacity by the project staff to continue as a research team and mount new projects on their own, not simply continue the existing project.

We considered that in addition to these four project outcomes it was also necessary to take account of a set of pre-conditions and of inputs during the life of the project. In this way we developed a model for project evaluation which would permit both generalisability across KELT activities (and no doubt others too) and at the same time allow for some measure of prediction of likely success based on the presence of the pre-conditions and the amount of input during the project.

Evaluation of language-teaching projects is a good example of the kind of activity applied linguists are called on to perform. What makes their contribution special, that is an applied-linguistics contribution, is in my view that they bring to the evaluation a readiness to generalise through model-making, as I have tried to illustrate in this abbreviated account of the study Tharu and I carried out in South India in 1990.

4.2 Literacy acquisition

In addition to critical (and sometimes sceptical) comment on current received opinion on language learning and teaching issues, applied linguistics also contributes its careful reading of published results in these fields. The study that is now briefly described, the critical literature review of biliteracy illustrates the applied-linguistic contribution to the ongoing debate on literacy in education.

As part of a project investigating schooled literacy in the second language (in this case, English in Australia for speakers of other languages) a critical literature review from an applied linguistic perspective was commissioned (BIP 1997). Given the prevailing view among English as a Second Language (ESL) practitioners of the need to establish prior literacy in the first language (L1), it was important to sift the published evidence carefully.

During the twentieth century, literacy has broadened its scope beyond reading and writing. The term 'multiple literacies' expresses one type of broadening by validating often unacknowledged skilled language practices. A plausible interpretation of the broadening to more and more domains is that literacy has extended its province from the apparently straightforward sense of learning the skills of reading and writing to the more all embracing sense of the demands of contemporary education. According to this interpretation, contemporary literacy and schooling are synonymous. What this means, of course, is that traditional ideas of schooling have also adapted so as to incorporate these wider demands. Surprisingly, therefore, literacy and schooling are still in step with one another. Just as schooling used to mean becoming literate in reading and writing, so present-day literacy means being schooled in multiple literacies.

Much of the discussion about becoming literate, both in the narrower sense of acquiring reading and writing skills, and in the broader sense of schooling, emphasises the 'rules of the game' aspect, that is seeing (and accepting) what it's for (where 'it' encompasses reading/writing and schooling).

An issue of concern in schools with multilingual populations is that of the role of the first language (L1), and particularly of L1 literacy, in the acquisition of second-language (L2) literacy, that is of literacy in the school language. Applied linguists become involved with this type of literacy question in two ways, first in helping define literacy in such a way that it is possible to distinguish between the skills of reading and writing and the wider sense of 'reading the world' (Olson 1994), and second in clarifying what is meant by being literate in the traditional skills, that is at what point or cut-off a learner is not literate. In discussions of the relationship between the L1 and the L2, the consensus seems to be that since literacy skills transfer from L1 to L2, L1 literacy should be taught prior to, or simultaneously with, L2 literacy.

There is a weak version of this view and a strong version. The weak version states that for full L2 literacy development it is desirable that there should be prior adequate development in L1 literacy. The strong version goes further, claiming that unless there is an adequate base of L1 literacy there can be no L2 literacy development. Views such as these derive in part from the earlier work of Jim Cummins (1984).

Those taking up the strong position emphasise one of two values of prior L1 literacy: the first is that literacy in a second language is easier because learners know what literacy is from their first-language experience. The second value makes the knowledge argument, that proper cognitive development is possible only where literacy has been acquired in the L1.

There is of course a sceptical view. That is that what is needed to acquire literacy in an L2 such as English is more and better instruction in that L2, in this case English. The underlying argument here is that there is no general connection between L2 literacy and the L1 and that a case-by-case approach should be taken when considering policy. School success, it is pointed out, depends on a number of factors, including attitude to schooling. In the morass of individual variation the school turns out to be uniquely powerful. What this suggests is that the good school can make all the difference to the acquisition of literacy in an L2, while the bad school can jeopardise the L2 student's chances. No surprise there! Interestingly, of course, it places the responsibility for an L2 learner's success as much on the school as on the student's attainments in the L1.

If there is a moral to the study of schooling in a second language, it is that there is no homogeneity, *except for the school*. Languages differ, learners differ, contexts of learning differ, and the L1–L2 relationship differs. It is incumbent on researchers and teachers therefore to take account of previous learning and at the same time not to assume that all previous learning in the L1 is necessarily what matters most for subsequent learning in the L2.

The contribution of applied linguistics to a study of schooled literacy in a second language is to demystify the role of the first language and to examine carefully just what influence it has, motivationally, cognitively and linguistically.

4.3 Pedagogical grammar

A pedagogic (or pedagogical) grammar we can define as a grammatical description of a language which is intended for pedagogical purposes, such as language teaching, syllabus design, or the preparation of teaching materials. A pedagogic grammar might be based on:

1. a grammatical analysis and description of the language;
2. a particular grammatical theory; and
3. the study of the grammatical problems of learners or on a combination of approaches.

Pedagogical grammars can be distinguished from analytical grammars. A pedagogical grammar is a grammatical description of a language specifically designed as an aid to teaching that language, such as the grammar textbooks used in foreign-language classes or the grammar instruction offered to trainee teachers. An analytical grammar attempts to account formally and logically for the structure of a language without reference to pedagogy, sequencing, levels of difficulty, or ease of explanation.

Few analytical grammars are suitable for pedagogy but developments in generative grammar, including case grammar, generative semantic models of language and accounts of linguistic discourse, indicate a renewal of interest in language as it is actually used in human interaction. Such grammars are therefore much more relevant to language learning and language teaching because they are less abstract than previous generative grammars. However, even these less abstract, more communicative grammars are still not intended to be pedagogic in the sense in which we are using the term, since the purpose of a pedagogic arrangement for a grammar is to afford the students tightly controlled practice in writing sentences and thereby to locate the source of their own writing errors. The successful textbook employing a pedagogical grammar approach will ensure that the items and exercises are arranged so as to promote understanding of the ways in which different grammatical devices combine with context so as to allow the writer (and speaker) to express the variety of intended meanings.

A pedagogical grammar therefore needs to be distinguished both from an analytic grammar and from other types of textbook. It differs from an analytic grammar in terms of purpose, which is to teach the language rather than about the language. It differs from other types of textbook in terms of organisation, in that it is arranged on pedagogical principles.

Using the technique of pedagogical grammar in response to a language problem facing him in designing communicative language teaching materials, Keith Mitchell (1990) describes his attempt to produce a description which anticipates learners' communicative needs 'by adopting meaning and use – semantics and pragmatics – rather than grammatical structure as its main principle of classification' (1990: 52).

Mitchell explains why Jespersen's analysis of the English comparative was in-adequate (while praising him for his far-sighted approach to language teaching, anticipating communicative ideas sixty years before they became fashionable). In doing so he demonstrates why the classic analysis which claimed that the following two sentences are equivalent in meaning was wrong:

1. Mary is as tall as her father.
2. Mary and her father are identical in height.

Mitchell points out that they are not equivalent because (1) means that Mary is either equal to her father in height or taller, while (2) means only that she is equal to her father in height.

Mitchell's analysis ranges from the logic of comparative structure through seman-tics and pragmatics to the lexicogrammatical possibilities inherent in the English language. In general terms his argument concerns the different ways in which the same concept may be expressed and at the same time the different but related con-cepts that are expressed in similar ways.

Mitchell concludes that:

'identity of degree', together with 'the average degree' and 'the ideal degree' are concepts that language users have not hitherto had much occasion to express, witness the relative grammatical and/or lexical complexity of the devices that have to be resorted to if one does want to express them. These can hardly be concepts that play any great part in the everyday categorization of human experience, otherwise speakers would have made it their business over the ages to ensure, as it were, that language provided a straightforward means for giving expression to them. It seems that when it comes to making comparisons quantifying properties of things in the world around us we tend to perceive these primarily in terms of differences, and even when we do perceive similarities we appear to like to leave room for the possibility of difference ... It seems therefore that everyday language operates with a much looser and more ambivalent concept of 'equality' than does mathematics.

(1990: 70)

Let us remind ourselves of Mitchell's purpose in dealing with this language problem, namely the design of a communicative-pedagogical description of English which would meet the needs of the syllabus designer and the materials writer. What he has reported on is clearly a small part of a larger task. In other words the 'problem' of how to teach learners how to express comparisons in English is only a very small part of the larger 'problem' of how to enable learners to access the resources of the English language.

But in this small-scale reporting what Mitchell succeeds in doing is to show how questions of this kind require the applied linguist to bring together recurring practical demands (how best to teach the language) with major theoretical issues (how the language deploys itself in order to permit meanings to be expressed). This particular engagement of theory and practice draws, it should be noted, more heavily on linguistic theory than my first two examples of programme evaluation and schooled literacy. The outcome of such an engagement is three-fold: it offers a resource to the syllabus designer and textbook writer; it informs our understanding of the ways in which pedagogy reflects learning and so assists with the theorising of applied linguistics; and it informs our understanding of the grammatical resource of the language and so has the potential to impact on linguistic theory itself.

4.4 Workplace communication

Away from education, the workplace is probably the major setting for necessary communication. Typically, it is the migrant for whom communication at work presents at the least misunderstandings and hostility and at the worst loss of job (or failure to obtain one). Those applied linguists who study communication in the workplace have a dual purpose: to extend our knowledge of language genre so as to add to the theoretical base of language variety; and to provide input to the design of language-teaching materials for use in training courses on workplace communication for migrants, or to provide advice for administrators about how to minimise mis-communication.

Those who work in settings which during the past twenty years have been the research sites for studies of workplace discourse include doctors, psychologists, commodity dealers and personnel managers. These studies have contributed to our understanding of institutional discourse and communicative relationships in the workplace. The problem for applied linguists who work in these settings is their tendency to underestimate the complexity of working with non-language pro-fessionals while avoiding being seen as both patronising and as irrelevant outsiders.

To be successful in these settings, applied linguistics needs 'a set of conceptual and analytic tools which are sensitive to the particular work contexts in which they work'.

Developing these tools is possible only by interaction between applied linguists and field professionals, the ambition being to achieve the integration of theory with practice (Roberts et al. 1997).

The 1979 film *Crosstalk* (Gumperz et al. 1979) set out to analyse and remedy cross-cultural communication in the workplace, with particular reference to the experience of Asian migrants in the UK. The film and its accompanying training methods are based on the analysis of differential features in the English of Asian-born speakers of English and in the English of UK-born speakers of English. What this analysis shows is that there are distinct cultural conventions used to infer meaning and attitudes. Use of such features (on both sides) causes misunderstandings and break-downs of communication:

> It is at the level of grasping the overall significance of what is being said and of drawing the correct inferences, that is of reading between the lines as to what is really intended, that the Asian-English system and the English-English [communication between two native speakers of British English] system of linguistic signals for information and attitude differ most.
>
> (ibid 1979: 9–10)

For example English-English people are confused by Asian-English lack of stress patterns and by their wrong use of turn-taking, while Asian-English people are confused by apologetic or polite and repetitive uses of English and by their appearance of not listening to what is being said.

In for example a job interview in which an Asian is applying for a post as librarian in a college, a number of 'indirect' questions were raised with the candidate concerning his reasons for his interest in this particular job. The point of this type of question was to determine whether the candidate saw the post for which he was being interviewed as part of a strategy of careful career development. The candidate, however, interpreted all questions of this sort as direct rather than indirect and therefore as challenging his right to want a job at all. As a result he found this line of questioning insulting.

The professionals involved in the interview were officials of the college where the applicant sought employment. They were the Vice-Principal, the Head of Department and the Chief Administrative Officer. The film and materials are based on the combined analysis by these officials and the project applied linguists of the form and purpose of typical job interviews and the ways in which these are linguistically encoded.

4.5 Critical pedagogy

This last example differs from those previously described in that it reports a general approach rather than a project grappling with a specific issue. The approach is indeed so general that it offers an alternative way of doing applied linguistics and in Chapter 6 we look at examples 1 to 4 from this alternative point of view. But in addition to permeating the whole field of applied linguistics, critical pedagogy (itself an aspect of critical applied linguistics) is a project in itself since it occupies space for both teachers and students of applied linguistics in their studying and in their research.

Critical pedagogy, and more generally critical applied linguistics, represents a kind of postmodern version of critical discourse analysis. As such it places the onus of action firmly on the subject, in this case the learner, student, reader. Alastair Penny-cook (1994a) describes the approach in Chapter 9 ('Towards a critical pedagogy for teaching English as a worldly language'). He takes as his point of departure: 'it is impossible to separate English from its many contexts and thus a key tenet of the discourse of English as an International Language – that it is possible to "just teach the language" – is equally untenable' (Pennycook 1994a: 295).

Pennycook is concerned to make clear that he is not proposing a prescriptive set of teaching practices; what he is doing is 'to lay out some general concerns in developing critical pedagogies of English' (ibid: 300). He recognises that his stance is ideological but points out that all education is political while usually pretending it is not: 'I would argue that all education is political, that all schools are sites of cultural politics' (ibid: 301).

Pennycook emphasises the importance of 'voice' which is used to refer to 'a contested space of language use as social practice … (it) suggests a pedagogy that starts with the concerns of the students, not in some vapid, humanist "student-centered" approach that requires students to express their "inner feelings", but rather through an exploration of students' histories and cultural locations, of the limitations and possibilities presented by languages and discourses … a critical practice in English language teaching must start with ways of critically exploring students' cultures, knowledges and histories in ways that are both challenging and at the same time affirming and supportive' (ibid: 311).

As a specific instance of the working out of critical pedagogy, Pennycook reports an experience when he was teaching English in China. He became aware that numbers of foreigners who purported to be teachers of English were in fact Christian missionaries. He decided that his students needed to be given the opportunity to consider this situation:

> In a course on 'British and American culture', a course that had always previously consisted of lectures on the political and education systems, festivals and holidays of the United States and the UK, I decided to add a section on American fundamentalism to the curriculum … it was important to make available to my students alternative readings of the United States that drew links between fundamentalism and right-wing politics and showed how the vast expansion of English language learning was being used by those who sought only to 'convert' their students and preach their right-wing politics. The object here was to give my students ways of thinking about connections between the language they were so busily engaged in learning and other cultural and political complexes about modernity, Christianity … anti-abortion campaigns … Chinese population problems and family policies, freedom of speech, and so on.
>
> (ibid: 313–14)

Pennycook is at pains to point out that this approach does not detract from his responsibilities to ensure his students' 'success' as normally defined. He sets out his creed:

> I am suggesting that first, we need to make sure that students have access to those standard forms of the language linked to social and economic prestige; second, we need a good understanding of the status and possibilities presented by different standards; third, we need to focus on those parts of language that are significant in particular discourses; fourth, students need to be aware that those forms represent only one set of particular possibilities; and finally, students also need to be encouraged to find ways of using the language that they feel are expressive of their own needs and desires, to make their own readings of texts, to write, speak and listen in forms of the language that emerge as they strive to find representations of themselves and others that make sense to them, so that they can start to claim and negotiate a voice in English.
>
> (ibid: 317–18)

It is important to note that unlike those who argue the case for linguicism (Phillipson 1992), Pennycook does not oppose the spread of English as long as it is approached critically: 'I believe that the spread of English, if dealt with critically, may offer chances for cultural renewal and exchange around the world' (Pennycook 1994a: 325).

5 DEVELOPMENT AND RESEARCH IN APPLIED LINGUISTICS

Finally in this chapter I want to consider examples of research and development work in applied linguistics. I shall cite four representative study areas to illustrate how applied linguists set about investigating the language 'problems' they encounter. In each case I shall discuss a developmental 'project' type approach and a research, investigative approach. These approaches are rarely easy to distinguish and they support one another, especially in an applied discipline. Nevertheless, the distinction is worth making if only because in some areas (for example second-language acquisition) the major thrust has been in research while in others (for example language planning) most work has been in development.

The four areas are language assessment, language planning, language-teaching curriculum and second language acquisition.

5.1 Language assessment

5.1.1 Development

The project described here (Elder 1997) exemplifies the real problem approach at the heart of applied linguistics. We can represent the process thus:

1. there is a social problem which needs resolution;
2. an applied linguist is invited as consultant; and
3. a solution (not *the* solution) is proposed.

In this case the problem was in education, not, as is so often the case, in English as a foreign or second language, but in the teaching of so-called modern languages in an English-speaking country, in this case Australia. There these languages are known as LOTEs (languages other than English) and for historical and geographical reasons (Australia's immigration policies after the Second World War and its location in the Asian-Pacific region) schools offer a very wide range of languages. In the State of Victoria, for example, students have the choice (not of course in every school) of some thirty-six different languages at the school-leaving examination, known as the Victorian Certificate of Education (VCE).

Apart from English, the choice of subjects students may offer at VCE is open. Performance on the 'best four subjects' of the VCE is used for university selection. This is very competitive and operates on a points system, known as the Tertiary Entrance Requirement (TER). In order to encourage the learning/teaching of LOTEs, candidates offering a LOTE are given an extra 10 per cent. This of course makes the selection of as LOTE attractive, at least for those who are good at languages. And there's the problem. Those who are 'good at languages' include students who have started the LOTE in school from scratch and those with a background in the LOTE from home exposure. These so-called 'background' speakers include on the one hand students from Italian and Greek migrant families who may by now have been resident in Australia for several generations and who may still maintain some use of the language at home. They also include students who at the other extreme have recently arrived in Australia from, for example, Hong Kong, Taiwan, Vietnam or Lebanon, where they may have already received some (possibly all) of their education in the medium of the LOTE they are now offering at VCE.

Does this home use (home both in Australia and, for the more recent arrivals, previous home in the country of origin) give them an advantage over those students who are candidates for the same LOTE but who have no home use, no family connection with the language, other than perhaps a parent who also studied the same language when he or she was at school? The considered view of the authorities has been that this does constitute an advantage for the so-called background speakers. Such a view appears to make sense: if you have studied in Mandarin (for example) for a number of years, you are already literate in the written script, you are familiar with a large number of Chinese characters, then you would seem to have a serious advantage over your peers (who may well be in the same class as you at school) who have studied Chinese for perhaps six years, whose literacy is limited and whose spoken Chinese is still formulaic.

For this reason those who declare themselves (on the basis of a questionnaire) to be background speakers are penalised at the TER stage. This is in practice more complicated since it is not that their TER is changed but that the university admissions officers are permitted to boost the scores of those who are not background speakers.

This is obviously a language problem. The contribution of applied linguistics was first to determine a methodology for categorising background and non-background speakers. A questionnaire was designed, the results of which were used to separate learners into four categories; reliability of designation was assured by multiple ratings. The second contribution was, on the basis of these categories, to examine the test results for bias. It was decided that if the tests were fair then background speakers would have no special advantage. In the case of the Chinese students it was found that they did. The question then was whether or not it was legitimate for them to have this advantage. What emerged was that the results could be interpreted in different ways depending on the point of departure, psychometric, educational or socio-political. Psychometrically speaking the test was not fair and it was biased. Educationally the test was fair, on the grounds that the background speakers did know more. Socio-politically, the score adjustment procedure was very unfair since ethnic minorities who were already disadvantaged because their English in many cases was not native-like were now also being penalised for native-like LOTEs, of which they were background speakers.

Applied linguistics in this project needed skill in devising a methodology for collecting and analysing the data. It also needed knowledge of the bilingual LOTE setting and an ability, based on experience and knowledge, to bring together the different points of view, psychometric, educational and socio-political.

5.1.2 Research

The role of language-testing research as an activity of applied linguistics is to further our understanding of language learning and illuminate the still uncharted space of language use. I do not share the ambition of some applied linguists to map out language use so that it becomes more and more systematised with its own rules of use. After all if that is what were eventually to happen then language use would be more and more taken over by language form, yielding itself to control by the rules of linguistics. That could eventually lead to a situation in which all language behaviour and knowledge are rule-governed, with nothing left to chance or to spontaneity. Because I am sceptical of this ambition, I am content with smaller successes, offering partial and temporary understandings.

In the 1980s one of the key research issues in language assessment was that of the so-called unitary competence hypothesis (UCH), or general language factor. This hypothesis, advocated by among others John Oller (1983), stated that underlying all language abilities was one primary factor, the general language factor. There was, of course, a deliberate connection with the 'g' of intelligence tests. As it turned out this hypothesis was eventually agreed to be too powerful, as Oller himself recognised. Language ability was not unitary but binary or multifactorial. But if language was not unitary, did that mean that there were separate abilities (and separate knowledges) for different areas of language, known in various contexts as styles, registers, genres, specific purposes, varieties, or rhetorics? The question of the separation of language varieties, itself a special case of the larger language question of the discrete nature of dialects and languages, is basic both to much practical language activity and to our theoretical understanding of what makes up language use.

Language teaching and language assessment in recent years have concentrated much of their efforts on the teaching and assessment of languages for specific purposes (academic, professional, occupational, medical, legal, economic and so on). Such work on English, known as English for Specific Purposes (ESP) took a directly counter-position to that of the unitary competence hypothesis since it seemed impossible that both could be upheld. With the abandonment of the unitary competence hypothesis then, it seemed that the ESP difference proposal must prevail. After all, are they not mirror-images of one another?

From an applied linguistics perspective this is not necessarily the case. It would indeed be possible for both to fail: no UCH and no ESP. If a multiplicity of language factors makes more sense of the evidence than does a unitary hypothesis, then it might also be the case that the multiplicity does not refer to specific purposes, all of which could be informed by one overriding purpose, but to (for example) more internal personal factors such as gender, age and motivation and less external social factors, such as professional academic and occupational purposes.

Research on the stability of specific purpose was initiated by Alderson and Urquhart (1985). Three studies were carried out, all studies used English proficiency tests but only in the third was the test the major investigation instrument:

> Study 3 was conducted using parts of the British Council's ELTS [English Language Testing Service] test, which contains specialised study skills modules aimed at different content area groups, e.g. 'Medicine', 'Life Sciences'. A student sitting ELTS chooses whichever of these modules is appropriate to his course of studies … Three ELTS modules were used … namely Social Studies, Technology and General Academic.

> (ibid: 196)

Quite deliberately the design of the study was a test rather than an experiment. There were two reasons for this. The first was that the tests were being used in a functionally appropriate way and would be viewed by the candidates as tests rather than as experiments. Artificiality was therefore somewhat controlled. The second reason was that these ELTS tests are 'social facts'. They are (or were in the mid-1980s) used as part means of determining adequacy in English proficiency levels for overseas students seeking admission to UK universities. Whether or not they are in themselves adequate statements about distinct registers of English, they were used as if they were. What the researchers did was straightforward, as so often good research is. They administered the tests of different ESPs to different groups of candidates with different kinds of 'background knowledge' who would normally have taken one of the modules.

Drawing together their results from all three studies the researchers concluded that 'academic background can play an important role in test performance. However the effect has not been shown to be consistent ... the studies have also shown the need to take account of other factors such as linguistic consistency' (ibid: 202).

But the most interesting conclusion they reach is the distinction they make between direct and overview questions with relation to accessing the content area under test. They report:

> when these students were familiar with the content area, they were able to answer direct and overview questions with equal ease; when this familiarity with the content area was lacking they could still answer direct questions, but their ability to answer overview questions was greatly reduced.
>
> (ibid: 202)

Although they do not say so the implication of this finding is that background knowledge matters: direct questions do not in themselves probe sufficiently into background knowledge whereas overview questions do. That is why in some of the comparisons they make there was no distinction on test results between groups who had background knowledge and those who did not, because what was at stake was a preponderance of direct questions.

This finding, properly muted though it is by the researchers, aware of the inadequacy of the tests themselves as valid representations of their content areas, does in fact match the earlier research finding we referred to, that is that the unitary competence hypothesis could not be supported. Similarly here what was indicated by this research was that there are indeed real differences between language varieties. The researchers carefully point to the need to distinguish between linguistic proficiency (which is the subject of their study) and linguistic competence. On the basis of their study (and perhaps too in the unitary competence research) what is established is that there are different proficiencies not that there are different competences. As Alderson and Urquhart say: 'the part played ... by linguistic competence ... remains unknown' (1985).

5.2 Language planning

5.2.1 Development

Natural resources (deposits such as oil and minerals, water, fertile land and fisheries) are at the disposal of states and subject to policies of various kinds. Populations are also resources, their abilities and, through education, their qualifications and skills. One such ability is the languages spoken in the community and those which the community wishes to promote. Whether the community has an explicit view of its language situation or not it will inevitably have a language policy which determines such matters as which language(s) are to be recognised as the official language(s) of the state, which languages are to be used as medium of instruction in schools, as the medium of broadcasting, in the legal system and so on. Official intervention by the state in some cases requires the institutionalising of a state body which oversees prescriptive issues, bodies such as the Academie Française and the Malaysian National

Languages Board. Even where there is no such official state body there will be some para-statal body (such as the BBC in the UK), publishing houses and newspapers that shape attitude and emphasise norms. Further there will be a policy, again explicit or not, indicating the official attitude towards minority languages used in the community and determining which languages are to be taught as foreign languages in schools. Such community (usually national) policies come under the general label of language planning.

The need for a national language plan is acute in newly formed communities which are faced with immediate decisions about which language(s) to select as the official state language. Newly independent states in the 1950s, 1960s and 1970s were faced with such a decision. In the main the majority chose to continue with the existing situation, which explains why so many former British colonies still use English as their official language, however many other languages may be current within their borders and however few nationals actually use English as their main means of communication. Inertia, continuation of their British connection, scarcity of resources to provide the necessary materials (textbooks and other reading materials) in an indigenous language, unwillingness to compel a choice among the competitor indigenous languages for selection as the new official language, reasons such as these have tended to continue the language status quo.

While the need always exists for language planning on a small scale, such as which languages to offer in a school curriculum over the next period, it is rare, even in the newly emerging states mentioned above, to be given the opportunity to develop a national language plan. Such an opportunity did arise in Australia in the 1980s where Joe Lo Bianco was invited to develop a National Policy on Languages. Australia was not a newly emerging state, but, like Canada which had some years earlier produced its own national policy of bilingualism, Australia did need to come to terms with its new multi-racial (and multilingual) population, following the large-scale immigration of the 1950s. At the same time it needed to adjust to its geo-economic reality of being a 'European' country in the Asian-Pacific region. And very late in the day there was the abiding recognition of the injury to indigenous communities whose languages were dying if not dead. What was needed, it was decided, was an informed view of the linguistic ecology of Australia which would allow practical and ethical decisions to be made. This is a classic applied-linguistics problem since it required a balance of political, educational and linguistic understanding. Such a combination can be found in the report by Joe Lo Bianco published in 1987 *The National Policy on Languages*.

The activity of language policy formulation is, writes the author:

known as language planning when explicit statements and programs are made and enacted to respond to urgent problems of a linguistic nature. Choices and priorities need to be made and set since language pervades all of public and private life. The context means that the federal nature of Australia, consisting of at least eight governments, influences the type of language planning possible in Australia. Therefore it is necessary that broad statements with clear principles be enunciated so that the language problems which face the country as a whole can be tackled at the various relevant levels by the appropriate authorities.

(Lo Bianco 1987: 189)

The proposed policy is comprehensive and takes account of what are called the 'language problems which confront Australia'. These, summarised, are:

English:
- inadequate past attempts to tackle illiteracy levels
- persistently high levels of inability to use/comprehend English among immigrants
- deficiencies in ESL for children

LOTEs:
- lack of take-up, especially among boys
- lack of recognition and use of migrant L1s
- decline of aboriginal languages

Also mentioned are the demands of tourism and the needs of interpreting and translating. In both cases there is insufficient recognition of the needs and possible opportunities.

The National Policy on Languages has been very influential in Australia. It is probably the case that it would not have had the impact it has had without its overarching applied-linguistic vision.

5.2.2 Research

The distinction between Development and Research is not easy to make, but there are differences. The essence of research is that it sets up a hypothesis (research question) which it attempts to investigate. What a development does, on the other hand, is to proceed on the basis of the best evidence available. The larger the enterprise, the more difficult it is to conduct research. The outcome of a research question can always be used to repeat the research in some revised mode. But if the enterprise is a national or semi-national plan/policy there is little likelihood that repetition will be possible. Development should of course draw on research findings and research outcomes but with national plans there is inevitably a dearth of relevant research. What can be done, as we saw with the Australian language policy, is to embed the thinking behind the plan in the nexus of considerations, all of which will have their own research to draw on.

Language planning – or language policy (Kachru 1981) – offers opportunities for research in applied linguistics, not so much in its careful reporting of plans, maintenance, survival, shift and so on but in its categorisation which permits methodical investigation. Ferguson's diglossia proposal (Ferguson 1959) and Stewart's functional language use idea (Stewart 1968) have been influential in language planning development. Here I want to refer particularly to Einar Haugen's 1966 essay on the relation between dialect and standard language.

What Haugen succeeds in doing in this discussion is to explain both what standardisation means in terms of the language–society interface and at the same time to provide a methodology for determining the extent to which a language code has achieved the status of a standard language. Haugen offers a table which has been much used and now underpins much of applied linguistic thinking about standard languages; it has helped explain why standard languages are necessary (see Table 2.1).

Table 2.1   Aspects of Standardisation

	Form	Function
Society	Selection	Acceptance
Language	Codification	Elaboration

(Haugen 1966/1972: 110)

Haugen argues that all standard languages are dialects that have become accepted, given status. (We can of course also say that they are dialects in power, dialects with an army; but that is a negative view since it is equally true of other characteristics of societies, from politeness to dress to housing and education, status tends towards the more powerful.) This is why linguists say that all languages/dialects are equal: what is meant is that potentially they are; it does not mean that they are equal socially. (It is not wholly clear that they are equal even linguistically, certainly not in terms of, for example, technical vocabulary, as we see when comparing Standard English with an unwritten language at this point in time.)

How does a dialect become a standard language? Haugen charts its normal progress (and it is its generalisability which makes his categorisation of theoretical value):

> The four aspects of language development … isolated as crucial features in taking the step from 'dialect' to 'language', from vernacular to standard, are as follows: (a) selection of norm, (b) codification of form, (c) elaboration of function, and (d) acceptance by the community. The first two refer primarily to the form, the last two to the function of language. The first and last are concerned with society, the second and third with language. They form a matrix within which it should be possible to discuss all the major problems of language and dialect in the life of a nation.
>
> (Haugen 1966/1972: 110)

Haugen's terminology may need explanation:

1. Selection of form: one of the existing dialects is chosen for standardisation purposes. The chosen dialect is likely to be the one spoken by the more powerful and better educated groups living in or near the capital.
2. Codification of form: the selected dialect is provided with a written grammar and a dictionary so that it can be used in official documents, taught in schools and learnt by foreigners.
3. Elaboration of function: where necessary, ways of talking and writing about

technology and other developments needed for modern education and commerce will be developed by an academy or language bureau. In the first instance it may be necessary to borrow or invent vocabulary lists.

4. Acceptance by the community: neither codification nor elaboration will succeed unless the community agree that the right dialect has been selected.

The relevance of Haugen's work to applied linguistics is that it provides a methodology for examining language in use. It abstracts and theorises from actual language data, the dialect continuum, the existence of standard languages, the decisions by society as to which dialect to select for standardisation purposes. It is this actualisation which gives it its robustness and which makes it an applied-linguistic endeavour. It is not linguistics alone, nor political science alone nor sociology alone. It is the bringing together of these viewpoints to focus on a language problem in society which allows us to call it applied linguistics.

5.3 Language-teaching curriculum

5.3.1 Development

The term 'curriculum' is used in its widest sense to include purpose and objectives as well as content (or syllabus) and method. An explicit curriculum can be seen as a statement of the means by which a set of objectives is to be achieved and at the same time an operational definition of how we should understand those objectives. Thus an English for Specific Purposes (ESP) curriculum will contain the content of a teaching programme, possible guidance on how to present that programme and at the same time represent by its instantiation what is meant by ESP.

The applied linguistics of curriculum studies may therefore be regarded as the language teaching specialism, which N. S. Prabhu sees as 'a matter of identifying, developing, and articulating particular perceptions of teaching and learning on the one hand and seeking ways in which perceptions can be shared and sharpened through professional debate in the teaching community on the other' (1987: 107).

This definition is given in his account of the Communicational Teaching Project, which he directed in southern India in the late 1970s and early 1980s. It was not, Prabhu states 'an attempt to prove a teaching method through controlled experimentation ... it should not be looked on as a field trial or pilot study leading to a large-scale implementation' (ibid: 103). It was, he writes, 'essentially an attempt to develop a fresh perception of second language teaching and learning. It drew on a pedagogic intuition arising from earlier experience, and deliberately sought further sustained experience, both to test the strength of the intuition and to be able to articulate it in the form of principles and procedures' (ibid: 109).

The impetus for the project was a profound dissatisfaction with conventional (English) language teaching in India, which has since the 1960s been of the structural-drill type (Prabhu uses the name Structural-Oral-Situational or SOS). This itself was an innovation on the earlier fashion of grammar–translation approaches. Since the SOS innovation was hard won, opposition to Prabhu's proposals for change was fierce. What he maintained was that 'the development of competence in a second language requires not systematization of language inputs or maximization of planned practice, but rather the creation of conditions in which learners engage in an effort to cope with communication' (ibid: 1).

Prabhu distinguishes sharply between his communicational competence and communicative competence (see below), which he regards as the ability to achieve social or situational appropriacy, as distinct from grammatical conformity. The focus of his project therefore was not on communicative competence but 'on grammatical competence itself, which was hypothesized to develop in the course of meaning-focused activity' (ibid).

The philosophy behind the project is that learners are meaning seekers. Grammar – competence – is best learnt through purposeful communication; the analogies used at various times are, first, the child learning his or her mother tongue where learning takes place through the search for meaning and not through formal instruction; and, second, the learner (first- or second-language learner) engaged on a content task such as a mathematics task. There, it was argued, the desire, the determination to solve the mathematics problem is so strong that learners will assist one another to negotiate their way to a solution. When tasks similar to a mathematics problem which use language but which are not language focused are presented then the challenge to find a solution will encourage language negotiation and hence language learning: learners 'when focused on communication ... are able to deploy non-linguistic resources and, as a result, not only achieve some degree of communication but, in the process, some new resources, however small, in the target language' (ibid: 29).

In other words, language is best learnt when it is being used as a means not as an end. This is a very nativist view and as might be expected met with opposition. Researchers maintained that the project was not experimental, and educators contested that those involved in the project, which was publicised as an innovation, could not be generalised to other contexts in India because those involved in implementing the project were quite untypical of the majority of classroom teachers.

However, as we have seen, Prabhu always denied that his work was experimental or indeed that in itself it was generalisable. He was not interested in revolutionising English teaching in India. What he was interested in was to develop a fresh perception of second-language learning. He argues that 'pedagogic innovation ... may be viewed as an act of renewing contact with innovation and re-interpreting experience through a fresh perception' (ibid: 109).

Not experimental, not available to the majority of classroom teachers: these are surely serious criticisms in spite of the disclaimers (Beretta 1990). Can a project that has so little claim to permanent effect legitimately be regarded as applied linguistics? If it is, is there a danger that critics will consider that applied linguistics is neither scientific nor relevant?

My response is that with the caveats Prabhu has offered, his work is of interest to applied linguistics because what it does is to elaborate on thinking about language learning. As such it will certainly not revolutionise language teaching in India but it may, as he very fairly observes, offer some insights, help us think again about our

normal practice. It is likely that the role of applied linguistics in curriculum development is as much in offering new insights based, however distantly, on theoretical
underpinnings from other disciplines as in offering ways of changing practice and
method.

5.3.2 Research

Research in curriculum tends to be within one specific area, such as assessment,
pedagogic grammar, background knowledge or genre comparison, rather than
overall method or content or teaching. What has influenced curriculum have
been speculative ideas, given the status of theoretical models and therefore at least
potentially researchable. I think here of communicative competence (Canale and
Swain 1980), notions and functions (Wilkins 1994), the graded levels of achievement movement and its associated unit credit scheme (Clark 1987). In all cases what
is interesting is that they have each drawn on the fundamental idea of the centrality
of interpersonal communication in language learning (and therefore teaching).

As a source for curriculum innovation as well as for research, communicative
competence has been unparalleled since 1975. Its first in-depth discussion by Dell
Hymes took place, it is well to remember, at a Research Planning Conference on
Language Development among Disadvantaged Children and was a deliberate
counterblast to what Hymes regards as the over-narrow emphasis given by Chomsky
to linguistic competence:

> The limitations of the perspective appear when the image of the unfolding,
> mastering, fluent child is set beside the real children in our schools. The theory
> must seem, if not irrelevant, then at best a doctrine of poignancy: poignant
> because of the difference between what one imagines and what one sees; poignant
> too because the theory, so powerful in its own realm, cannot on its terms cope
> with the difference. To cope with the realities of children as communicating
> beings requires a theory within which sociocultural factors have an explicit and
> constitutive role; and neither is the case.
>
> (Hymes 1971)

Communicative competence is based on the notion of appropriacy, an attempt
to build a model for 'the rules of language use without which grammar would be
useless' (Pride and Holmes 1972: 278). Hymes's powerful insight combined with
the trenchancy of his portrayal made possible major development and research in
applied linguistics, akin to the Restricted and Elaborated Codes proposed by Basil
Bernstein (1971) and the interlanguage hypothesis by Corder in the 1980s (Corder
1981). In sociolinguistics, in second-language acquisition, in curriculum design,
in language assessment, the construct of communicative competence has been of
major importance. Whether it has enabled us to do better (teach more effectively, for
example) is another matter. But as an explanatory device, illuminating what is done
and at the same time examining what it means, communicative competence is a good
example of applied linguistics as explanation and as inspiration.

5.4 Second-language acquisition

5.4.1 Development

The example selected to illustrate development in second-language acquisition studies is that of the Lexical Frequency Profile, a measure of vocabulary in the writing of second-language learners. As Laufer and Nation (1995) point out: 'there has been interest in such measures for two reasons – they can be used to help distinguish some of the factors that affect the quality of a piece of writing, and they can be used to examine the relationship between vocabulary knowledge and vocabulary use' (ibid: 307).

The development of a computerised instrument can be seen as a response to the common need to evaluate the role of vocabulary in language learning. It is likely that the Laufer and Nation study builds upon the revival on interest in vocabulary among second-language teachers. This revival – interestingly – represents a return to a more traditional applied linguistics view of the importance of vocabulary as against the centrality of grammar. At the same time, what vocabulary control indicates is a concomitant awareness of genre, of those words that group together in a discrete domain.

The Lexical Frequency Profile uses a frequency list against which to match the vocabulary of the submitted written work. Profiles based on running texts of 200+ words have been shown to provide stable results. The measure is, it is claimed, valid and reliable. Furthermore, the computer program allows for different frequency lists to be used and it is therefore possible to produce a different profile for different proficiency levels; the authors propose two different measures, one for less and one for more proficient students.

The Lexical Frequency Profile appears to be a robust response to the need for quick, reliable and valid estimations of writing proficiency and at the same time a useful indicator of the role of vocabulary in language learning.

5.4.2 Research

Second/foreign-language learning and teaching is expensive and it is also very often wasteful, in that many of those who embark on a course of instruction abandon it before they have reached some useful take-off point. Whether there is an optimum age to start learning a second/foreign language (see Chapter 4) is therefore of considerable practical importance. It is also of theoretical importance because it bears on the question of the critical or sensitive period (which takes place some time during puberty) for engaging with a new cognitive load. Furthermore, it relates to our understanding of what it means to be a native speaker (Davies 1991a). It is assumed that only those exposed to a language in early childhood are native speakers of that language. It is further assumed that if there is exposure to more than one language during early childhood, then it is equally possible to be a native speaker of more than one language. But later exposure, it is thought, cannot produce a native speaker.

There are, of course, serious problems in defining a native speaker so narrowly –

for at least two reasons. The first is that there are indeed so-called exceptional learners who start learning a second language in later life and who do somehow attain native-like mastery, in some cases so perfect that their provenance cannot be distinguished from that of a birthright native speaker. The second reason is that those birthright native members differ among themselves. Not only do they have different accents, they also have different grammars (Ross 1979), quite apart from their very different control over performance skills in the language: in writing, speaking and so on.

However, the sensitive period position has been difficult to counter for second-language acquisition, even thought its legitimacy properly belongs to the acquisition of the first language. Birdsong (1992) has challenged the view that ultimate attainment (native-speaker ability) is not possible for exceptional second-language learners. Bialystok (1997) has shown that on the basis of her experiments it is not only the exceptional learner who is capable of such attainment.

She accepts that 'the general success of younger learners in acquiring a second language is true' (ibid: 133) but points out that the evidence does not therefore mean that 'this advantage is the reflection of a sensitive period in learning' (ibid). She rejects the casuistry of those who wish to add qualifications to the claim that a second-language learner can become a native speaker: as she writes: 'there either is a maturational constraint on second language acquisition or there is not' (ibid: 134).

And she concludes that it is not in fact only the exceptional learner who can overcome the problems of reaching ultimate attainment after the sensitive period. Indeed, it is quite a normal feat: 'it is prudent to assume that successful second-language acquisition remains a possibility for all those who have learnt a natural language in childhood and can organize their lives to recreate some of the social, educational and experiential advantages that children enjoy' (ibid: 134).

Research such as Bialystok's is unlikely to have direct application to second-language teaching. But that is of course not its purpose. And yet it belongs firmly within applied linguistics since it takes a problem of language in use (or several problems) such as what is the optimum age to start acquiring a second language, what sort of attainment can be expected of a learner, whether native-speaker attainment is possible, and so on. These are real problems and what research such as Bialystok's does is to investigate them, reflect on them and provide an explanatory framework that may be used for later developmental studies.

6 CONCLUSION

In this chapter I have considered the kinds of language problems that applied linguistics addresses. I have also discussed the marriage in applied linguistics of practical experience and theoretical understanding, of developmental and of research directions. In Chapter 3 we explore further the relation between the work of linguists and applied linguists in relation to three areas of shared interest: language in situation, language and gender and clinical linguistics. We discuss the distinct triggers for their research questions as well as their investigative procedures and the skills and knowledge they each draw on.

Chapter 3

Language and language practices

'Two Voices are there, one is of the sea,
One of the mountains; each a mighty Voice.'
(W. Wordsworth, 'Thought of a Briton on the
subjugation of Switzerland', 1807.)

1 INTRODUCTION

The relation between linguistics and applied linguistics is explored in relation to areas of shared interest. To highlight the distinction, I first consider the very different approaches made by linguists and applied linguists to the way people use language, what is often referred to as the study of language in situation. I then explore in some detail two further areas, language and gender and clinical linguistics. An activity such as clinical linguistics or language and gender may be practised by both linguists doing their application and by applied linguists, and it is therefore important to consider the distinct triggers for their research questions (which, in the case of the applied linguist, are more likely to be institutional 'problems') as well as their investigative procedures, the skills and knowledge they each draw on.

It is a commonplace that there are different ways of looking at the same 'thing'. I am not here referring to the issue of epistemic relativism (the idea that all referents are socially constructed, that there is no thing-in-itself), which we have raised in Chapter 2 and return to in Chapter 7. What I have in mind is that there can be different views of the same phenomenon; it is not that the phenomenon is thought not to exist or to be socially constructed in different ways but that it can be explained variously, depending on the vantage point you take up. For example suicide, the famous Durkheim phenomenon, has been of interest to both psychologists and sociologists (as well as of course to those working in other disciplines, penologists, medical researchers, theologians and so on): to the psychologist, suicide is of interest because it is, as Durkheim himself said, the most individual of all actions. And it is of interest to the sociologist because suicide is a social act, an act that denies all value to the society where it occurs. The fact that rates of suicide and trends in suicide are, as Durkheim showed, different across societies but stable within any one society emphasises its societal significance.

We might say, therefore, that what distinguishes psychology and sociology (at least in part) is not that they are interested in different phenomena but that they have different ways of addressing and explaining the same phenomena. Much the same is true of history and political science or of physics and branches of engineering. And the different ways of addressing and explaining, what we have also called differing vantage points, have two faces, that is that both the looking towards the topic differs and the looking away differ. This is particularly the case when one of the viewers is practice oriented, as in engineering. Far more than in the psychology–sociology opposition, here the whole purpose of the activity, of looking towards the phenomenon, is dedicated to looking away, back to the engineering 'problem' that the engineer needs to solve.

Such multiple perspectives are common experience. The mother looks at her successful grown-up son and feels maternal pride; the girlfriend looking at the same person feels attraction; his employer is delighted that his confidence in the young man's abilities is being fulfilled; the sports coach sees unfulfilled athletic promise … and so on. These are all 'true' versions of the one person: what makes them different is the purpose and the stance of the person who is observing.

We find the same variation in attending to language. The literary critic and the grammarian may both look at the same historical text, the one seeing an early example of a poetic genre, the other the key to an unsolved problem in the grammar he or she is writing of that language. In the distinction we have drawn between linguistics and applied linguistics there is the same difference of viewpoint.

The linguist will experience a discussion among elders in an Australian aboriginal community, where only very few still speak the first language (L1), and will think of vocabulary lists and informants to help to write a grammar. The applied linguist, listening to the same discussion, will consider policy issues (should/can the language be maintained?) and whether to advocate a bilingual programme in the schools (English plus the local language) or an English-only programme. And if English whether to recommend some use of aboriginal English, the equivalent in Australia of North American ebonics (Fillmore 1997).

2 LANGUAGE IN SITUATION

Both the linguist and the applied linguist concern themselves with so-called language situations. By a language situation is meant an evaluation of the role of language in a social setting: thus language as a medium of instruction in Canada; the maintenance of Welsh since 1960; English spoken by males and females in a middle- and a working-class district of Melbourne; the role of Mandarin in Hong Kong since the Chinese take-over; the interpreting and translating policy of the European Union; the relation of language and religion in Indonesia. The approach of the two scholars is likely to be very different. What the linguist is concerned with, above all, is either the testing of a theory or the careful description of the detailed situation.

In a survey of the use of English in Melbourne, the purpose of the linguist's research and the subsequent report might be to demonstrate that the theoretical approach of William Labov (1994) has once more been confirmed. In his socio-linguistic studies in the USA and those of his students and disciples all over the world the model followed has been that of the very stable yet dynamic social influence on language. In other words, middle and working class, males and females differ in their accent and in particular in very specific phonetic features and yet in all cases over time those accents change. But typically they change systematically so as to maintain the same social distinction among the groups. Just as groups dress differently, so they speak differently. That seems to be the point. The linguist's task is to collect the appropriate data needed to test the theory, the argument of course being that the more such studies are carried out and produce significant results, the stronger becomes the likelihood that the theory is well founded. Such studies are very like the kinds of research carried out in the physical and biological sciences, where younger researchers provide evidence of their successful apprenticeship by replicating the same or very similar studies by their elders.

What the linguist is doing in these types of study is applying a research instrument in an applied area, that is taking the theoretical linguistic model and placing it over a social setting. The question asked is does this setting support the theory. Now for the linguist this is not theoretical linguistics; it is twice removed since it involves non-laboratory investigation and it takes into account social factors. This then to the linguist is an example of linguistics applied, a situation in which to apply linguistics.

A second example of the linguist operating in a language in situation type of research is with the census data. Social scientists are typically interested in decennial census data since they provide evidence of stability and change in society. For the linguist the chief interest is in the so-called language question, which in many set-tings asks such questions as: which language do you speak at home? It may also ask which languages you speak and/or write in other settings and which language you consider to be your mother tongue. Results of such language survey type questions are then collated to produce tables of frequency and incidence. One such collation of results is found in the work of E. Annamalai (1998).

What Annamalai does is to collect survey statistics of the numbers of mother-tongue speakers in India and to relate those statistics to linguistic definitions of the various language groupings and families. His process of sifting reduces the number of 'mother-tongues' in India from the 4000+ reported names to a more manageable c. 200. He writes:

[T]he people of India have reported 1652 mother tongues (1961 Census). These mother tongues as reported in the census are not languages in a grammatical sense but are tokens of group identity in a sociolinguistic sense and they include names of villages, castes, occupations etc. Some of the mother tongues may be languages, some may be dialects and some may be indicators of speech variation not even having the status of a dialect. The census abstracts these mother tongues, which are themselves an abstraction arrived at after eliminating spelling variations, spurious names etc from the actual reported names exceeding 4,000, into languages on the basis of linguistic distinctiveness. According to this abstraction of the 1961 census figures, there are about 200 languages in India (Govt of India 1964). They belong to four language families, viz Indo-European (54 languages and 27% of the languages), Dravidian (20 and 10%), Austro-Asiatic (20 and 10%) and Sino-Tibetan (84 and 42%); the rest are foreign languages and unclassified languages (22 and 11%). They vary in population size from less than 25 (Andamanese) to more than 250 million (Hindi) as per the 1981 census.

Of these languages, 101 are tribal languages belonging to the above four families (Indo-European 1, Dravidian 9, Austro-Asiatic 19 and Sino-Tibetan 63, unclassified 9) (Govt of India 1964). It may be noted that all of the languages of the last two families are tribal and about half of the Dravidian languages are tribal. They vary in population size from 5 (Andamanese) to 3,130,829 (Santali) according to the 1961 census and in status from being a preliterate language to being a language of state level administration and college level education like Mizo (a Sino-Tibetan language) and Khasi (an Austro-Asiatic language). The number of tribal languages is an abstraction of 304 tribal mother tongues in 1961. There are 613 tribal communities (Govt of India: 1978) speaking these languages. But not all of them have a tribal language as mother tongue. Of the population of tribal communities (29.9 million in 1961 constituting 6.9% of the total population of India), only 57% speak a tribal language as mother tongue (i.e. 12.8 million). For 43% of the tribals, the mother tongue has shifted to a non-tribal language, which is largely the dominant language of the region (Annamalai 1994).

At the national level, no language is a majority language with speakers exceeding 50% of the country's population and in that sense all languages in India are minority languages. At the state level, however, there are majority languages, whose population may vary from 96% (Kerala) to 63% (Manipur). 18 languages are listed in the Constitution for certain specific purposes, and independent of these specified purposes, they benefit most from the power and resources of the State. These 18 languages constitute 95.8% of the population in 1981. There is thus a collective majority (Annamalai 1994).

Now this is very clearly one type of application of linguistics in that it provides a description of a language situation based on an interaction between the classification of the linguist and the interpretation of the Census of India's officials, themselves it would appear influenced by the views of linguists. But the account goes further because it also attempts to interpret the data by concluding that there are no 'majority' languages in India. All languages enjoy 'minority' status at the national level and therefore 'there is a collective majority'. In other words the language situation in India represents a majority through minorities, a kind of multicultural-ism of languages. Notice that this is an interpretation which is put bald on the record. There is no argument and even less no thesis. Nor does it take any account of the other influences on the language situation, in particular the political, the religious, the social class, the level of education, the influence of the media and so on. These are all part of the language situation of India and all have something to say about the definition of 'a language'. Annamalai uses the term 'language' as though it was a given. But that is not the case, even in linguistics. It is less so in sociolinguistics, where the definition of 'a language' is seen to be as much political as linguistic. The gross number of 1,652 (or 4,000), which is reduced first to 200 and then to 18, is strictly a political rather than a linguistic categorisation. But we are presented with these data as though the status of 'a language' was perfectly clear. Such linguistic classification is based on the 'language family' tradition of classification and assumes that languages change over time by contact only with other languages, rather like the human genetic descent paradigm.

But this is only part of the story and while for the linguist such philological arguments are understandably sealed off from other factors, this surely cannot be the case for an applied linguistics account of a language situation which must take these other factors into consideration. Indeed it explains the applied linguist's reaction to such an account as that set out above: what relevance does this have for me?

Such a reaction is of course that of the applied linguist whose interests are also in language situations. For the applied linguist does not approach the language situation of India (or anywhere) with the intention of describing it in order to say what it looks like. That is not the applied linguist's interest. The applied linguistic interest is not descriptivist but it does have an analogy to the linguistic approach mentioned above, which asks how far this new set of data relates to (tests out) some supposedly overarching theory. Where the applied linguist starts is with a necessary question, necessary in the sense that it arises as a problem demanding action within the language situation. So what sort of question(s) is the applied linguist likely to pose with regard to the language situation of India?

Language situations do not exist in a vacuum or in a laboratory. They exist in nation-states and affect (and are affected by) all the institutions that exist within a modern state: administration, education, law, medicine, religion, business, commerce, media, tourism and hospitality, entertainment, sport and so on.

For the applied linguist working in India the questions have to do with the social facts of the situation:

- communication within and across these institutions
- access to a vehicular language by various groups
- the extent to which linguistic autonomy of the States restricts mobility
- the role of English in the creation and maintenance of an Indian elite
- the extent to which Hindi is increasingly dominant through its control over resources
- the gap between official language policy and the situation in rural and urban schools
- English as a symbolic rather than an instrumental policy

Thus the applied linguist's approach to the last issue (English as a symbolic rather than an instrumental policy) might be concerned with (at least) two problems:

1. Why is English taught so widely in India when its results are so unsatisfactory?
2. How can the teaching of English be improved?

With regard to the first question, the applied linguist would note that English is taught throughout India, mostly ineffectively. Also that increasingly in those States where Hindi is not the official language (in the southern States, for example) selection of the necessary three languages in the curriculum usually means the mother tongue, the State official language (e.g. Tamil) and then English. This seems to be a reaction to the Constitution requirement that every child should study English and Hindi (the two national languages of India) plus the local language. English is therefore the preferred language. And that in spite of its lack of success for learners. Why so? Is it the triumph of hope over experience (as Dr Johnson described second marriages)? Is it resistance to the spread of Hindi? And why are the results so bad? Is it some kind of inertia because in reality the majority of the needs of India institutionally are served by the substantial private educational sector in which typically the medium of instruction (not simply one of the second languages) is English?

With regard to the second question, the applied linguist would first collect empirical evidence that the teaching of English does indeed need improvement – of course what is meant here is substantial improvement since always and everywhere all teaching can be improved. Then on the reasonable assumption that the teaching of English is in need of considerable improvement (see the discussion of the previous question), various factors would need to be isolated. The teachers: who are they, what training have they received, how good is their proficiency in English, what is the status of the teacher in this society? Then the resources (including textbooks and so on), the curriculum, the assessment system, the attitudes towards learning English as opposed to (1) being seen to be studying it and (2) knowing it.

These then are the kinds of practical issues the applied linguist would pursue in relation to this question about the symbolic versus instrumental status of English in India. Similar approaches could be made to the other issues set out above which would interest the applied linguist (but not it seems the linguist) in relation to the language situation of India.

What I want to do now is to take the two more specialised examples, those of Language and Gender and of Clinical Linguistics and to examine in some detail what linguists and applied linguists find of interest in these topics, how their purposes differ, what kinds of techniques the two approaches use and what skills they draw on in their pursuit of these topics.

3 LANGUAGE AND GENDER

There appears to be a permanent tension in all linguistic-driven studies of language between change and stability, between variation and stasis, between difference and sameness, the individual and the group. In general we can suggest that it is on the change aspect that the linguist focuses while the applied linguist is more concerned with the sameness aspect. Thus the linguist has traditionally been interested in the diachronic characteristic of language (much as the biologist is primarily concerned with species evolution), while the applied linguist takes greater account of the synchronic. Of course the linguist deals in grammatical rules and in lexical entries but these are always to be seen as somehow temporary, open to question and primarily belonging to one idiolect or another. This is why the effort to standardise a language is not a primary linguistic activity: when linguists concern themselves, as they do, with standardising (or language engineering as it has somewhat dismissively been called) then they shift into an applied mode. This is also the case for dictionary writing, and even more clearly for language-teaching textbook writing. But for applied linguists these stabilising projects are the very stuff of their professional activity since they see their professional responsibility as that of providing more efficient uses of language by society, now.

This change–stability difference we see clearly in the extensive work on language and gender in recent years. We should note in passing that gender here does not refer to the traditional gender of grammatical analyses where it stood for a distinction many languages make among word classes. To some extent grammatical gender does coincide with biological sex, but only partially. A useful distinction contrasts male/female for sex with masculine/feminine for grammatical gender.

The distinction is sometimes made in sociolinguistics between the influence of society on language ('society in language') and the influence of language on society ('language in society'): by society in language is meant the systematic influence of social forces on language (e.g. a language variety unique to a social class such as the royal court or the adoption of a new phonetic or prosodic feature such as the high rise tone, which we discuss below); by language in society is meant the influence of language on various social institutions (e.g. language planning for education, the choices made by the media – newspapers, broadcasting, television, or the internet – or which languages to use in various settings), the role of language in religion (e.g. the connection between the written holy text and the spoken vernacular). And given the primary concern of linguistics in language-in-itself, which, we have argued, means language in flux, it is inevitable that of the two ways of relating language and society, the focus of the linguist's attention should be on the first, on the impact of society on language and on the ways in which social forces cause language to change. In the same way, the applied linguist's concern for stable states means that he or she is more likely to focus on the influence of language on society and on the extent to which that influence can be gauged and controlled so as to facilitate human inter-action through language.

A similar reciprocal distinction may be made between gender in language and language in gender. (This is hardly surprising since the language–gender relationship is often treated as a subcategory of sociolinguistics.) Gender in language therefore is more the concern of the linguist, while language in gender more that of the applied linguist. As we shall see, their concerns are not discrete: linguists do become involved in applied work when, for example, they advocate the use of 'inclusive language' (on which more below). Similarly, the applied linguist may well, out of interest or as part of necessary ongoing research, get involved in the study of gender influence on language change over time, such as the feminisation of homosexual speech. But we should also recognise that if the applied linguist does become involved in such 'change' research, his or her purpose is not to address the linguist's central concern with language change; rather it is to provide support for some project which could be used to promote the separate status of homosexuals' speech, such as a dictionary or forensic tape models. While recognising the overlap, let us proceed by examining the two concerns at their polarities.

So far we have used 'gender' as though it was the normal term. But is it? Why gender rather than sex? For the linguist's interest in language-in-itself there is strictly no need to make the sex–gender distinction that is nowadays widely made, according to which sex is biological and gender is social, which is to say that, whatever the sex of an infant, the gender it grows into is attained through a process of socialisation. Since therefore gender is already a secondary influence, based first on biological sex and then on various social processes, the linguist is likely to see gender (in this sense of socialisation) as less important than the major sex distinction: what interests the linguist, we might suggest, is the maleness and the femaleness of language. Of course some biological males will be socialised as females and vice versa; of course the male–female distinction is never absolute; and equally of course linguists in their reporting may well refer to the distinction they are making as that of gender rather than that of sex because they, like all of us, prefer not to offend particular sensitivities. Whether it is called sex or gender in language, then, what are the kinds of areas that are of interest to the linguist?

3.1 High-rise intonation

In recent years, attention has been drawn to the increasing use of a particular type of rising statement intonation in what are traditionally known to be falling-tone accents. This is the use of the 'high rising' contour ... this usage ... has certainly been a very noticeable feature of Australian and New Zealand English, at least since the 1960s, and its greater frequency in the latter country suggests that it may well have originated there.

(Crystal 1995: 249)

Why is it used? Why should a statement end with an intonation pattern which would normally be associated with the function of a question? Any explanation needs to take into account the descriptive findings of several recent linguistic studies. One such study found that women used it twice as much as men (but teenagers, the working class and ethnic minorities also used it frequently). The tone appears to be preferred by the less powerful members of society.

It acts as an (unconscious) expression of uncertainty and lack of confidence, perhaps even of subservience and deference ... Explanations for its use vary but one influential view is that women have come to use the tone because of their subservience to men: other non-powerful groups have then followed on.

(ibid)

3.2 Leading change

Women in the lead of language change is exactly what Labov (1966, 1994) claimed in his sociolinguistic results. It is what Chambers and Hardwick (1986, in Crystal 1995: 342) found in their study of changes affecting the diphthong /au/ in Vancouver and Toronto. The phonetic quality of the Canadian production of this diphthong (known as 'Canadian raising') has long been well known as a major distinction between Canadian and American spoken English. This distinction, according to Chambers and Hardwick, is now disappearing. They found that the distinctive feature of the vowel was often replaced by one whose quality was either further forward in the mouth or more open (non-raising) or both. The effect was to make the production of words such as ('house', 'about') more like versions of the diphthong used in the USA. But what is relevant for our purposes is that 'fronting correlates with sex in both cities, with women the leading innovators' (Crystal 1995: 342).

3.3 Different language?

We have referred above to social class differences in language (use). Similar differences have been reported with regard to gender differences whereby men's and women's speech differ. 'At one extreme,' comments Holmes (1991), 'the sexes use different languages, as reported for longhouse groups in the Amazon Basin, where language differences assist in maintaining exogamic divisions … At the other, sex differences involve fine phonetic discriminations and relative frequencies of occurrence, rather than absolute differences in women's and men's usage' (Holmes 1991: 207).

She notes that in societies where there is clear societal sex-role differentiation there are likely to be sex-exclusive linguistic differences, while in societies 'where sex roles overlap, it is more common to find sex-preferential differences' (ibid).

3.4 Use of standard

Many sociolinguists have reported the use by women of more standard (as opposed to vernacular) variants than men (e.g. in English the standard 'ing' as opposed to the vernacular 'in' as in talk*ing*/talk*in*). Indeed Trudgill (1983: 162) refers to this finding as 'the single most consistent finding to emerge from sociolinguistics over the past twenty years'. Explanations as to why this is so vary from women's social status being more dependent on appearance, to the vernacular having more masculine connotations. Both the explanations and the findings themselves have been challenged by feminist sociolinguists (Milroy 1987) and various other proposals put forward, such as the importance of social networks, of solidarity among women (and presumably men) and of variants (such as glottalisation) used predominantly to signal gender affiliation. What all these findings indicate is that sex (or gender) does indeed operate as a major trigger of social dialect choice. It is not necessary, it seems, to seek explanations in terms of power or even solidarity: what the findings reveal is that both men and women find ways of marking themselves as men and women in the ways that they use language. Furthermore, they continue to do so and therefore if the other sex catches up, as it were, by taking on the standard forms or the high rise tone or the fronting, then they move on to some other distinguishing marker of difference.

3.5 Politeness

Other markers of difference that linguists have researched include politeness features, which appear to be sex-exclusive in languages such as Japanese but possibly sex-preferential in English; conversational interaction where the finding that men are more combative and women more supportive tends to find approval; cross-cultural differences and attitudes to women's talk. Attitudes are, it is claimed, manipulable: the study of attitudes in social psychology and elsewhere tends to be at the meeting-point between the more theoretical and the more applied. So it is here. An interest in language attitudes is one that linguists and applied linguists share. For linguists an interest in language attitudes can offer explanations for the type of female lead in language change to which we have referred. For the applied linguist the same interest can be used to explain success/failure in language learning.

3.6 Boys and girls

A somewhat similar interest in sex differences (particularly in the earlier years) requires applied linguists to study language achievement by boys and girls – by language achievement here is meant second/foreign-language learning as well as schooled literacy in the mother tongue or L1, by which here we mean the school language, understood as the medium of instruction in all areas of the school work. Just as in the studies mentioned above, the common finding here is that females are ahead: girls do better than boys in all verbal areas of the school. The explanation typically offered is that girls are more verbal than boys, that this is hard-wired into the brain: indeed it is curious that the ubiquity of this explanation for what goes on in schools does not reach over into those other areas of male–female differences. I suggested that there was really no need for an explanation – that noting the difference was enough, but even so it is surprising that the explanation of achievement differences, the view that females are more verbal is not used to explain why females are more advanced in language change.

Applied linguists have certainly taken a keen interest in this school difference between boys and girls: and it must be stressed (and it is worth doing so because it acts as a distinguisher of the interest between linguists and applied linguists) that their reason for that interest is not that they are primarily interested in the language of boys and girls but that they are interested in how boys and girls use language so that they can take action to improve the teaching and learning of both groups or to facilitate intercommunication between boys and girls.

3.7 Language in gender

We have used the word 'manipulable' in relation to the acting on language attitudes in order to try to change them and we have suggested that this intervention goes to the heart of the applied linguist's interest in language and gender. While the linguist is, as we have seen, concerned with the role of gender in language, the ways in which gender (or indeed sex) affects both language structure and language use, the applied linguist's professional role as interventionist means that he or she is concerned with the language–gender relationship the other way round, with language in gender, paralleling the impact of language on society.

What impact does language have on gender? The most obvious answer is that it promotes and, above all perhaps, enshrines unequal power relations, including of course negative stereotyping of women. It should be pointed out that making such a direct causal link, when all that we can be sure of is that there is a correlation between language and power, is disputed. It is further disputed that changing the language will necessarily change the power imbalance. Language, it may be argued, is merely the messenger not the message. Nevertheless, there is recognition that being politically correct, which is what wishing to change the language of gender has been mocked for being, has the merit of compelling awareness of the power imbalance which the inertia of a fixed power relationship, enshrined in a fossilised terminology, hides from us all. The rationale is similar to that of exploring language attitudes with a view to changing them, a view which takes for granted that attitudes are malleable and can be changed so as to promote good intergroup relations. Similarly, while power in itself is notoriously hard currency, language can be changed through engineering: such change may do no more than create a temporary awareness of the inequalities, but it may possibly do more and help ameliorate them. Whether or not this is true, considerable effort has in recent years been directed at attempting to make the language more equal with the intention of redressing the gender–power relation.

3.8 Sexism

> Some of the most important linguistic changes affecting English since the 1960s have arisen from the ways society has come to look differently at the practices and consequences of sexism ... There is now a widespread awareness, which was lacking a generation ago, of the ways in which language covertly displays social attitudes towards men and women. The criticisms have been mainly directed at the biases built into English vocabulary and grammar which reflect a traditionally male-orientated view of the world and which have been interpreted as reinforcing the low status of women in society. All the main European languages have been affected, but English more than most, because of the early impact of the feminist movement in the USA.
>
> (Crystal 1995: 368)

Bringing sexism in language into consciousness, at least among the educated, has not been difficult. No doubt Crystal is correct in suggesting that the feminist movement has spearheaded this development. The effect has been to encourage change by individuals who are sensitive to the issue and by organisations which wish to promote an ethical stance (or unkindly avoid litigation for sexual harassment). Implementing change, however, has not been easy.

In vocabulary, words of masculine gender which are commonly used to refer to people, both male and female, have been targeted. Thus, 'chairman' becomes 'chairperson' or 'chair' and 'policeman' 'police officer'. Marital status for men is not marked linguistically: 'Mr' being neutral as to whether married or not. The introduction of 'Ms' for women (with some success) attempts to equalise in terms of address. Special vocabulary for women in professions where there is no need for gender distinctions is now disfavoured: thus 'actor' not 'actress', 'waiter' not 'waitress'. It is frequently pointed out that sexism is implicit in the unmarked status of the male form whereby morphological processes take that form as the base and add affixes ('-ess', '-ette', '-ine') to signal female. What is not in question is that languages typically contain far more terms to describe women than men, usually derogatorily, and that even when they are not at first derogatory they tend over time to acquire negative connotations (e.g. harlot, tart).

In grammar the focus of change has been on the third-person singular pronoun in English, which is always marked for gender. Holmes points out that

> [E]xperiments exploring people's perceptions report that 'man' and 'he' are consistently interpreted as referring to males, despite generic contexts. The problem arises when a pronoun is needed in combination with a sex-neutral noun (such as 'patient') or an indefinite pronoun (such as 'anybody'). Alternative solutions are to use a hybrid (e.g. 'he/she') or the plural ('their'). Thus the following solutions are among those found: all have their critics:
> 1. If a patient needs attention urgently, he should ring his bell.
> 2. If a patient needs attention urgently, he/she should ring his/her bell.
> 3. If a patient needs attention urgently, he or she should ring his or her bell.
> 4. If a patient needs attention urgently, they should ring their bell.
> 5. If patients need attention urgently, they should ring their bell.
>
> (Holmes 1991: 214)

The long history of attempts to establish an epicene pronoun in English is well documented by Baron (1981) and there is some suggestion that preferred usage now is for 'they' as an alternative generic pronoun.

Discourse patterns also have been subject to scrutiny, with attention given to such inequalities as order of mention ('boys and girls', 'man and wife', 'I now pronounce you man and wife', 'Lords and Ladies', though 'Ladies and Gentlemen' is ignored as somehow slipping through the sexist net) and value of mention (e.g. 'the bomb was responsible for the deaths of seven people including one man'). Changes to existing texts are less common and no one seriously attempts to rebowdlerise Shakespeare. But those texts that claim a universal appeal, such as the Bible, the Prayer Book, have been carefully edited so as to offer a more inclusive language of mention and address

(Doody 1980). We might speculate that such changes are in the direct line of the increasing vernacularisation of religious texts on the grounds that just as the early translations into German, English and so on were attempts to make congregations feel that they owned those texts in ways that they could not when they were only in Latin or Greek, so the further inclusivising takes account of the reality of many congregations which are (in Christian churches) largely made up of women, who find themselves excluded by the traditional male-dominated language of the Bible.

Change, however incomplete, there certainly has been, and it has been remarkably quick. It has affected writing far more than speaking and in the written language it is likely to be permanent since publishing companies and other normative bodies now often insist on the avoidance of sexist language.

It may be that changes in English are easier than in languages (such as French) where there is greater morphological marking of grammatical gender. Even so, it is the case that in often very different ways all languages exhibit sexist language and the thrust of this language in gender movement has been to encourage first consciousness-raising and change where that is possible.

To what extent are applied linguists (rather than linguists) involved in these interventions? The answer is a great deal, first of all through participation in proposing and encouraging and explaining the changes (e.g. Cooper 1982; Holmes 1991; Cameron 1985), and second through offering a radical critique.

After all, what the applied linguist is able to do is to bring into consideration about language problems not only the linguistic view, or the feminist view but other views too, including what effect change may or may not have and to what extent change will be acceptable. The linguist's single-minded interest in language change and the effect that has on the internal structure of language means that he/she is more likely to assume that deliberate change, especially when it appears so desirable, will be effective and will change the structure permanently. The applied linguist on the other hand is more likely to be sceptical and to acknowledge that deliberate change has never been easy to bring about and that in any case even if the language changes, that does not necessarily change the power inequalities, which is the main thrust of the movement to rid language of its linguistic sexism.

3.9 Applied linguistics and linguistics applied

In spite of their main interest in gender-in-language, linguists also work at the other end on language-in-gender, where their theoretical concern with the change in language that is led by gender becomes a concern to intervene against the perceived injustice of linguistic sexism. Interestingly, and of course paradoxically, the act of intervention contravenes what we have suggested is their linguistic concern, that is with change. That is to say: if language is of its nature variable, over time and space, which might be called the linguistic creed, then any attempt to fix it, what Swift referred to as 'ascertaining', will necessarily fail. What must happen, surely, is that even those changes which are accepted very soon become overtaken by new non-deliberate changes, which may very well return the language in gender relation to the status quo, unless in the meantime those non-linguistic power relations themselves change and so render nugatory their operationalising in language.

The skills the two professional groups call on in these areas are not all that dissimilar; it would be surprising if they were since (as we have seen before) the linguist may also work at the applied end and the applied linguist may research the area of some aspect of gender in language – although, as we have seen, always with some ameliorative outcome in view. But at the poles the skills and techniques are different: the linguist will analyse, survey and interview. The applied linguist will test, observe and, above all, evaluate. But more than anything the applied linguist, unlike the linguist, will examine the language in gender situation in context and consider any proposed remedy in terms of the history of the area and of the effects on the stakeholders' interest in the language of that situation. We might propose that the linguist operates deductively and the applied linguist inductively; while reminding ourselves that that famous opposition is in the event untenable since each requires the other; neither can stand alone.

4 CLINICAL LINGUISTICS

On the face of it clinical linguistics is very definitely applied work since it sets out to diagnose what problems there are in an individual's communication system and then attempts to provide appropriate remedies. The best-known practitioner is the speech therapist (or pathologist) who works with childhood speech defects (caused for example by a cleft palate) and with adult aphasias (caused by strokes and by road and other accidents). But there is more to it.

The speech therapist's work draws on descriptive work in language acquisition and language loss, including sophisticated speech synthesis using state of the art computer technology, on phonetic and grammatical accounts of deficit, what we might call (drawing on the analogy of pedagogical grammar) a deficit grammar, that is to say an algorithmic inventory drawn up to exemplify the areas of loss most likely to be experienced by the therapist's patients (e.g. the protocols of Anthony et al. (1971) and of Crystal et al. (1975/1976). The linguist's interest is, once again, primarily in change: to what extent is non-acquisition (as exemplified by the child with some speech impairment) systematic in that it relates regularly (but negatively) to so-called normal acquisition. Similarly with loss (whether through age, illness or trauma): to what extent does loss mirror acquisition so that it is possible to establish a relationship between the two? While such research is of obvious applied interest since it would allow swifter and more precise diagnosis both of children's defects and of adults' traumas, it also is of profound concern to the linguist's understanding of what language is through knowing what it is not. The path is through changed states to failure of changed states to what it is that causes language to exist at any one time as a system and which enables it to change into another system.

Where does the applied linguist fit into clinical linguistics? If my premise is accepted, then what drives the applied linguist is an interest in achieving stable states and in improving (and ameliorating) communication. Thus the applied linguist will have two roles in clinical linguistics (and thus, of course, overlapping with but at the same time separate from the role of the linguist who becomes involved in applications here). The first role is that of the speech therapist him/herself. And the second is that of the trainer of speech therapists. Indeed the two go together, because once we accept that the applied linguist has a role in the training of speech therapists then the trained speech therapist becomes, by definition, an applied linguist.

4.1 Language impairment

Language impairment means the absence of some part of the language faculty: we say 'part' advisedly since the absence of the whole of the language faculty is probably found only in completely vegetative states. Impairment can occur at any age: the child may be born lacking some physical or mental attribute which prevents or slows the development of so-called normal language. At any age an individual may suffer loss of control of part of the language faculty through illness or accident. And some losses which occur throughout life following trauma of some kind occur regularly (though not universally) among the elderly, brought on by the normal process of ageing, which after all can be regarded as a form of trauma.

4.2 Kinds of impairment

Among young children the common impairments concern physical disabilities such as cleft palate, emotional states which cause stammering, and mental retardations which slow down normal speech acquisition. There are also special conditions such as dyslexia and dysarthria, which may or may not be altered states of consciousness, but clearly, whatever their cause, require intervention and treatment. Then there are the large-scale physical disabilities of the young (though also acquired, again through illness, in later life), disabilities such as blindness and deafness. Accidents (industrial, traffic and so on) and illness (e.g. stroke) bring about particular physical impairments in parts of the brain and so cause various types of aphasia. These aphasias may (but need not) affect whole language repertoires among bilinguals and multilinguals, in the sense that if, for example, speaking (or one component of speaking) is lost, then it is lost in every language of the repertoire. What the elderly – usually the very elderly – may experience is loss through gradual attrition of the components of their language repertoire. Thus, they may lose the ability to nominate and to recall proper names. Such loss again typically affects the whole repertoire of bi- and multilinguals. But a further humiliation of the bilingual old is that they commonly regress to an earlier state so that later acquired languages among adult migrants, for example, are lost and only the language used in childhood remains. In all such cases what we observe is the application of the rule of Ribot: first in, last out.

4.3 Linguistic analysis

The linguist's interest in these altered states is precisely in their alteration: what is it that makes them different (what has changed) from the normal state? 'Before intervention can take place,' writes Crystal, 'the specialist needs to have identified exactly what the nature of the disability is. This requires an analysis of those areas of language that are particularly affected – whether structural (in phonetics, phonology, graphology, grammar, lexicon, discourse) or functional (language in use) ... Effective intervention presupposes the accurate identification of where the problems lie' (Crystal 1995: 434).

And in order to carry out the analysis of those areas of language that are particularly affected what the specialist needs is a comprehensive map of 'normal' language development and a diagnostic set of tools to employ in pinpointing accurate identification of where the problems lie. (Note that diagnostic instruments for the language impaired are mirror images of the proficiency and achievement tests used to chart normal development in language learning.)

'The target of intervention,' Crystal continues, 'is to bring the deficient language from where it is to where it ought to be. A knowledge of the stages of normal language acquisition ... is therefore also a prerequisite of successful intervention.' And he concludes, 'The specialist needs to be aware of which teaching techniques and strategies are available and appropriate' (ibid).

Crystal has here identified three particular kinds of skill for the specialist: linguistic analysis, disability diagnosis and pedagogic know-how. The linguist's interest is clear in the first of these because of the major involvement of linguists with charting the process of language acquisition, originally in the L1 but increasingly now in the L2 as well. In the second area, diagnosis, we find the linguist's and the applied linguist's interests overlapping since for the linguist the development of diagnostic instruments is where they shift into an applied mode (but observe below who are the authors of such instruments) and for the applied linguist the construction of such instruments is central to what they consider to be their normal professional activity. And then in the third area, that of pedagogy and of remedial intervention, we are clearly in the area of the applied linguist and not of the linguist. At least that is the case if my claim that practising speech therapists are (like language teachers who have gone through courses in applied linguistics) applied linguists.

4.4 The language problem

For the applied linguist, interested in clinical linguistics, the issue is: what is the problem? At its simplest the problem appears to be that there are in society individuals who are linguistically (or communicatively) impaired. This is 'a problem' because the prevailing view of society is that to treat the impaired (in school, the community, in work) as though they were not impaired would be socially unjust and (probably) inefficient. From an economic point of view such people are a nonreturnable cost which might be reduced if their impairments could be alleviated or remediated. Such people therefore need treatment and it is at that third of Crystal's stages that the applied linguist's action starts. But before the problem can be addressed, two further stages are required. The first is to determine who it is that needs the treatment. This is an issue that looms much larger for the applied linguist working in speech and language therapy services than it is for the applied linguist working in language teaching. Since the language teacher works with so-called normal children and adults the service offered is for all: of course there are situations in which selection is made, on the grounds for example of need, ability, aptitude and so on and in those circumstances assessment of some kind may be carried out. But for the therapist applied linguist it is always the case that a selection must be made in order to determine just who are in need of treatment: it is as though what the therapist operates is a negative correlative of what the teacher uses; his/her diagnosis is of the absence of ability while the teacher who is using selective measures operates on the basis of the presence of ability. Accurate selection of those in need of treatment is therefore necessary, and for that to be successful appropriate assessment instruments are needed. But even before such instruments can be produced there is a further more fundamental stage and that is the mapping of normal developmental stages. When the linguist moves into application in clinical linguistics what he/she does is to work from a chart of normal development. If the applied linguist needs to look behind treatment for the purposes of assessment, then it is likely he/she will operate with a chart bringing together normal and impaired development. This suggests that a clinical/deficit grammar resembles a pedagogical grammar.

4.5 The crucial difference?

Is it then the case that the linguist moves from theory to description and then to application? Not of course in all cases, for individual linguists themselves take up different positions in their professional work along the line. The applied linguist, on the other hand, starts from the problem which requires practice of some kind and then in order to attack the problem moves back towards theory, taking in description and clinical methodology (including instrumental methodologies such as assessment procedures) along the way. Is this the crucial linguist–applied linguist distinction?

4.6 Theoretical arguments

Let us look at two areas of theoretical argument which are important to clinical linguistics. The first is the linguistic theory on which the analysis of language, to which Crystal refers above (structural and functional), is based. The linguist involving him/herself in clinical linguistics is likely to choose a theoretical model that allows for the kinds of application necessary, in other words it is likely to be a model that takes account of both structure and function and is less concerned with current disputes of theoretical concern simply because they prevent the kind of full descriptive apparatus (they pose too many doubts) that the application will need. Such a linguist is therefore likely to make use of a more traditional-type grammar or a functional grammar, which may not be up to date but will serve the purposes of clinical work.

The second type of theoretical interest is that of the study of aphasia:

> Two main and opposing approaches were evident in the late 1800s and early 1900s and are still evident now. Indeed, they form the basis of ongoing discussion which continues up to the present day.
>
> (Kerr 1993: 102)

> The first was a physically based approach which held that different anatomical structures were responsible for particular language functions. These could, there-fore, be selectively impaired by damage to discrete areas of the brain. The thrust of study was to determine where different language functions were located, in order to 'map functions on to anatomical structures and thus be able to predict localisation of lesion according to surface language symptomatology. Thus Broca (1865) and Wernicke (1874) mapped expressive and comprehension skills on to the third frontal convolution of the left hemisphere and the temporal convolution of the left hemisphere, respectively.
>
> (ibid)

> The opposing approach viewed aphasia symptomatology as indicative of a single underlying disorder of language, manifested in different ways in different patients … The rationale was the belief that aphasia symptomatology, however diverse, was an outward sign of one underlying deficit, which could vary in severity and be further complicated by additional sensory, motor or other impairment.
>
> (ibid: 103)

> Current theories of acquired language disorder include both traditional theories, and many remain strongly localisationalist. However, recently emerging disciplines such as cognitive neuropsychology and the study of functional communication attempt to enlarge our understanding of language impairment and its functional effects and show a move away from traditional theoretical frameworks. They reflect a rejection of the supremacy of neuroanatomy.
>
> (ibid: 104)

What is striking here is not that theoretical discussion of aphasia continues to develop: it would be surprising if it did not; what is striking is how far apart these two areas of theoretical concern are. The first is clearly central to the linguist's professional interest; the second far removed. Indeed it is unlikely that the linguist will have much interest in aphasia unless he/she has already specialised in clinical linguistics. In practice it appears that some phoneticians have indeed done so but remarkably few grammarians. In other words those who do are already committed, in some sense, to an applied linguistic view of language.

For the applied linguist the situation is both more difficult and easier: more difficult because he/she may not have the linguistic theory at hand to apply; easier because for him/her both the linguistic and the aphasic must be understood but neither has priority over the other. The applied linguist therefore who gets involved in clinical linguistics is less likely than the linguist to be dominated in his/her thinking by any linguistic theory: theory then becomes the servant and not the master.

So if the linguist does make a linear approach to practice from theory, the applied linguist surveys the field from the position of practice and then takes account of any theory/description that has a bearing on language. This does not make applied linguistics non-theoretical but it does mean that it is not mono theoretical.

4.7 Combined approach

Those who have produced the necessary instrumentation for diagnostic assessment are not in the main linguists (but see Crystal et al. 1975/1976) but applied linguists (including speech therapists who have been trained in applied linguistics), phoneticians, medics and engineers. Thus Anthony et al. (who produced the Edinburgh Articulation Test 1971) included an engineer, a medical doctor specialising in neuro-pediatrics and two speech therapists. Laver et al. (1981) who produced a normative Vocal Profiles Analysis scheme included a phonetician and two speech therapists. Wirz writes that current practice tends to favour approaches more from cognitive psychology (Byng and Coltheart 1986) than from medicine, which in the past was heavily dominated by the anatomical (and therefore localisation) view of impairment. She characterises the development in the twentieth century from individual diagnostic to comparative group assessment with a return to a greater (and better informed) study of the whole communicative person. In all of this linguistics plays a part, but a small part. We see in the training of clinical linguists such as speech therapists both a parallel with the development of applied linguistics in their need to draw on a wide variety of informing disciplines and in part an insight into the role of applied linguistics within speech therapy itself, since for many (but not all) practitioners, speech therapy is a branch of applied linguistics.

Wirz (1993) writes of 'the richness of variety that offers the speech and language therapist the challenge in any assessment undertaken' (Wirz 1993: 14). That richness of variety is also necessarily seen in the training the therapist receives. Crystal (1995: 434) writes of a 'broad-based course of study, including medical, psychological, social, educational and linguistic components, as well as the fostering of personal clinical and teaching skills'.

Courses can be broad-based in two ways: either by ranging widely across many subject areas (medicine, psychology, sociology, education and (applied) linguistics) or by taking for granted a wider than normal frame of reference to any one subject. Thus the applied linguistic approach to clinical linguistics is likely to consider impairment as an aspect of loss, itself the negative inverse of positive language retention in the individual. The parallel type of loss in society is represented as language decay or language death (when a whole language dies through abandonment by its speakers, most commonly through death), while the parallel social retention is referred to as spread. All parameters may be regarded as aspects of language shift. Now placing shift as the superordinate means that applied linguistics has admitted its own interest in language change. But we should make two comments here. The first is that applied linguistics comes to this theoretical construct not from above but through the need to explain and understand different types of loss; and the second is that the applied linguist remains not fundamentally interested in shift in itself: what he/she is doing is attempting to understand it better in order to stabilise it, however momentarily, and so orient and remedy the impaired to that stable moment.

4.8 Individual and social loss

What this allows us to do is to link individual language loss with social loss, that is loss by groups, both L1 and L2. Those who lose their L1 do so usually through contact with some (politically) dominating language group. This may happen through in-migration (e.g. Celtic language speakers, Australian aborigines, American Indians) or by out-migration (e.g. Singaporean Chinese, Guyanan Indians). But of course it may also happen through disappearance of all L1 speakers, although this usually takes place not in isolation but in the context of the earlier example. In other words, it is not that the people themselves die out; their children and grandchildren survive, and may indeed multiply, but they have shifted language to that of the more politically powerful group (Irish to English in Ireland, Latvian to Russian in Latvia).

Why do speakers shift language, and does this have any bearing on the clinical linguist's concern with individual language attrition?

Where there remains a rising generation who have the choice of continuing with the traditional language and shifting to the new, the unwelcome answer is expediency: the old is regarded by the young as lacking utility against the challenge of modernism, not having the prestige associated with consumerism and technology, having outmoded cultural values and so on. Of course there are always counter-positions whereby a strong challenge can be made to such a movement for change from traditional religion and culture (for example in Islam), But the opposition needs to be very strong indeed to have a more than marginal influence and it is difficult to think of any compelling force other than a fundamentalist religion which is strong enough to do so.

The reasons for social loss may not be informative about the reasons for individual impairment, although the attempt to look more carefully at the cover-all explanation of expediency and subject it to analysis does relate to the wider scope now attributed to clinical linguistics which 'may be said to encompass the functional effects of impairment on communicative adequacy and social interaction, and includes the study of emotional factors and normal interaction' (Kerr 1993: 105).

But it is in the areas of just what is lost socially and individually through impairment that we do find common ground.

What is lost as language shifts is that the L1 becomes increasingly influenced by the L2. Thus there is the acculturation of proper names, whereby, for example, Chinese Christian children may be given Christian (that is Western) proper names; there is the loss of productive word formation so that borrowings (and even more new formations) are based not on the morphology of the L1 but on that of the L2; there is lexical loss leading to a lexical creep of L2 words into the L1; there is phonological loss such that new formations are given L2 phonological shape (Dorian 1981).

To what extent does this mirror loss in impairment? In loss brought on by old age in the L2, there is some similarity, in particular in the well-known area of naming, if only because there is somewhere else (the L1) to go, although of course it is in the reverse direction from language shift. However, both with the monolingual elderly and with those suffering from acquired language problems such as aphasia, there is typically nowhere else to resort to (even if the aphasic patient is bilingual since the impairment is not language specific) and so the damage is as much psychological as linguistic and treatment must adjust accordingly.

5 CONCLUSION

I have argued in this chapter that there appears to be a permanent tension in all linguistic studies of language between a focus on stability and a focus on change. To that end I have looked at three areas of common interest to both linguists and applied linguists: language in situation, language and gender, and clinical linguistics. Linguists and applied linguists work in all three areas and while their work can overlap (e.g. developing assessment instruments for speech therapists, encouraging more inclusive language to combat sexism in the area of language and gender) their orientation is janus-like, looking in opposite directions, with language change as the linguistic agenda driving the linguist in search of evidence regarding linguistic theory, and language stability, the providing of more efficient means of communication in the society we live in now, motivating the applied linguist.

In Chapter 4 I focus on the major role of applied linguistics in language teaching, especially the teaching of second languages and therefore with language-teacher education. This role is dominant in the field and is seen by some as being the proper concern of applied linguistics.

Applied linguistics and language learning/teaching

Homines dum docent, discunt.
(Even when they teach, men learn.)
(Seneca, *Epistula Morales*, 7/8.)

1 INTRODUCTION

In the last chapter we considered three areas of common interest to both linguists and applied linguists and attempted to distinguish the purposes and procedures of the two professions. I proposed that linguists and applied linguists typically look in opposite directions, with language change as the linguistic agenda driving the linguist in search of evidence regarding linguistic theory, while the applied linguist is motivated by the providing of more efficient means of communication in the society we live in. I turn next to the field of language teaching and learning: this is dominant in applied linguistics, in the sense that more applied linguists specialise in this field than in any other. There is a view, held by some linguists and applied linguists, that language teaching and language-teacher education are the only proper concerns of applied linguistics.

The chapter begins with a presentation of the arguments for and against confining applied linguistics to a concern with second-language teaching and learning. Then I take the examples of two 'problems' in the field, first the optimum age problem (which we have already raised in Chapter 2) and second an investigation into the validity of a large-scale English language proficiency test, the English Language Testing Service (ELTS) test, the predecessor of IELTS (see below), and in particular the construct used in the design of that test, that of English for specific purposes. These two 'problems' are considered from the point of view of a number of relevant factors, opening up a discussion on what it is that needs to be taken into account when the applied linguist is faced with a problem in language education. Finally, I consider the methodology used by the applied linguist in operating on a problem and to that end I take as examples four areas of importance in language teaching, second language acquisition, proficiency language testing, the teaching of languages for specific purposes and curriculum design.

2 CLAIMS

In spite of the widening range of activities undertaken by applied linguistics and in spite of the general agreement about the reach of its provenance claimed in the Statutes of the International Association of Applied Linguistics:

> L'Association a pour but de promouvoir les recherches dans les domaines de la linguistique appliquée, comme par exemple l'acquisition, l'enseignement, l'emploi et le traitement des langues, d'en diffuser les résultats et de promouvoir la coordination et la coopération interdisciplinaires et internationales dans ces domaines.
>
> (Article 2 of the AILA Statutes 1964)

> (The Association's purpose is to promote research in the areas of applied linguistics, for example language learning, language teaching, language use and language planning, to publish the results of this research and to promote international and interdisciplinary cooperation in these areas.
>
> Article 2 of the AILA Statutes 1964)

and proudly asserted in Kaplan and Widdowson (1992):

> the application of linguistic knowledge to real-world problems ... whenever knowledge about language is used to solve a basic language-related problem, we may say that applied linguistics is being practiced. Applied is a technology which makes abstract ideas and research findings accessible and relevant to the real world; it mediates between theory and practice.
>
> (ibid: 76)

and in Crystal (1992: 24), also opting for the more inclusive approach:

> the use of linguistics theories, methods and findings in elucidating and solving problems to do with language which have arisen in other areas of experience. The domain of applied linguistics is extremely wide and includes foreign language learning and teaching, lexicography, style, forensic speech analysis and the theory of reading.

and in Wilkins (1994):

> [T]he study of the uses that man makes of the language endowment and of the problems that he encounters in doing so is the subject matter of applied linguistics.
>
> (Wilkins 1994: 162)

there remain the cautionary voices concerned to restrict its scope so that it does not appear that applied linguistics claims to be a theory of everything! For example:

> [T]he majority of work in applied linguistics has been directly concerned with language teaching and learning.
>
> (Strevens 1994: 81)

and Wilkins again (1994):

> the field which has so far generated the greatest body of research and publication, namely that of language learning and teaching.

(ibid: 163)

and again:

> [I]n practice applied linguistics has developed so far as an enterprise principally dedicated to creating a better understanding of the processes of language, especially second language, learning.

(ibid:164)

A position he welcomes on the grounds that otherwise: 'In its widest sense no coherent field of applied linguistics exists' (ibid: 163).

3 A PERSONAL ACCOUNT

Alice Kaplan's 1993 evocative account of her own love story with learning and teaching French reminds us that not all language learning is doomed. At the same time, she is blunt about the difficult task of being a language teacher: '[L]anguage teachers are always in search of the foolproof method that will work for any living language and will make people perfectly at home in their acquired tongue' (ibid: 130).

Kaplan has gone beyond the lure of method having seen its infinite regress:

> I was told the story of language teaching when I was learning to become a teacher. Once upon the time, the story goes, all languages were taught like Greek and Latin. Learning was based on grammar rules and translation. You talked in your own language about the dead language you saw written down. Then in the late nineteenth century came the Direct Method, the ancestor of Berlitz. You spoke in class in the language you were trying to teach; you worked on pronunciation; you practiced grammar out loud.

(ibid)

Based on grammar rules and translation: the dead hand of linguistics has long weighed heavily:

> From the forties on, people looked to linguistics to revolutionise language teaching: language classrooms would be 'labs' with scientific data and results; the emphasis would be on speaking, speaking like natives and learning like native speakers do. In the late 1950s, Noam Chomsky argued that children acquire language more or less automatically by the time they are five and whatever makes it happen can't be duplicated by adults – it has nothing to do with situation. Chomsky's insight did language teachers absolutely no good: they couldn't duplicate genetic processes, and they couldn't hope to reproduce childhood as a model for second-language learning.

(ibid: 130–1)

Given the ease with which new methods arise and are abandoned one after another, it is surprising how attracted language teachers are to new methods. The reason, Kaplan suggests is that: 'Language teaching methods make for a tale of enthusiasm and scepticism, hope and hope dashed. Every once in a while someone comes along and promises a new language method ... Whatever the method, only desire can make a student learn a language, desire and necessity' (ibid: 131).

In spite of the extent of the activity and the attention given to training in method, the fact is, as Kaplan points out:

> Language teaching is badly paid, little recognised, and much maligned. It is left up to native speakers for whom it is stupidly thought to be 'natural', therefore too easy to be of much value. PhDs want to move on from language teaching to the teaching of literature, and theories of literature. Language teaching is too elemental, too bare. You burn out, generating all that excitement about repetition, creating trust, listening, always listening. In literature class you can lean back in the seat and let the book speak for itself. In language class you are constantly moving, chasing after sound.
>
> (Kaplan 1993: 139)

The history of language teaching is, indeed, the history of method. Like fashion in dress/clothes, method in language teaching emerges and disappears, and if one looks far enough it recycles itself after a decent interval. As staleness is to fashion so is failure to method. Since reliance on method alone must of necessity lead to failure, it is inevitable that all methods will be challenged by new or revived alternatives. As Kaplan recognises in the comment already quoted: 'language teachers are always in search of the foolproof method' (ibid: 130).

Language learning and language teaching are 'problems' because they are so often ineffectual. The temptation is always to seek new and therefore 'better' methods of teaching, better methods of learning. Such an unthought-through solution results from faulty diagnosis, which itself derives from a lack of objectivity. The informal foreign language learner who is not making progress is all too easily persuaded that what is needed is to change the methods of learning. And that is also true in formal instruction where the teacher becomes dispirited because the methods in use are not working. Again the solution is to change the method. And for a time the new methods such as direct, mim-mem, communicative, cognitive, technological (Stern 1983) work but then the novelty, the very method effect, begins to wear off and the learning, lacking the halo effect of newness, reverts to its customary lack of progress.

What applied linguistics offers, where its coherence (*pace* Wilkins 1994) lies is in its recognition that the question to ask is not how to improve the learning, but what is it that is not being improved, in other words what it is that is supposed to be being learned. The 'how to improve' question comes from a teacher training tradition where solutions are understandably method directed: what do I do in the classroom on Monday morning? and the answer so often is: learn a new method.

The how question also derives from an approach via linguistics (as Alice Kaplan pointedly notes), the 'linguistics-applied' approach, whereby the diagnosis has to do with the need for the teacher to understand more about linguistics and then the improvement will come from attention to methods, better use of the old or adoption of new. The reason for such naivety in linguistics is that to the linguist knowledge about language will of itself improve language learning while knowledge about language and skill in teaching and learning are unrelated. That is not the case with the applied linguist for whom knowledge about language and skill in teaching and learning are seamlessly linked, since learning and teaching are themselves aspects of knowing about language in the context of second-language acquisition and it is through understanding them better that improvement will come.

That knowledge is partly quite traditional; it is knowledge about *language* in itself, dealing here with language systems; then knowledge about *a language* (usually the one that will be or is the target of teaching), dealing here with language structure; and finally knowledge about language in its interactions, dealing here with acquisition, with cognition and with society.

What this means is that some of the content of a course in applied linguistics which will be of benefit to second language teachers (and by extension to second-language learners) will offer linguistics. But it will not be the whole course (possibly 30 per cent), it will not be identical with courses given to graduate linguistics students and it will take into account in the provision of tasks, workshops, examples and so on, the professional activity of the majority of the students (language teaching). It is important at this stage that students perceive an applied linguistics course as vocationally driven and planned and that their own profession, for example language teaching, is not dismissed or trivialised as uninteresting or not worthwhile.

4 APPLIED LINGUISTICS AND INSTITUTIONAL PROBLEMS

In Chapter 3 we suggested that 'language problems' are the key to understanding applied linguistics. Many of these problems will manifest themselves in individual interactions (my failure to make myself understood when asking directions in a foreign language, your hasty judgement about your interlocutor's social status in the first few seconds of a telephone conversation, and so on) but the applied linguistics enterprise engages itself with such problems only when they are considered by society to be matters of institutional concern. The applied linguist is therefore called on to intervene, to train, to explain and possibly to solve recurring problems in the school, the hospital, the workplace, the law court or the television studio.

Applied linguistics as an enterprise is therefore a research and development activity that sets out to make use of theoretical insights and collect empirical data which can be of use in dealing with institutional language problems. It is not primarily a form of social work with immediate access to individuals in the happenstance of their ongoing social communication, although its findings may of course be helpful to counsellors and teachers faced with these particular problems.

The starting-point for applied-linguistic activities is typically to be presented with an institutional language problem. The purpose of the activity is to provide relevant information which will help those involved understand the issues better; in some cases on the basis of the information it will be possible to offer a solution to the problem. More likely is an explanation of what is involved, setting out the choices available, along with their implications. In earlier chapters we have discussed some of these language problems and indicated certain of the choices that would face those interested in finding a solution. We have suggested that if they are to contribute to a solution, all choices must be fully informed by the local context.

We distinguish this problem-based view of applied linguistics from other views which begin from theory. The applied linguist is deliberately eclectic, drawing on any source of knowledge that may illuminate the language problem. Proceeding eclectically is legitimate because for the applied linguist language problems involve more than language. They involve (some or all of) these factors:

- the educational (including the psychometric or measurement)
- the social (and its interface with the linguistic, the sociolinguistic)
- the psychological (and its interface, the psycho-linguistic)
- the anthropological (for insights on cultural matters)
- the political
- the religious
- the economic
- the business
- the planning and policy aspect
- and, of course, the linguistic, including the phonetic.

We turn now to a consideration of two 'problems', that of the optimum age for starting to learn a foreign language and that of the validation of a language proficiency test so as to consider the factors that the applied linguist needs to take into account when faced with a language problem.

4.1 Optimum age

First the age of starting a foreign language. What is the right age to start language learning? This is a question often asked by administrators, politicians, parents, as though there is one right answer. Is there – other things being equal? We can only attempt an answer when we have asked some preliminary questions, such as what is the language learning for? Which students are to be involved? Is there one through system or are there several (for example primary, secondary, tertiary)? If there are several, do they interlock with one another? What method is envisaged, will it be foreign language instruction, content based, immersion, and if immersion, which version (see below)? Which language is being studied? Has the choice been made on the basis of its prestige or its distance from the students' home language, which may determine how difficult they find it? What prospects do successful language learners in this situation have of further study, use of the language(s), jobs and so on. What possibilities exist for visits to the target language country? How is success measured? Who are the teachers? Are they well trained, and how proficient are they in the target language?

One approach to the optimum age question has been the appeal to the sensitive age or critical period view: this view considers that developments in the brain at puberty change the way in which we learn. Before puberty we acquire languages (one or in a bilingual setting two or more) as native speakers. After puberty we learn in a more intellectual manner as second- or foreign-language speakers. This idea, based on the sensitive or critical period hypothesis, if true (and it has been difficult to refute), would support a universal optimum age for starting a second or foreign language, namely as early as possible, in order to allow for possible acquisition as a native speaker. (See the discussion in Chapter 2 of research by Bialystok.)

An early start for second- and foreign-language learning at school is not unusual. Foreign-language teaching in the elementary school in the USA, French in the UK primary school, languages other than English in the Australian primary school: these are well-known examples of the willingness among educational planners to (1) extend the length of explicit language learning and (2) take advantage of the greater plasticity of young children in automatising new skills and internalising new knowledge. Such aims are plausible. Why then the doubts and the reversals of policy such as the on–off programmes found in the UK? Why the doubt, among professional language educators as much as among administrators, that spending longer teaching a language and starting earlier are not necessarily beneficial? How could they not be?

Research into second-language learning suggests that there may be no optimum age since adults can learn as efficiently as children and indeed more quickly. What matters are local conditions. To illustrate the applied linguist's insistence on the need to take account of local conditions I refer to three very different contexts: an Australian private girls' school; the Nepal government school system; and French immersion in Canada.

4.1.1 Presbyterian Ladies' College (PLC)

This school, in Melbourne, is a large independent girls' school (N=1200) with both primary and secondary departments. It offers six languages at secondary (Years 7–12). One foreign language, French, is also offered in the primary school (Hill et al. 1997).

Observations by the language teachers had indicated that after two years in the secondary school girls who had studied French in the primary school appeared to be performing at the same level in all four skills as those who had begun French in the secondary school. The only observed advantage for early starters was in pronunciation. Differences of course there were, but these appeared to be individual rather than group related.

The primary campus of PLC offers French from pre-Prep (three-year-olds) to Grade 6 and the senior campus both Beginners' French and Continuing French in Years 7 and 8 and then combines the two streams in Years 9–12.

The usual practice at PLC is to separate beginners from continuing learners in order to maintain and develop the advanced skills of the more experienced learners.

As has been said, by the end of Year 8, in the view of the teachers, there is no longer any need to keep the two strands separate. Both use the same textbooks in Years 7–8; both start at the beginning of new texts in Year 7. It is, however, expected that the continuing learners will treat the earlier parts of the textbooks as revision and move faster than the beginners.

If the critical period hypothesis is correct, then we might expect those children who start French early (in the primary school) to be at an advantage when they reach the secondary school. They appear not to be. Teachers are sceptical (indeed secondary teachers are often sceptical of primary school language learning). They may be wrong to be sceptical but to the applied linguist their scepticism is one factor in the situation: it contributes to the 'language problem' as do the qualifications of teachers in the primary and secondary department, the teaching materials used in both, the measures used to determine progress and the aims of the French teaching programme in the primary and the secondary schools, whether they are in harmony or not. It is possible that what counts as doing well at French in the primary school (being communicative in the spoken language for example) differs from doing well in the secondary school (accuracy in the grammar of the written language, perhaps).

The situation of a private girls' school, with its own primary and secondary departments, where there is keenness to learn French and resources are ample is on the face of it an ideal setting for the critical period to operate. It appears not to. For the applied linguist this is a problem that invites explanation and that neatly combines theoretical interest and practical involvement.

4.1.2 English teaching in Nepal

Until the early 1960s English was widely available in the Nepal school system; the basic medium of instruction was Nepali but English was taught everywhere as a foreign language and there were private schools in which English was the medium of instruction. In the early 1970s Nepal withdrew from English for purposes of nation building (it should be noted that Nepali, the national language, is itself a colonising language, introduced only about 300 years ago). English medium schooling was forbidden. But English did not go away. In the 1980s the ban was lifted, to avoid the unfortunate situation whereby middle-class parents were procuring English for their children by sending them to English medium boarding schools in Darjeeling, itself a Nepali-speaking enclave in India. It was decided by government that to avoid this embarrassment English should be officially reintroduced. A Survey of English Teaching by three applied linguists was commissioned in 1983. Its findings were disturbing (Davies 1987).

No school teacher in the sample studied possessed adequate English proficiency (by which was meant ability to read at an unsimplified level). For that reason, and in order to avoid the huge waste of time and resource devoted to English for the majority of children who drop out before they have gained any usable language skill, the Survey's recommendation was that English should begin in government schools as late as possible, well up in the secondary school.

However, there were, as the Survey team acknowledged, counter-arguments which were political rather than psychological, that is they were about the perceived role of English in Nepal rather than about the critical period. The Ministry of Education had to recognise the powerful local views on the need to entrench English early: one of the King's chief advisers stated that in his view English should start in the first year of primary school. The fact that there were no qualified teachers (and no prospect of any coming forward) was unimportant. The Ministry was of course well aware of its own government's acceptance of the local political imperative. In a situation where English represents modernity and the key to professional advancement, starting English in the secondary school would be seen as deliberately penalising the children of the majority, most of whom never reach secondary school (about 50 per cent of primary school entrants dropped out at the end of the first year). It was essential, so government officials argued, for English to start as early as possible, not primarily to teach English but to provide the appearance of equal opportunity.

Making decisions about English teaching in Nepal is more than a language problem. What the applied linguist is able to do is to clarify the choices and explain the parameters of those choices, what the implications are of starting English at different ages. In this local context (as in any other) there is no one general recipe (such as the critical period) that can be served up to determine the way forward.

4.1.3 Immersion language teaching

Over the last twenty years, immersion language teaching in Canada has been widely celebrated as a success story in bilingual education. What immersion means is the teaching of the second language as the medium of instruction. This use of the second language as medium is much older than the Canadian enterprise, and is still the practice in many colonial situations such as anglophone and francophone ex-colonies.

But it is important to examine carefully just what is claimed for this Canadian version of bilingual education. Its applied linguistic evaluators are very careful to make clear just what those claims are and just what constraints must be put on those claims (Swain and Lapkin 1982). These restrictions remind us that immersion education cannot easily be transferred to other situations where the same conditions do not pertain.

Canadian immersion programmes of various types (early total, early partial, late partial, beginning in Grade 8) have all been shown to be successful in terms of their objectives. But they require the presence of four factors:

1. The parents of the students need to be involved in establishing and ensuring the continuation of the immersion programme.
2. The immersion students (and their parents) must be members of the majority community in the local bilingual setting.
3. Both students and their parents must have a positive attitude towards the target language and its speakers.
4. The immersion programme must be optional.

In other words, immersion language teaching has worked well in Canada (primarily in Ontario) not only because it has offered the kind of resource-rich exposure to French that is not possible for English in Nepal, but also because the learners, like their parents, are members of the majority community of English speakers who desire to learn the language of the minority French-Canadian community. Transposing the immersion project to a country like Nepal would be hazardous. Once again we can observe that the role of applied linguistics is to describe and evaluate language problems within their own contexts.

4.2 Factors relevant to the optimum-age problem

The range of factors taken into account was hinted at above in our discussion of the optimum age for starting a second/foreign language in an Australian secondary school. In relation to that school they include:

1. **the educational** The project described was school-based, and therefore subject to the relevant institutional constraints of what can be done in the school setting, including what kind of measurement was acceptable, tests, interviews and so on.
2. **the social and sociolinguistic** It was necessary to consider the status of the school, girls only, middle class, including a large proportion of migrant parents, independent and therefore not constrained by State regulations with regard to textbooks, hours of instruction, teacher qualifications, examinations, size of class, choice of target language, school resources available; attitudes of stakeholders to foreign language instruction, and especially to French which, in the Australian context, is seen as less instrumental than for example Indonesian or Japanese.
3. **the psychological and psycho-linguistic** At issue was the relevance of the sensitive or critical period, as well as the relevance of the age of starting a foreign language to the mode of learning; at issue also were findings from studies of second-language acquisition research.
4. **the anthropological and cultural** Two aspects here were particularly relevant, the issue of the language classrooms in the school under study as independent cultural communities and the need to investigate these communities using ethnographic techniques; and the role more generally of culture, in this case French culture, however interpreted, in supporting and facilitating the learning of the language.
5. **the political** Quite apart from its role in Australia as still the most prestigious foreign language taught in schools and therefore potentially advantaged as against other foreign languages, even those with large numbers of bilingual or 'background' speakers, French in Australia has in the last three years been under strain because of the French Government's insistence on carrying out controlled nuclear explosions on one of its last colonial territories in the South Pacific. As a result, some Australia-based French restaurants and other

businesses suffered during this period. It was therefore relevant to investigate whether this negative attitude carried over into school French language learning.

6. **the religious** Unlike Italian, which has a largely Catholic client base and Hebrew, which is studied largely by Jews, French seems to be neutral with regard to religion.

7. **the economic** Given the current emphasis in education on marketing products for customers, it was necessary to investigate whether French was seen as instrumental, that is vocationally well placed, and what reasons children and their parents might have in choosing French rather than another language, since the school offered a choice of six languages in its secondary department.

8. **the business aspect** More relevant perhaps in a private language school which tailors its courses to the fluctuations in student demand and market share.

9. **the planning/policy aspect** Within the context of a national language policy, it was necessary to consider the school's overall curriculum in order to determine whether there was indeed a plan which incorporated work in the primary and secondary departments or whether the various components at the two levels had evolved unplanned. It seemed likely that the teachers who raised the problem in the first instance were convinced that there was no single plan which encompassed both primary and secondary departments; the question that needed addressing therefore was whether this was the case and to consider whether it was necessary to bring to bear techniques derived from the planning literature.

10. **the linguistic** Relevant here were the materials used to teach French in the primary and secondary departments as well as in the two streams, Beginners and Continuers in the first two years of the secondary department. It turned out that both streams used the same textbooks. Relevant also were the models of French, in particular whether native-speaking teachers (and which kinds of native speaker) were used at the two levels and in the two streams. It was also important to examine the judgements made of the children's spoken French by their teachers, and whether similar judgements were being made at the primary and secondary levels.

5 DOING APPLIED LINGUISTICS: THE PROCESS

Taking into consideration so many factors, such wide-ranging eclecticism by the applied linguist is open to criticism on (1) the grounds of superficiality (trying to look at everything and as a result observing nothing very much), (2) the lack of a strong theoretical base, and (3) what may be the excessive demands on professional training. The criticism of its lack of a strong theoretical base was discussed in Chapter 3 and the issue of the demands on professional training will be considered in Chapter 6. These are all related matters but it is important to say something here about the criticism of superficiality.

What the superficiality criticism means is that if the attempt is made to take account of so much information, appealing to the various factors mentioned above, then the result must be the collection of too much data for sifting to take place and for the necessary priority ranking of the various pieces of information to enable a way forward to be planned.

But this is to ignore the way in which applied linguistics activities actually proceed. Yes, an analysis is made which takes account of the various factors we have mentioned; but then the first elimination takes place because not all factors will be thought to be relevant: as we saw with our example earlier in this chapter on the optimum age for starting French in a private girls' school in Australia, where the religious factor was discounted. Those factors which are seen to be of direct relevance are then investigated and data collected for analysis.

As in any applied profession (e.g. general medicine) the data are not necessarily collected or analysed by the same person: applied linguistics has its own specialisms which provide for professional expertise where necessary. Thus there are within applied linguistics those who specialise in pedagogic grammar, curriculum planning, applied sociolinguistics, programme evaluation, language testing, language-teacher training, second-language acquisition research, applied stylistics, language planning for education, computer-assisted language learning, language-teaching methodology, language in the workplace, languages for specific purposes, bilingualism, cross-cultural communication, clinical applied linguistics, forensic language studies, and so on. In addition there are textbook writers, lexicographers, interpreting and translating specialists, as well as theoretical and descriptive linguists, whose advice and expertise may be called on.

6 FACTORS RELEVANT TO THE ELTS EVALUATION

In this next section of this chapter, I examine in detail an applied linguistic project in the field of language testing so as to clarify further the factors taken into account, the sources of knowledge appealed to, the skills drawn on and the stages followed. Necessarily, this project has its own particular features and will therefore be typical only in some aspects of projects undertaken by applied linguists. Following this examination, and to conclude the chapter, I consider the methodology used by the applied linguist in operating on a problem and to that end I take as examples four areas of importance in language teaching, second-language acquisition, proficiency language testing, the teaching of languages for specific purposes and curriculum design.

6.1 Background

Language testing reaches into many if not most applied linguistic activities. Assessment is central to all institutional language activities where there is frequently appeal to a language standard or norm.

The language problem to which this testing project belongs is that of the educability of tertiary students in a non-native language medium. The students in question were overseas or foreign students aiming to study at British universities. The problem arose because a number of such students had been found part-way through their studies to have inadequate English to proceed to a satisfactory conclusion and so graduate at either the undergraduate or more usually the postgraduate level.

The organisation where this issue became an institutional language problem was the UK para-statal British Council, a non-governmental body entrusted with the task of allocating scholarships and so on to selected students in a variety of disciplines wishing to attend British universities. Subjective judgements by its officers as to whether a prospective student's English was adequate had been found to be unreliable. English proficiency tests had been commissioned, the first used until the late 1970s (Davies 1965) and the second operational in the early part of the 1980s. This second test, known as the English Language Testing System (ELTS) test, had been designed in response to the push from the communicative movement to communicative language teaching and in consequence communicative language testing, and had based itself on the need for specificity in advanced language assessment.

What in practice that meant was that those students wishing to study a life science, such as biology, would be tested on materials (in English) drawn in part from the life sciences area. Similarly, those students wishing to study engineering would be tested on materials drawn from the technology area. There were six of these specialist areas, enough it was thought to cover the needs of most prospective students. This ELTS test was used widely in the early 1980s, administered through the British Council in some eighty different countries. It was noticeable that the comparable American test (Test of English as a Foreign Language, or TOEFL), which had been in use unchanged since the mid-1960s, made no concession to ways in which different contexts influence language use.

By the mid-1980s it had come to be felt that ELTS was unnecessarily complicated. Its very specificity caused more problems than it solved since it was by no means clear to prospective candidates (or their teachers, British Council officials and so on) which special module of ELTS they should take since they might well be in the process of moving from one specialism to another between the undergraduate and the graduate level: should they seek to be tested in the area of their previous study or in their future study area?

Again, the promise of specificity was open to complaint since in any one area (e.g. the life sciences) the range of topic and specialist language was so huge that what was clear to one biologist might well be opaque to another, making the text under test as difficult for him/her as for someone from, say, social studies. One consequence was that in order to avoid overspecialisation within the specialist area, test constructors aimed at generality, which inevitably made the texts they chose less and less specific. As a result the chosen texts could become so general as to lose all trace of the very specificity they were supposed to contain. Perhaps this meant that the whole notion of a specific test should be abandoned and a return made to the situation in which TOEFL (and the previous British Council test) had originated, that is a general test of English proficiency, the same test of 'academic' English for everyone (Alderson and Urquhart 1985, discussed in Chapter 2 above).

The language problem presented by the British Council to its applied linguistics consultants in the mid-1980s was what to do about the ELTS test. Should it remain in use as it was, should it be revised, should it be rewritten? An evaluation was needed, drawing on as wide a range of information as possible.

The detailed investigation of ELTS (Criper and Davies 1988) then carried out is described below; and in order to clarify its relevance to our discussion of the enterprise of applied linguistics, I record my discussion under the various heads or factors we have already noted.

6.1.1 *Educational (including the psychometric) factors*

ELTS was a proficiency test used in an educational setting, that is at entrance to a British university. The educational questions that needed investigation were: to what extent the test was being used at undergraduate and postgraduate levels, and for temporary attachment by senior academics; and whether it was suitable at these different levels; to what extent it was in use (and found suitable) in different faculties, and whether it was (as had been intended) being used differentially so that test scores deemed proficient in one faculty (or university) were rated not sufficiently proficient in any others. Again, many universities had provision for remedial English tuition for their foreign students; what was the extent of this provision and what use was made by those involved of the ELTS results? Both sensitivity to the ways in which tertiary institutions operated and an understanding of their role and complexity was called for in the project.

In addition, there were other skills that were required. One of these was the analysis of the ELTS test in terms of its relevance to the content of the specialist areas it purported to test. For example, what connection, if any, was there between the test materials in the life sciences module and the textbooks, lectures and so on in university departments of biology, bio-chemistry, botany and so on? And how far were these likely to be constant at the different levels, under- and postgraduate? For analyses of this kind it was necessary to draw on the expertise of those skilled in teaching life sciences at the different levels. The applied linguist could not be expected to carry out the content analysis but he/she would expect to interpret the results.

Another essential skill, which appears to be unique to the testing area but in practice is relevant everywhere in applied linguistics research, is that of familiarity with measurement (the psychometric aspect of educational studies) and with elementary statistics, to which must also be added the skill of data entry and of statistical analysis by computer. Those applied linguists who are consulted about testing projects (as with this ELTS project) are likely to have all three skills, the psychometric, the statistical and computer literacy. If not, then they must call on colleagues or external consultants.

But for the purposes of understanding the working of any test these skills are all essential since they provide the necessary evidence about the test's workings, often called its validity and reliability. Using these skills it was possible to examine the extent to which ELTS gave its users the decisions they needed, in particular whether it enabled them to make the right choices of candidates, those with adequate English for their studies.

It was also important to investigate whether there was even-handedness across modules, so that one module (say the life sciences module) was no harder than any other (say the social studies module). If it was harder, then it was possible it was right that it should be, but this was a matter for empirical investigation: if the English of life sciences is truly more difficult than the English of social studies, then it is appropriate that the tests should mirror this distinction. If not, and one was in fact more difficult than the other, then we had established a case of irrelevant bias which should be corrected.

ELTS contained four parts, tests of the four skills: reading, writing, listening and speaking. The results offered a profile score (skill by skill) and a global score, combining the four skills. It was important to determine the extent to which the profile scores provided useful (and usable) information to the test users (university departments etc.). Here again what was needed was a statistical analysis across a wide range of candidates of the various scores and a survey (through interview, question-naire etc.) of the actual use of these different modes of reporting to the institutions.

Since ELTS information was already being used in a large number of tertiary institutions, it was necessary to check how the information was being used. Were the so-called profile scores (separate scores for the four skills of reading, writing, listening and speaking) being used or were institutions interested only in the overall global score?

By the time of the evaluation teachers of English as a foreign language (EFL) were already beginning to consider the needs of those candidates intending to take the test. Inevitably, courses in EFL, both the more general and those specifically designed to provide pre-ELTS tuition, were taking account of what the test involved. The question for the evaluators was whether such washback from the test was beneficial in terms of its influence on EFL teaching or whether it was likely to exert a largely negative influence, for example by overstressing the practice of multiple-choice test questions.

6.1.2 Social (and its interface with the linguistic and sociolinguistic) factors

ELTS was predicated on a committed view of language variety, itself deriving from the more theoretical notions in sociology of role and status, and in sociolinguistics (or sociology of language) of the significance of situation in determining language use (situation being understood to include all aspects of setting, including the speakers and their relationships to one another), as well as the more practical com-municative competence view that language learning (and therefore its assessment) should be communicative, by which was understood being appropriate to its purpose.

The theoretical and practical reasons for the design of ELTS appeared convincing at the time of its construction. But when it came to the evaluation it was necessary to look closely at the rationale for its design, and in particular at the validity of the notion of discrete language varieties. For this part of the investigation, again it was necessary to call on subject specialists but also to undertake an empirical investigation which compared performance on the same subject modules by students with different specialist backgrounds, and the opposite, different subject modules by students from the same specialist backgrounds.

It was also necessary to examine the claims of communicative competence and estimate the extent to which a test could ever be truly communicative, given the requirements of the communicative competence idea, that it be spontaneous and non-predictable.

Here too it was necessary to look at differential performance on ELTS by various groups (for example males and females, younger and older students) as well as by speakers from different language backgrounds. A continuing controversy (which we come back to under politics below) was whether those who could lay claim to an education in their own countries in English medium should be excused the test.

6.1.3 Psychological (and its interface, the psycholinguistic) factors

Levels of proficiency beyond early and intermediate acquisition have not been prominent in second-language acquisition research as a topic worth pursuing. And yet studies of advanced writing, of vocabulary acquisition, of pragmatic interference and of discourse handling, these are all relevant to the study and the assessment of advanced proficiency. The ELTS evaluators needed to analyse how far the test designers had looked at these different areas of language studies and had incorporated these ideas in the ELTS test. What became clear during the study was how little is known about levels of proficiency and what it is that distinguishes one level from another in terms of language function. It was also necessary to take note of how much English was used in different countries, the question being whether those from settings with poor resources should be tested separately, on the grounds that more important than the present proficiency of candidates from those settings was their aptitude for gaining future proficiency within a resource-rich environment, for example in a UK university.

6.1.4 Anthropological factors (for insights on cultural matters)

Since the ELTS test was being used throughout the world and therefore open to scrutiny across cultures it was important to examine whether any of its content could be thought offensive.

Medicine, for example, might be regarded as neutral in this regard since the whole point of overseas students attending medical courses in the UK was (presumably) to learn Western medicine. But in the West itself there is disagreement as to what should be studied and what is legitimate medical practice. There are severe differences of opinion among those involved in medicine about such topics as abortion and euthanasia. In some countries, mention of contraception is unacceptable and should probably be avoided in such a widely used test.

The attitude that if these students actually come to the UK to study they will not be able to escape from discussions about contraception as well as medical explanations of its uses and patients' enquiries about its efficacy, these are all true but not the point. Culture is context bound and what the test must try to achieve is a judicious balance between a valid sampling of what students in a particular discipline need to do once started on a UK university course and an avoidance of giving offence to the students and their home communities. This may be censorship but it is sensitive self-censorship since it recognises local norms and does not try to change them. If that is thought to be desirable, then the ELTS test is not its vehicle.

Another use of anthropological skills is in the exercise of ethnographic techniques in researching how students study in a foreign language medium and the extent to which they do so in distinct ways. Evidence from this type of study is confirmatory or not of the test scores and may show that what the test is testing is not exactly (perhaps not even remotely) what the students themselves know and are capable of. This is another approach to the issue of test validity.

6.1.5 Political factors

Political insights at the national level meant careful attention to issues such as test exemptions. It was always accepted that a student from, say, New Zealand would not be expected to sit the test on the grounds that New Zealand is an English-speaking country. But whether the same dispensation applied to countries such as the West Indies or India was an open question. And there were uncertainties too about blanket exemption for countries such as New Zealand, since it was always possible that a candidate from New Zealand (with New Zealand citizenship) might have been educated in, say, Thailand and have used New Zealand only as a base for university applications.

It was necessary, therefore, to consider the question of exemption carefully and to recommend offering exemption not on the basis of nationality or provenance but on the basis of individual educational history. Given the complicated history of English medium education in the colonies and ex-colonies, this would not avoid all objections but it was probably fairer than country-wide exemptions. An issue that clearly needed addressing was whether all exemptions should be completely removed so that everyone not schooled in the UK should be required to take the test.

Political sensitivity was also necessary on the more local scale, that is in terms of the extent to which ELTS was in practice being used as a normative instrument. Those whose applications were processed by the British Council were in two large categories, British Council scholars whose admission depended on their satisfying the Council's own fairly strict guidelines, and other students who had gained admission to a British university direct and whose English was being tested by the British Council simply as an agent of the admitting university. The issue here was whether the admitting university had any serious interest in the level of English of its incoming students or whether it was ignoring the test results on the grounds that a student would be able to pick up adequate English once admitted. More crudely in such cases, it was not so much the English of an overseas student that mattered as the fees they paid. Fees increasingly dominated UK university activities through the 1980s and 1990s, as market forces became more and more important.

6.1.6 Religious factors

Religious considerations were relevant only in so far as the test raised the kind of religio-cultural concerns mentioned above in the section on the anthropological factor. If the test was to be acceptable across all religious settings it was important that it did not contain any material which might be offensive to one or other religious group. In addition to the obvious avoidance of references to the deity and to those closely associated it was also relevant to query any mention of those social issues which are considered taboo in some religious contexts, matters to do with sex and the family for example.

6.1.7 Economic factors

A cost-benefit analysis was necessary in order to determine whether the cost of the test outweighed its usefulness. The test was expected to pay for itself, candidates were charged a fee. But processing of the test in the receiving institutions was not paid for and there were administrative costs that needed to be taken into account and balanced against the costs of remedial English programmes in these institutions. The fundamental question was whether there was any benefit to institutions in selection based, in part, on present English proficiency; and this was influenced by the amount of reliability that could be placed on the test results. Even if they were 100 per cent reliable, there would still be costs. But since no test has complete reliability, it became necessary to compute, in financial terms as far as possible, what contribution a flawed instrument made to the output of university overseas students. This is similar to the questions discussed in medical reports on the proportion of False Positives to False Negatives acceptable from the use of a new drug.

6.1.8 Business factors

This factor related closely to the previous one of economics. The ELTS test was developed at a time when government money was still available for the monitoring of overseas students. As this support was progessively withdrawn, it became clear that ELTS would have to operate more and more as a business operation which would sell its services to universities and other receiving institutions, as well as to test candidates. It was also to be hoped that a future development would expand the test's use to universities outside the UK. And indeed that was what did happen: the successor to ELTS, the International English Language Testing System (known as

IELTS) is a joint British-Australian operation. (The original plan was that Canada would also participate, but that did not come about.)

6.1.9 Planning/policy (including the ethical) factors

A number of issues to do with planning and policy have already been mentioned and will not be repeated. But there is an additional aspect which was emphasised in the evaluation, and that was the need to plan the integration of the proficiency test with the universities' remedial programmes, so as to ensure that those false positives who were admitted would be given proper attention. The evaluation of ELTS made clear that a one-off proficiency test, often administered months before a student arrived in the UK, was unsatisfactory and what was necessary was an integrated programme of assessment and teaching, the assessment becoming increasingly diagnostic so as to inform the remedial programmes. This type of integrated programme required resources and these it was difficult to argue for in a climate of reduced resources.

Here there was also the ethical factor to consider in that overseas students who were increasingly being charged larger and larger direct fees for tuition were not necessarily being given the kind of English support (including assessment) they could properly expect to receive. From the point of view of assessment, it has been interesting to observe how those involved in this field have in recent years become more and more concerned about the ethics of their activity. We shall come back to this issue in Chapter 6.

6.1.10 Linguistic and phonetic factors

We have already considered some of the linguistic aspects under educational and the sociology/sociolinguistic, above. But there is an even more central linguistic aspect and that is the issue of sampling. Like any proficiency test, ELTS is meant to represent the language: those whose results indicate satisfactory proficiency are deemed to possess enough English for their study. This is a very large assumption. No proficiency test is likely to take up more than, say, three hours of test time and yet that test is expected to predict whether a student can cope with a year or three years' study, including very complex spoken and written material.

It was also assumed in the non-specialist components of the ELTS test that a proficiency test should target language use in the community, on the reasonable grounds that a student who coped easily with English communication in life outside the university, interacting with other students, communicating in the local shops, solving accommodation problems, seeking medical attention, going to the cinema, managing an English-speaking daily life, would be more likely to succeed in his/her studies. These are all large demands from a test. What this means is that the samples of English use that are put into the test must be very carefully chosen on the basis of their normality and frequency within the language. Anything odd or idiosyncratic, or even jokey, is best omitted. Judgements of the samples in the ELTS test required careful analysis on the basis of linguistic knowledge of the English language, the kind of analysis that is necessary for selecting the materials contained in a pedagogic grammar.

In addition, judgements were necessary of the spoken component of the test. These in part related to the voices used for the listening sections and in part to the ways in which the students' own speaking was measured, how far the question of intelligibility was raised, and of course intelligibility to whom. Just as the touchstone for the written materials in the test was the standard language, so the question which raised itself with regard to the spoken components of ELTS was what sort of norms should be applied to the judgements made of the candidates' own speech. To this extent the language problem which led to the evaluation of ELTS was indeed a problem involving language as much as it involved the other factors to which we have drawn attention.

7   INVESTIGATING THE PROBLEMS: THE METHODOLOGY OF APPLIED LINGUISTICS

Faced with such fundamental problems concerning language learning and teaching, problems such as how to plan for the optimum starting age for language teaching in a school or education system, problems such as how to assess language learning success most validly, and how to know whether or not this is being achieved, applied linguistics has developed a series of methodological approaches to the collection of relevant language data. Several of these have been referred to in earlier discussions. What I propose to do now is to consider four areas of applied linguistics that have very direct relevance to language learning and language teaching. What 'relevance' means here is that for the applied linguist these are areas that in different ways bring together the language, the learner and the context. The four areas all connect with what it is that is supposed to be being learned. The four areas are:

1. Second-language acquisition research: what are the stages of second-language learning?
2. Language proficiency testing: what are the markers of successful language learning?
3. Teaching of LSP: what does the learner need to know?
4. Curriculum design: what does the teacher need to know?

In all four of these areas in which applied linguistics has particular relevance to language teaching and language learning, the thrust of applied linguistic activity is to extend our knowledge of what it is that the learner is learning: stages, markers, needs, or plans. But equally the ambition is to determine not only the linguistic evidence – if that were the case we would be concerned here with linguistics applied. Instead, in addition to the evidence from linguistics, the applied linguist is also and equally interested in the learning and the context. So it is second-language acquisition in context, language proficiency testing in context, teaching of language varieties in context, curriculum design in context.

Let us consider second-language acquisition (SLA) first. Here we are less concerned with the very specialised form of SLA research which has developed in the last decade and which moves one branch of SLA research towards a parallel study with Child Language Acquisition and therefore is less interested in context than the more traditional SLA research.

Similarly with language proficiency testing. Here again the linguistics-applied temptation is to move the enterprise more and more towards a factorial and/or cognitive study of the mind and its language faculty (Oller 1998), while the applied linguistics concern is with the delineation of indicators of successful contextual language learning.

Again with the teaching of language varieties. Here the distinction is perhaps easier since where linguistics-applied research is towards the separation of language varieties into discrete codes and/or texts. That is not what applied linguistics is interested in. For two reasons: first, because uncontextualised varieties are essentially uninteresting for a study of language in use; second, because second-language learning takes place in context and therefore it is crucial that for teaching purposes the context of their use should be highlighted.

Curriculum/syllabus design: such activity should for applied linguistics purposes be context sensitive. A completely generalised curriculum would be too abstract to be effective.

In all cases therefore the applied linguist attempts to bring together the language, the learner and the situation. That is the challenge and that is the value of applied linguistics to language teaching and language learning. But there is another aspect too and that is the role of the applied linguist as critic. Here I am not thinking so much of the critical applied linguistics that we sketched in Chapter 2 and return to in Chapter 7. Rather I am thinking more traditionally of the proper role of the academic which is always and everywhere to be sceptical.

7.1 Second-language acquisition research

Research into second-language acquisition began in a very traditional applied linguistics way by investigating the problem of learners' errors. All language teachers (and probably all language learners) are aware of the fact of error: an error is a gap (filled or unfilled) in a learner's knowledge of the target language. So much is obvious and always has been to language teachers who have sought explanations for error: is it linguistic, to be accounted for by contrastive analysis so that an error is a confusion of some kind between one or more component of the L1 and the L2 (the target language); or is it psychological, to be accounted for by learning theory of some kind?

The applied linguistics contribution has been (1) to put these two kinds of explanation together and (2) to look at the system of error without seeking causes (note that this is as we suggested in Chapter 3 the normal applied linguistic approach, looking at states and not at change over time and space). These together yield a synchronic explanation of second-language learning stages.

Starting then from a problem, what error means, SLA research has developed its study of the learner's language (or 'interlanguage') into the most abstract of applied-linguistic projects. So much so that applied linguists (not just language teachers) have begun to query what the current paradigm has to offer to the amelioration and improvement of communication, which we have suggested is the overall aim of applied linguistics.

It may be that indeed SLA research has shifted from being an applied linguistic activity to being more of a linguistic-applied one and that would explain the increasing research time given to investigating cognitive models based on L1 universal grammar theory. If this is the case then SLA research is no longer part of applied linguistics, and it may be that this is a natural process whereby language problems when studied can become formalised, a kind of colonisation by linguistics, a widening of its empire. Similar progression could be attributed to discourse and to stylistics: both concerned with problems of analysis of texts longer than the sentence and now in some measure both subsumed within a greater linguistics where they are on the applied side (linguistics applied) or at least in the no man's land between linguistics applied and applied linguistics. And more recently corpus linguistics seems to have taken the same route, since it is in some sense a linguistic formalisation of ideas about genre and different kinds of language text, as we see below in the discussion of the teaching of LSP.

7.2 Language proficiency testing

Testing is more a normal part of language teaching than of other curriculum subjects because the language teacher is concerned with skill as well as with knowledge. This means that there is more need for testing. Testing is further complicated by the unusual presence of a living criterion, the native speaker. In History, Physics and so on there is no equivalent, no body of persons who represent ultimate attainment. Of course there may be an individual, an Einstein or a Gibbon, whose scholarship is universally recognised as a model for us all; but even that is not really comparable because no course of instruction sets out to emulate such scholarship whereas in many language-teaching operations the goal is the native speaker.

What language proficiency testing is about is the setting of appropriate targets for varying levels and uses of language. Such tests aim to provide the rigours of test guidelines, while ensuring that the right kinds of language behaviour are included and in appropriate quantities. The applied linguistic interest in language proficiency testing is now central but that was not always the case. What has become clear over the last thirty years is the role of the test in encapsulating both what the learner needs to know for a particular purpose and what amount of that knowledge counts as success. This is a major contribution both to the practice of language learning and teaching, and to the theoretical understanding of language learning and language need.

Furthermore, language proficiency tests both model the native speaker and at the same time provide an alternative means of setting goals for learning. They operationalise language learning precisely by setting explicit goals, which is another way of stating that language tests make language learning accountable by establishing what it means to 'know' the language. They do this by sampling the relevant areas of language to be learned and guarantee that their sampling is correct through their documentation on reliability and validity. And here is the major distinction between tests of proficiency and tests of achievement (or attainment): tests of proficiency sample the language that is being learned; tests of achievement sample the teaching programme (syllabus, course, textbook etc.) that has already been agreed, a sample then of an existing sample.

We can distinguish six kinds of information that language testing provides. The first is in research in which language testing is used to provide hypotheses in relation to our understanding of language and language learning. The status and concept of language proficiency, the structure of language ability and the natural order of language acquisition have been much discussed by language testers using language testing techniques to produce data which furthers discussion. Such issues are primarily intended to add to our knowledge and understanding of language and language learning, though no doubt they also have an applied potential in language-teaching programmes.

The second use of language testing in experiments is a subset of the first use, in research. But there is an important difference. In the research use we are thinking of research into language testing; in the experimental use we are thinking of tests as criteria for language teaching experiments, for example in method comparison.

The third use, which is reflexive, and much discussed as a responsibility of testing, is used less than it could be, that is the washback effect on the syllabus of language testing (Clapham et al. 1997). The implications of test results and their meaning are employed as a critique of the syllabus and the teaching; while the testing structure, the content and method of the tests themselves influence the teaching. We are concerned here with teaching to the test, for it is always the pejorative aspect of washback that is implied, but we stress that there is a positive side to this. The implications are, first, that teaching is influenced by testing and, second, that testing has an important responsibility – to ensure that its influence is constructive.

The fourth use of language testing is measuring progress among learners, the most common type of test being the achievement test.

The fifth use is in selection of students on the basis of either previous learning or in terms of some more general language-learning ability or aptitude for the next stage of education or a particular vocation. What is of interest here is the interaction between use for progress and use for selection, that is to what extent a valid test of progress is in itself a valid test for selection purposes.

The sixth use is in relation to evaluation of courses, methods and materials. This is a special use of testing which must cope with the learner variable, distinguishing it from the evaluation of the materials, programme and so on.

Language assessment provides a triple message:

1. A message about skill, to what extent learners have reached adequate proficiency, however that is defined and the role of language tests in developing more specific and detailed indicators of adequate proficiencies.

2. A message about development, which appears at first sight only to be psycho-linguistic since it seems to suggest a progress along a very clear and obvious path towards ultimate attainment. That obviousness is not true even of native speakers, who may have very different endpoints. Attached to this message about development for all language learners is an indication of the identity which the learner chooses (usually unconsciously). Information about develop-ment therefore provides an indication – through assessment – as to both the psycholinguistic and the sociolinguistic provenance of the learner.

3. A message about knowledge. Language users, both native speakers and non-native speakers, distinguish themselves in terms of their awareness of language. This shows itself both in the range of acceptability judgements they are prepared to make and in the extent of their conscious metalinguistic reflect-ing upon language, which in turn demonstrates itself in knowledge about language and in areas of ludic creativity. Such a reification of language does seem to discriminate both among native speakers and among non-native speakers; it does, of course, have some bearing on our first message, that of skill, since there may well be an element of knowledge within skill which deter-mines differential proficiency (Davies 1990: 11).

7.3 The teaching of language for specific purposes (LSP)

Richards et al. (1985) define LSP thus:

> second or foreign languages used for particular purposes and restricted types of communication (e.g. for medical reports, scientific writing, air-traffic control) and which contain lexical, grammatical and other linguistic features which are different from ordinary language … In language teaching decisions must be made as to whether a learner or groups of learners require a language for general pur-poses or for special purposes.

Such definitions are overbland. They take for granted the discreteness of LSPs and of registers. But except in the most restricted spheres (e.g. knitting patterns) where the LSP conforms to a kind of ritualised speech, there is no discreteness, there is always overlap. Here is an excerpt from an encyclopedic article on a branch of cognitive psychology:

> Marr and Poggio (1979) implemented the same two constraints, of smoothness and uniqueness, in a quite different non-cooperative stereo algorithm that used multiple spatial frequency tuned channels and a coarse-to-fine matching strategy. The key idea here was to exploit the fact that only a few edge points, and hence only modest ambiguity problems, arise in very coarse channels. Matches obtained in these can then be used to guide matching in more finely tuned channels. Ambiguities in all channels are reduced almost to zero by suitable coupling of spatial frequency tuning to the disparity range allowed for matching. This requires that the high spatial frequency channels have very narrow disparity ranges, and

that they therefore need to be 'put in the right place to look' if they are to find the correct matches. The algorithm does this by generating appropriate vergence eye movements driven by the coarser channels.

(Frisby 1990: 251)

Now I am an educated native speaker of English. But, like most people, I tend to read material that is already somewhat familiar. The content of this Cognitive Psychology topic (the computational theory of perception) is quite new to me and I find the excerpt above hard to process. Of course, it will be said, this excerpt of some ten lines is part of a larger whole and if I were to read the whole article with care then I would be in a stronger position to understand the quoted section. While this is no doubt true, its very obviousness underlines the problem facing the second-language learner who wishes to access this article. To propose that he/she read the whole article is one version of the advice that in order to understand a text in a subject area you need to understand the subject first, or in order to understand this excerpt you need first to read not just the article it is taken from but also the whole of the encyclopedia the article is taken from. This is the submersion version of advice! For of course if you are not already familiar with cognitive psychology then reading the encyclopedia will probably also require the understanding you don't yet have – remember you are a second-language learner of English. Catch 22 indeed!

In my case it is just possible that if I were to read the whole article and check the cross-references to other articles I might then be able to understand the quoted excerpt. And in practice when an excerpt of this kind is given to a second-language learner it will almost always be the case that the student in question will have already studied cognitive psychology, either in the L1 or in English and will therefore have the background knowledge in the subject needed to make sense of the explanation of the computational theory of perception, even if the actual information is entirely new. If all or most previous study of cognitive psychology has been in the L1 then there may be some language problems with the English of this entry that will need attention. But if the matching of the subject matter to the needs and interests of the learner has been done well then there will be an advantage in providing a text of this kind, either as part of the content of the psychology class or as an exercise in the English support class or possibly in both.

The basic assumption then behind programmes dedicated to teaching languages for specific purposes (LSP) is that language function, purpose, area and so on require the use of a special variety of the language; this was the argument we referred to in the discussion on language and gender in Chapter 3. Different domains of social life can be equated to different language varieties. The growth of LSP (ESP for English) over the last thirty years has been considerable but it is of course not new. German for Scientists/Chemists/Engineers was in vogue long before for non-German-speaking scientists who needed access to scientific materials written in German. What has changed is that English has taken over the former role of German in science and of just about every other language everywhere else. That is the first reason, the continuing of a tradition in a new medium. The second reason targets

English: it represents a reaction against the literary materials widely used for the teaching of English as a foreign/second language.

The applied linguistics contribution to this activity has been two edged. On the one hand it provided the necessary skills in textual analysis, the writing or practice materials and of tests in LSP; it experimented with the evaluation of courses using LSP as against those which used non-specific language materials (e.g. general English). On the other hand it offered a sceptical commentary, criticising the lack of a clear model of variety which showed the differences between one variety and another. Furthermore it showed that the differences between one variety and another are likely to be in terms of frequency of the use of different features rather than in completely differential use. Of course there would always be certain vocabulary items that would be specific. But those who had background knowledge in the area would already be familiar with these terms or at least would acquire them very quickly.

A major contribution of applied linguistics to language learning and teaching studies has been to develop materials purposely written for the language teacher. This is the case of LSP, as we saw in Chapter 2, with pedagogical grammar. The role of applied linguistics is to mould a relevant content area for the needs of its target audience, in this case experienced language teachers (Howard and Brown 1997). It is a form of simplification, as all language-teaching materials are.

7.4 Curriculum design

Language teaching is not confined to the classroom: if it were then the idea that teaching is and should really be about method would have more force. But language teaching in reality also takes in the necessary education of the teacher, the preparation for the teaching, the follow-up from the teaching, the whole professional activity of the teacher, which means also the continuing education that keeps the teacher in touch with developments in the field (Richards and Rodgers 1986). Language-teaching responsibilities also take in the support systems to the teacher, the training of new teachers, the in-service education of teachers, the textbook writing, the assessment systems, the evaluation projects, the curriculum design and planning, and the research into language teaching. All of these are part of the wider understanding of language teaching and may of course be carried out by those who are also engaged in class teaching or may have been so in the past. What a curriculum provides for the language teacher is a plan, based on a view or philosophy of language and of learning.

According to Richards, Platt and Platt (1985), curriculum design (also curriculum development) refers to: the study and development of the goals, content, implementation, and evaluation of an education system. In language teaching, curriculum development (also called syllabus design) includes:

1. the study of the purposes for which a learner needs a language (needs analysis);
2. the setting of objectives, and the development of a syllabus, teaching methods and materials; and

3. the evaluation of the effects of these procedures on the learner's language ability.

Nunan quotes Stenhouse with approval (Nunan 1990: 76):

The uniqueness of each classroom setting implies that any proposal – even at school level – needs to be tested and verified and adapted by each teacher in his own classroom. The ideal is that the curricular specification should feed a teacher's personal research and development programme through which he is increasing his understanding of his own work and hence bettering his teaching ... It is not enough that teachers' work should be studied: they need to study it themselves.

(Stenhouse 1975: 143)

What Richards and Rodgers (1986) suggest is that while a curriculum often is the plan and the philosophy, a syllabus contains the details of the content to be taught and the methods to be used. Curriculum may of course encompass syllabus: 'Traditionally the term syllabus has been used to refer to the form in which linguistic content is specified in a course or method. Inevitably the term has been more closely associated with methods that are product centered rather than those that are process' (Richards and Rodgers 1986: 21).

At its most basic the applied-linguistic contribution to curriculum design is to provide a plan which encompasses a sequenced series of teaching stages and goals, ensuring that the basic grammar, vocabulary and pragmatics are included in the time available. A useful (but not essential) addition would be to provide lesson materials that are both interesting and challenging, but this is not primarily the applied linguist's responsibility, unless he/she is also engaged as a textbook writer. This aspect of the applied linguist's work matches the older formulation of methodics, which made central to the work of the language-teaching methodologist, the three-pronged task of selection, grading and sequencing. While it may be the case that all language features are equally difficult, it is the applied linguist's professional job to sequence them in such a way that progression (and inclusion of what has preceded) seems appropriate. And while scorn has been heaped on the proposal that such teaching materials should be 'teacher-proof', the underlying intention is laudable, given the very broad range of professional teaching ability and skills available in an educational system; given also the range of proficiency in the target language among those teachers.

8 CONCLUSION

In this chapter I first considered the arguments for confining applied linguistics to a concern with second-language teaching and learning. Then I discussed two 'problems' in the language-teaching field: first, the optimum-age problem and, second, an investigation into the validity of a large-scale English-language proficiency test, the English Language Testing Service (ELTS) test. These two 'problems' were considered from the point of view of a number of relevant factors, opening up a discussion on what it is that needs to be taken into account when the applied linguist is faced with a language problem. Finally, I considered the methodology used by the applied linguist in working with a problem, and to that end I took as examples four areas of importance in language teaching: second-language acquisition, proficiency language testing, the teaching of languages for specific purposes and curriculum design. The chief role of applied linguistics in the field of language teaching and learning is, as elsewhere, to ask the right questions about the enterprise under discussion in its own context and at the same time to ensure that in spite of its particularities, the enterprise is approached as an example of the general system of language teaching to which it belongs.

Chapter 5

Applied linguistics and language use

'Language is only the instrument of science and words are but the signs of ideas.'
(Samuel Johnson, Preface to the *Dictionary of the English Language*, 1755.)

1 INTRODUCTION

This chapter is parallel to Chapter 4, where we examined the role of applied linguistics in language teaching and learning. We move on in Chapter 5 to survey areas outside institutional language learning: correctness, forensic linguistics, applied stylistics, lexicography and artificial languages (or language treatment). The role of applied linguistics is to recognise that these problems often cause deep passions and may need to be viewed as issues in which language plays only a part. The examples chosen for discussion are: language correctness because of public fear and outrage at what is perceived to be a decline in standards; forensic linguistics in order to determine the authenticity of oral and written texts for both defence and prosecution purposes; applied stylistics on the grounds of the need to teach literature to foreign learners; lexicography which determines what to include and what to exclude in dictionaries for home and school; and language treatment (the creation of artificial languages) because of the central interest there in communication across frontiers.

As in Chapter 4, we propose here that the chief role of applied linguistics is to ask the right questions about the context in which a language problem is embedded and then to generalise to other contexts where the same problem can be shown after analysis to exist. In that way a systematic approach to language problems can be made which will both explain and at the same time provide a set of options for action.

2 PROBLEMS

Language matters so much in our everyday thinking, our learning outside school, our communicating with one another that it inevitably arouses passions and creates problems. Applied linguistics exists to try to explain the passions and suggest solutions to the problems. To some extent, as we shall see, the passions and the problems are connected so that explanation of the passion is itself part solution of the problem.

What are some of these problems? There are problems of language use, the well-known ones of what it means to be correct (and whether it matters), of whether some accents are better than others, of the language disadvantages some children face at school because of their social class or ethnicity, of understanding instructions on domestic appliances and on official documents (such as tax forms). And then there are the lesser known problems of institutionalised misunderstandings such as police transcripts, doctor–patient communication, the language–content relation among subject specialists (e.g. chemical engineers, information scientists), and authenticity in simultaneous interpreting.

In each case what we have is what appears at first sight to be a straightforward language problem. That of course is true, but that is not all there is. In the first place the problems are about language and its users or its context; in the second place, they often concern our feelings about ourselves, our insecurity and our identity, our children and their future, our attitudes to others, including our prejudices, our view of truth and of community.

The role of applied linguistics is to recognise that these problems (often) cause deep passions and need to be viewed as more than language issues. Thus debates about the teaching of reading are often presented as a polarity (for mother-tongue speakers) between the phonic method (sounding out the letters) and the whole word (or whole-language) method and (for second/foreign-language learners) between the use of simplified reading materials and authentic reading materials. Which is right? Why do these debates arouse such passions? Are the opposing views in the event incommensurable?

The well-known problems of language usage may be similarly deconstructed. The notion of correctness, of using correct English/French and so on arouses strong feelings, especially among those who contribute to the letter columns of newspapers. For them (as indeed for all prescriptivists) the problem is one of simple error that language use is always right or wrong. And yet a more engaged analysis, an approach from applied linguistics, will ask questions about the currency of alternative forms and about the role of language change. Such an analysis may suggest that the appeal to correctness may be a vain attempt to restore a form or a meaning which is already lost or disappearing (such as 'It's I' now lost to 'It's me', or 'uninterested' now replaced by 'disinterested', or 'different from' now losing ground to 'different to').

Just as errors, both of grammar and of word choice, are condemned as simply wrong by those who wish to uphold standards, so some accents of English (e.g. Birmingham, Broad Australian) are stigmatised as ugly and uneducated. There are, of course, no intrinsic grounds for such stigmatising, any more than there are for racial prejudice. Those who see accent prejudice as solely a language problem are inclined to wax indignant, to maintain that all accents are equal (forgetting perhaps the continuation of the *Animal Farm* motto: but some are more equal than others). For them, therefore, there is no problem: society has the duty to behave differently and overcome its prejudices. The applied linguist, however, is likely to recognise that it is indeed a problem and that it extends beyond language, reflecting social and political (and possibly ethnic) values. Accent stigmatising is *par excellence* a socially embedded language problem. Maintaining that it is a real problem, that some accents are more valued socially than others, does not mean approval any more than it lays claim to a solution. In attempting to make sense of language problems, by contextualising them, applied linguistics does not necessarily solve but it does hope to explain.

The accent problem parallels the educational code problem whereby working-class children (we might extend the involvement to ethnic-minority children) are said to be disadvantaged educationally because the code of communication they use at home is different from the school code, which is largely verbal and is close to the code of the middle-class home. As such the middle-class child has little gap between home and school, while the working-class child has a chasm. The model in which Basil Bernstein (1971) put forward this proposal in the 1970s was heavily attacked from two quarters: first, because these 'codes' were not describable linguistically and, second, because the proposal appeared to attack the language of the working class. And yet the model appealed greatly to teachers, since it offered an explanation of why working-class children often performed less well at school. In consequence, Bernstein's model of restricted (working-class) and elaborated (middle-class) codes became common knowledge in educational circles, especially among teachers of English.

In fact, Bernstein had never claimed that his model was primarily about language: for him language was only part of the communication code, which also involves context and social role and sense of self. Indeed, what he was proposing was a kind of applied-linguistic model while what he was mistakenly attacked for was for appearing to be talking only about language. Or perhaps there were other reasons for the attacks, since similar proposals in the USA (by, e.g., Brice Heath 1983) have not been so pilloried.

Problems with instructions and information (on machinery and appliances, on official forms) are of two kinds: inadequate translations from the maker's language into the user's language and inadequate conceptualisation of the nature of instruction and of the need to make the language of instructions accessible to all readers, whose literacy skills will vary hugely. Consider this advice from a telephone directory: 'HYPHENS: Names which contain a hyphen are treated as two words and are sorted according to the first name. The second name is treated as initials. This does not apply to hyphenated names which begin with a prefix.'
Examples follow:

A-Grade Machines
Afnan G.
Agar L. F.
Agar-Lyons B.
Agar P. M.
AGRA Products
Alfonso M.

Some of the examples have hyphens, some don't; there are no obvious prefixes. Given the mass audience for whom local telephone directories are intended, this advice is somewhat opaque.

Organisations such as the Plain English Movement offer a kind of applied-linguistic approach to such problems, proposing ways (both verbal and non-verbal) in which the language may be simplified and the reader's attention engaged.

Institutionalised misunderstandings may not be so well known but for those affected they can be overwhelming. One such problem concerns the interaction between the police and members of the public who are involved in some way in police investigations, both witnesses and accused. The taking of a statement by the police (analogous to the taking of a clinical history of a patient by a doctor) gives considerable scope for error, ranging from complete fabrication of what was supposedly said to a biased interpretation of what was meant by the interlocutor to a genuine misunderstanding. Such errors need not be deliberate, even though they sometimes are. More likely perhaps is the situation in which the police are convinced of the guilt of an accused and therefore find themselves impelled to an interpretation of what was said which could lead to a conviction. In the days before tape recordings of statements were mandatory, the room for error between what was said and what was actually written down was wide. The written statement was signed by the accused, of course, but even then error was possible: the accused might be only partially literate, the transcript could be altered later.

Once again for the applied linguist the language problem involves a context which needs to be taken full account of: the police and the accused are locked into a communicating system which means that what is said is less important than what is expected. An applied-linguistic analysis of the encounter will take account of more than the verbal exchanges. It may suggest that on the basis of the transcript there are different interpretations of what was actually said and also that one side's interpretation of what was meant is not the only interpretation (see the discussion of forensic linguistics later in this chapter).

Doctor–patient communication has a similar tendency to error. The extreme case is where the doctor and the patient (or the patient's relative) interact in different languages (although this gap may be bridged by an interpreter). But in the case where both appear to share the same language we have resonances both of the code disjunction between middle and working classes mentioned earlier and of the specialist register of medicine, which may well be alien to many patients whatever their social class. The problem for the doctor (as with the police investigator) is that one part of examining a patient is done by talking. The room for misunderstanding between a figure of authority and a client is considerable, as is the room for wrong diagnosis, based on a misunderstanding or an inadequacy of what is said and a conviction that the doctor 'knows' what is wrong.

What the applied linguist can do here is to underline the importance of paying more attention to what the patient says (recommending interpreter services where necessary) and explaining to those involved in medical training that there is typically a disjunction between what is said by the patient and what is meant. In the case of medical language what this means is that it is possible (and probably necessary) for doctors to put their meanings into simpler language. It also indicates that medical meanings and content can be put over in different ways according to the audience.

In the case of specialist scientists, such as the chemical engineer or information scientist, problems frequently arise in graduate studies where the student has only partial proficiency in the language of instruction (usually English). The solution which concentrates on the language is simple: learn more English. But for the applied linguist there are other considerations, such as whether the demands of the institution in regard to English are valid demands, whether the student needs to be proficient in written English in areas other than those of his/her specialism, whether the apparent problem concerns language use outside the institution rather than having inadequate English for the course itself. Analyses of this kind are likely both to indicate what, if anything, is needed and at the same time explain why, in many cases, students' English does not appear to improve.

A criticism of simultaneous interpreters is that they range widely from the speaker's meaning. As a straightforward language problem, the solution is obvious: provide better interpreters. But it is worthwhile asking ourselves what is expected of simultaneous interpreters and then what 'better interpreters' would do. Much simultaneous work takes place at international conferences interpreting speeches made by delegates. Such speeches are of two kinds: the first is the set speech where there is normally a written transcript (already translated) which acts as the authentic account of what was said. The second is the impromptu speech: here there is normally no written transcript (although one may be made available later). What matters here is not that the interpreter takes account of all that is said; surely what matters is that the main point is transmitted. All good simultaneous interpreters will provide that. That is what matters: all else in simultaneous interpreting is show and symbol, making public the value to themselves and to the groups they represent of the delegates' own languages. Once again we need to view the 'language' problem in the context of the international meeting, where what is paramount is the amour-propre of all delegates: simultaneous interpreting offers that display, getting it right is less important than getting the gist across. The applied linguist is conscious of this language embedding, and while sympathetic to the need for an accurate rendition, is also alert to what is practical and to what is needful.

Language problems in the institutionalised settings of school, work (including the office, the hospital, the factory), conferences, the media and so on, are very rarely problems only of language. In many cases they involve individuals and groups who have problems in interacting with one another and in making decisions about policy. These problems may manifest themselves in language but their origins are only partly there. Of course this does not mean that in explaining and attempting solutions we ignore language. It may be that intervening on the language is the quickest way to bring about change. But no intervention will be successful that does not take account of the context in which the language problem is embedded.

We discussed in Chapter 3 how in practice we can distinguish between Linguistics and Applied Linguistics. Linguistics, we might suggest, looks through a telescope holding the large end to the eye, focusing solely on language to the exclusion of all else: language problems are seen as wholly linguistic problems. Applied Linguistics looks through a telescope with the small end to the eye, and so views language as part of the whole. The linguistic view is the laboratory view, the applied view is the real world view.

3 LANGUAGE CORRECTNESS AS AN APPLIED-LINGUISTICS PROBLEM

Being correct for the user of English means conforming to the rules and conventions of Standard English. The learner of English as a second or foreign language must first master the rules; thereafter he/she too must cope with the conventions (or norms) which are the basis of English instruction at school for the first-language user. Guides on how to be correct or, more usually, how not to be incorrect, abound, as do morality-type injunctions on the need to maintain correctness. They range in target from the prescriptivist alarms of letter writers to newspapers about stereotyped points of grammar (is 'none' singular or plural? is 'whom' a dying inflected form? do we write 'try to' or 'try and'? is it wrong to split an infinitive?) to the pedagogic approaches of textbook writers, whose interest is very much in the canons of the grammar and vocabulary of the contemporary standard language. They range also from the manuals on clear thinking and rhetoric (and their equivalent modern textbooks on communication studies) to the sociolinguistic interest in linguistic class markers and feminist observations on the need for an inclusive language which encourages its users to be non-discriminatory.

Let us look at some examples of concerns in these various areas and then consider the ways in which these are of interest to the applied linguist.

3.1 Old shibboleths

Complainants about slippage in Standard English sometimes use as evidence the increasing loss of differentiation between two apparent alternatives, for example 'disinterested/uninterested'; 'try to/try and'; and 'owing to/due to'. In the last example 'owing' is considered to be normally adjectival but functions as a compound preposition in a sentence such as: 'Owing to the bad weather we were delayed.' Traditionally prescriptivists have made the point that in this adverbial use 'due' cannot be substituted for 'owing'. It is therefore acceptable to write: 'the delay was due to the bad weather' but not: 'due to the bad weather we were delayed'.

And yet, as Peters (1995) remarks, this prepositional use of 'due to' is not new and there is therefore no need to perpetuate the shibboleth against 'due to'. Here Peters helpfully reminds us of two fundamental points: first that a standard language changes over time and no power can stop it: what may have once been a necessary distinction between 'owing to' and 'due to' is no longer valid. The second point paradoxically states that at any one point in time it is necessary for those whose job it is to prescribe (teachers, textbook writers, syllabus planners, newspaper editors and so on) do just that, prescribe what is acceptable and what is not. How they do that is to use their own judgement, recognising that there will always be differences of opinion. It is understandable therefore why those whose job it is to arbitrate in these matters tend to be conservative. At the same time those with good sense recognise that constructions which may be considered as wrong by many people now may well be regarded as quite acceptable in the next generation.

It matters that we are sensitive to the way others feel about language use. For example, some people feel strongly that prepositions should not end sentences. But perhaps, as Bishop amusingly reminds us, we should not be too serious about it:

> I lately lost a preposition;
>   It hid, I thought, beneath my chair
> And angrily I cried, 'Perdition!
>   Up from out of in under there.'
>
> Correctness is my vade mecum,
>   And straggling phrases I abhor,
> And yet I wondered, 'What should he come
>   Up from out of in under there?'
>
> (Morris Bishop, 'The Lost Preposition')

3.2 Effective writing

Another demonstration of correct English is said to be effective writing, which displays clear thinking. Writing a coherent text longer than a sentence is one of the hardest of all the skills schools set out to teach. The role of the applied linguist here is to take on the second of Peters' tasks and act prescriptively by explaining what is wrong with early written drafts and in what ways to make the draft clearer.

Given the difficulty of constructing a good piece of writing, it is not surprising that even well-known writers can fail to achieve the clarity they desire. Here is a short piece which opens the Preface to H. G Wells' *The Common Sense of War and Peace*, 1940, which it is not difficult to find fault with:

> For the greater part of my life I have given most of my working time to the problem of the human future, studying the possibility of a world-wide re-organization of human society, that might avert the menace of defeat and extinction that hangs over our species. This has been my leading pre-occupation since I published *The Time Machine* in 1893. I have never thought, much less have I asserted, that progress was inevitable, though numerous people thought to fancy that about me.

The passage seems to have been hurriedly dictated, and not afterwards revised. Wells does not trouble to define the meanings of his words, confident that most of his readers will have read at least one or two of his important works and be able to make the definitions for themselves.

Here are some critical comments which are quoted as examples of applied linguistics at its most interventionist. They are followed by a proposed redraft of the passage:

1. 'the problem of the human future'
   (Comment: Wells gives no clue as to whether he is speaking in terms of a few months, a few generations, or millions of years.)
2. 'that might avert the menace of defeat and extinction that hangs over our species'
   (Comment: does this mean that individual men and women might become physically immortal?)
3. 'the menace of defeat and extinction'
   (Comment: a menace of defeat by what? Flood, fire, disease, exhaustion of food and fuel supplies, moral degeneration? The concept 'extinction' contains 'defeat', which could have been omitted.)
4. 'my leading pre-occupation since I published *The Time Machine*.'
   (Comment: any pre-occupation is a leading one; the 'pre-' in the word denotes priority.)
5. 'I have never thought, much less have I asserted'
   (Comment: how much is less than never? He means: 'I have never asserted, nor even thought.')

Redraft

Ever since 1892, when I began to write *The Time Machine*, the two chief subjects of my literary studies have been the process of moral and physical degeneration that now threatens to make man extinct in a few hundred years, and the various theories of world-wide social reorganization that have been designed to arrest this process. Many people fancy me to have asserted, at some time or other, that nothing can prevent the beneficent progress of civilization from continuing indefinitely. They are wrong.

This redraft is taken from Graves and Hodge (1943: 211–14), from which the above comments are also taken. And since in one sense making a text 'more correct' is to redraft it so as to make it better, more effective in its context, then perhaps we should accept that 'correct English is simply good English and incorrect, bad' (Warburg 1966: 87). After all, for the applied linguist, being correct matters, not only for the sake of clarity but also because language is embedded in social life.

3.3 Social class markers

When parents say of their teenage children that they don't understand their language, what they probably mean is that young people use somewhat different vocabulary; also perhaps that the topics they talk about are not those current among their parents' generation. This difference is an example of the general case that different groups mark their speech in ways that distinguish it from that of others, sometimes in grammar, more often in vocabulary and most of all in pronunciation. At the same time these different groups share the same common language, which allows them to communicate readily with one another, but in subtly different ways, recognised by everyone, salient socially not linguistically.

One of these group distinctions is that of the linguistic markers of social class, which in English has been satirised as marking the U(pper)–non-U(pper) distinction. Examples from Ross (1978) include:

bicycle or bike	(U):	cycle	(non-U)
present	(U):	gift	(non-U)
expensive	(U):	costly	(non-U)
what?	(U):	pardon	(non-U)
money	(U):	lolly	(non-U)
sofa	(U):	settee	(non-U)
writing-paper	(U):	note-paper	(non-U)

Does it makes any sense to regard the U usages as more correct than the non-U? This is indeed what Ross suggests. He uses the terms 'upper class (abbreviated U), correct, proper, legitimate, appropriate … to designate usages of the upper class; their antonyms (non-U, not proper, not legitimate etc.) to designate usages which are not upper class' (ibid: 91).

Surely these examples are so unimportant that the argument must be fatuous. But that of course is Ross's point, that these variants are linguistically trivial and therefore do not hinder communication across the class divide but at the same time mark the social distinction very clearly. Ross calls them 'philologically trivial and, apparently, almost all of a very ephemeral nature' (ibid: 104). Socially, however, they are not at all trivial because, if Ross's argument is to be accepted, the non-U speaker can never convincingly become a U speaker. The non-U speaker may learn to use U usages but always too late since new ones emerge to maintain the social difference.

This is not, however, the case with the use of non-discriminatory language, since the campaigns in its favour take for granted that it is possible to become non-discriminatory language users. In so doing, we are also choosing what may be regarded as more 'correct'.

3.4 Non-discriminatory language

Non-discriminatory language attempts to be neutral as to group membership. Its neutrality distinguishes it from discriminatory language, which is defined in a recent booklet issued by the Equal Opportunities Unit of the University of Melbourne as: 'that which creates or reinforces a hierarchy of difference between people … including sex and gender, race, ethnicity, class, sexuality, age, political or religious beliefs and physical, intellectual or psychiatric disability' (EOU 1998: 5).

The purpose of the booklet is to 'expose how language can be used in discriminatory ways' (ibid: 4). It discusses topics such as false generics ('man' used to mean both men and women), compounds with 'man' that can be perceived as exclusive (e.g. 'manmade', 'manpower'), the use of clichés and stock phrases that may reinforce invisibility of the out-groups (e.g. 'man in the street', 'man of letters/science'), occupational titles which convey assumed gender or class norms (e.g. 'cleaning lady', 'groundsman'), paternalism whereby less powerful groups are infantilised (e.g. 'waitress', 'comedienne'), discriminatory humour (e.g. ethnic and racial jokes), quoting discriminatory material (here the commentary suggests the use of 'sic' to draw attention to the fact that the discriminatory words are a quotation).

The lists of U/non-U terms are intended as statements of fact. Non-U speakers are not supposed to see them as accusations, although that is probably how they do see them. The campaign for non-discriminatory language use goes further, further even than the pedagogic guides whose mission it is to prescribe Standard English. The EOU booklet is proscribing rather than prescribing.

3.5 Correctness and the applied linguist

The correctness issue presents itself as a language problem to the applied linguist in two ways. First, as an issue which, as we have seen, is constantly drawn to the attention of students in particular and of the public more generally. The applied linguist has a professional responsibility to take a serious interest in all aspects of the issue, including public concern. Second, the applied linguist, in person or in writing, is properly called on for guidance about the choices of usage students, and indeed all of us, must make. Is the response again to be that these decisions are unimportant because the matter seems so often apparently trivial?

The theoretical linguist's view is that these are not linguistic questions but either unimportant 'performance' errors or social ones and in both cases outside their concern. But for the applied linguist they are very much questions that belong within applied linguistics and to them the applied linguist has three responses.

The first is theoretical and has to do with what people's concern for correctness means, and the answer of the applied linguist is, somewhat unexpectedly, that it represents just how systematic is speakers' use of a language. It invites the applied linguist to: 'address the major question: why does language exhibit such a great degree of regularity?' (Taylor 1990). Such a view necessarily widens the more restricted linguistic concept of language, suggesting ways in which applied linguistics may support and improve the somewhat impoverished abstraction of language which today acts as the focus of linguistic attention.

The second response follows on from the first in that it recognises that for the applied linguist these pre- and pro-scriptive views are themselves all part of the correctness problem and that to dismiss them as irrelevant or uninformed or indeed trivial is to turn away from the real use of language to the laboratory. The applied linguist may be sceptical about the stern calls for a non-discriminatory language use, on the grounds that language engineering is often ineffectual, but he/she does recognise that the motivation to ameliorate the wrongs of society is genuine and is part of the current politico-linguistic context. Discriminatory and non-discriminatory choices need to be presented by the applied linguist as options available to language users and attention drawn to the implications of one or other choice.

Third, the applied linguist must be more than objectively critical (and sceptical) in the sense of making informed assessments of the correctness issue. As a teacher and trainer of teachers he/she must also take sides and legislate for students and others as to which language choices are at this point in time more or less standard. In doing so he/she may be wrong, of course, but that is to recognise that even the informed are themselves caught up in time's linguistic turn.

What is significant about my choice of these three factors is the acceptance by applied linguists of the need to act as a bridge between their language expertise and the skills and knowledge in the specialist area in which resides the language problem they are addressing.

4 SOME FACTORS IN FORENSIC LINGUISTICS

Forensic linguistics has been defined as the stylistic analysis of statements made to the police by those accused of criminal activity.

4.1 Example 1

In 1991 two applied linguists were invited to act as expert witnesses in the Country Court of Victoria in Australia in a case involving an accused person of non-English-speaking background who had been charged with assaulting a police officer (Jensen 1991). At a preliminary hearing the counsel for the defence attempted to establish that the accused should have had the assistance of an interpreter at the time of his arrest and police interview. The police record of interview contained a detailed confession of guilt, and was thus a key item of evidence in the case for the prosecution. If this item of evidence could be shown to have been unfairly obtained (and separately, obtained under duress) it would be excluded from evidence before the jury and result in the accused being acquitted. This in fact is what happened.

I want to look now at this example in the light of the relevant factors.

4.1.1 Educational

During evidence in court it was necessary for the two applied-linguistics witnesses to convince the prosecuting counsel (and the judge) that their educational qualifications were such that they could be accepted as expert witnesses in their field.

4.1.2 Specialist professional knowledge

The applied linguist who works on languages for specific purposes (e.g. English for chemical engineers, Japanese for tourist guides, German for musicology) must seek advice on the content of those disciplines from specialists in these fields. Similarly, with forensic linguistics, the applied linguist needs advice about the workings of the law, insofar as they affect the way in which evidence is to be given. Such advice will of course be given by the relevant specialist, in this case the lawyer for the defence or prosecution, depending on which side the applied linguist is appearing for. In addition, if the case concerns an area with its own specialism (financial probity, perhaps, or aircraft parts), the applied linguist will need information from specialists in these areas on how to interpret the content of the transcripts which he/she is analysing stylistically.

4.1.3 Linguistic and phonetic

Since the applied linguist is called on to support one or other counsel as an expert witness rather than as the chief investigator in forensic language problems, it is likely to be the linguistic and phonetic factors that he/she must concentrate on. What is typically at issue here is whether it is probable that the accused said or wrote what he/she is recorded as having said or written. Such assessment requires careful judgement of the accused's level of English proficiency as well as a thorough stylistic analysis of the transcripts so as to infer whether someone at the proficiency level of the accused was likely to have made those statements and whether the transcript showed consistency of proficiency. In the case in question the applied linguists' evidence was accepted and the accused acquitted.

4.1.4 Professional expertise

Equally interesting was the need for the two applied linguists to establish that their professional field could itself be regarded as a distinct area of scholarly expertise. Unless this was established to the satisfaction of the court, their evidence could not be heard, on the grounds that experts are permitted to offer opinions only on matters which the average person of good common sense (e.g. a jury member) is incapable of assessing (the so-called rule of common knowledge).

4.2 Example 2

When the applied linguist acts as consultant in a police case, the task set is often to compare different versions of what purport to be texts from the same person. These may be different accounts by the police and by the accused of the events in question; they may be two texts which may or may not have been produced by the same person, one perhaps written and the other perhaps spoken. What the applied linguist is called on for is to provide expert evidence on an individual's speech behaviour where this is relevant to the crime of which he/she is accused.

John Gibbons reports on an Australian case in which he has been involved:

> The man involved immigrated from Lebanon in adulthood and spoke a limited amount of English as a second language. He was arrested by police and charged in relation to an alleged drug deal in his house which involved friends and relatives. He was interviewed by police and the interview was recorded in typed form – the police record of interview (PRI). When the case came to trial I was contacted by the man's defence to check the fidelity of the PRI. In order to obtain comparison data I recorded two interviews with him and transcribed them – the Transcript. Soon after, a third description of events was obtained by his counsel using the services of an interpreter – the Statement.

(Gibbons 1995: 175–6)

Gibbons was able to show that the PRI and the Transcript were sufficiently different for the defence to be able to question the veracity of the PRI:

There are two characteristics that differentiate these accounts. In the Transcript the speaker's limited proficiency in English means that he has difficulty in linking clauses, so he presents them in a string, and depends on the listener to construct their relationships. To add the linkages found in the PRI risks misrepresenting the relationships between ideas. The other noticeable difference lies in the frequent repetitions in the Transcript, for example 'I never seen him in my home' is repeated three times, and 'No visitor' is given in addition. This appears highly redundant, but it is of course a common form of emphasis, particularly among second language speakers; and indeed repetition is a codified form of emphasis in some languages. So, similarly, this omission risks misrepresentation … a related difference between the Transcript and the PRI is that the PRI is entirely lacking in affect or rhetorical effects. By comparison the Transcript is more vivid.

(ibid: 183)

Gibbons points also to the clarity and dignity of the speaker when interviewed in his first language through an interpreter. All in all there is good reason to query the PRI as being a doctored version by the police of the accused's account of what happened. He concludes: 'allowing second language speakers to communicate their version of events is not a simple matter … there is a risk of misrepresentation if their words are not accurately transcribed'.

The police force with which Gibbons was working (New South Wales) have been influenced by advice such as his and have introduced videorecording of statements. Gibbons hopes that they will also accept the need for interpreters, difficult though it may be to arrange, 'to reveal a second language speaker's full and accurate account of events (as well as giving a more accurate impression of their intellectual maturity)' (ibid: 183–4).

5 APPLIED SYLISTICS

'Stylistics occupies the middle ground between linguistics and literature.'
(Widdowson 1975: 117)

That may very well be the case but it does not resolve the ambiguity basic to all stylistic endeavour, which is whether its purpose is (in both literary and non-literary texts) to examine and describe the ways of working that the texts exemplify; or whether in addition it is to add to our understanding of the meaning of those texts. Freeman (1970: 14) fudges the issue: 'modern linguistics can make substantive factual and theoretical contributions to our understanding of the poetic process'.

It may be that contemporary approaches to the reading and to the criticism of literature avoids commitment on either of these options. Since there is no one meaning in any literary text and since the reader is free to interpret in an individual and unique way, then that freedom of interpretation will not be constrained by increasing his/her understanding of the poetic process. What this also does is to steer between those opposing views of literature, the one that literature is a particular use of the ordinary language for purposes of imagination and heightened sensibility; the other that literature makes us of a language variety which bears no relation to so-called ordinary language. The question the stylistician addresses is not whether this text is in English or in some special English code which deserves its own grammar. The question addressed is how does the writer gain the effects that this text seems to produce?

The interest in linguistics by scholars in literature and other disciplines can be illustrated by Levi-Strauss's announcement in his inaugural lecture at the Collège de France in 1961 that he saw anthropology as part of semiology. This was part of what might be called the Saussurean turn, which summarises the attraction for the propositions put forward by Saussure in his Cours de Linguistique Générale. A more recent but equally influential writer, Stanley Fish, has developed a theory of reading or of reading literature which is liberating from the traditional views of literature as some special almost magical type of language which could only be approached in some recondite hermeneutic way. Fish makes it clear that reading literature is precisely that: it is about how to read a genre and not about cherishing a set of literary objects; furthermore that the reader's response is what needs explaining. Culler makes the point:

> If one claims that the qualities of literary works can be identified only in the structure of the reader's response, then literary theory has a crucial and explanatory task; it must account for responses by investigating the conventions and norms which enable responses and interpretations to be as they are. No longer need one maintain, in the face of the evidence, that the language of poetry is objectively different from the language of prose. The same sentence can have different meanings in poetry and prose because there are conventions that lead one to respond to it differently.
>
> (Culler 1981: 123)

Recent treatments of stylistics have moved on from the study of the form of linguistic utterances to a wider interest in pragmatics or, as it is sometimes called, pragmastylistics. Such an approach is no longer confined to the treatment of speech acts as though they were our sole pragmatic indicators. What it does is to attempt to provide 'a framework for explaining the relations between linguistic form and pragmatic interpretation and how the style of a communication varies as the speaker aids the hearer to identify the thought behind an utterance, and the implicit interchanges with the explicit' (Hickey 1990: 9).

Hickey (1990: 9) proposes that 'the very concept of style assumes a special significance in the area of creative literature, for that is where it finds its "highest" expressions. How a reader responds to a literary work may, in fact, be the very test of its "texture" or even its value, and such response constitutes the subjective aspect of style … while the linguistic surface of the text, being the stimulus of any response, represents the objective side of the same phenomenon' (ibid: 157).

The necessary emphasis on reader response makes sense when the readers are all highly educated native speakers of the language of the text. But in the majority of cases in which applied linguistics interests itself, most of the readers are either unwilling readers or have both inadequate target language proficiency and limited cultural knowledge on which literary texts typically draw. And since the purpose of a course in applied stylistics is not primarily to foster literary appreciation or even an interest in literature for its own sake (such aims may be pursued elsewhere in a general course of applied linguistics), it becomes necessary for the teaching to provide both the information that will be lacking to the second-language reader and also to find ways of simulating the interaction with the text by the student which the ideal reader would give. To this end various methodologies of presentation have been worked out, of which Enkvist and Leppiniemi's (1990) is one. Their conclusion (drawn from one of their protocols) that the reader should 'use your imagination to create your own world of a poem' (ibid: 205) fits very nicely our own view of the role of stylistics in an applied linguistics course, or what we should now really call applied stylistics: the aim is not, it must be repeated, to appreciate literary texts, it is not even to provide readings of literary texts; rather it is to show how a linguistic approach to the language of literature can be fruitful in meshing with the responses of the (typical) reader. In other words it provides an extension to the student's skills of reading. Providing the means to enable the development of these skills itself requires a high degree of skill which does not in itself depend on the institution of an education system. In other words applied stylistics (which can be equally well be applied to non-literary texts) can be used in journalism as well as in textbooks, in advertising as well as in simplified readers. As Cook reminds us, what stylistics emphasises are 'patterns of formal features and deviations from normal use. Literary stylistics ... has closely scrutinised the linguistic idiosyncracies of particular texts, and speculated upon the connection between linguistic choices and effects upon the reader' (1998: 205). Applied linguistics scrutinises and speculates, but its primary contribution to stylistics appears to lie in the analysis and then in the design of specialised reading materials.

6 LEXICOGRAPHY

> 'Neither is a dictionary a bad book to read.
>   There is no cant in it, no excess of
> Explanation, and it is full of suggestion.
>   The raw material of possible poems
>   And histories.'
>   (Ralph Waldo Emerson, 'Dictionary Poem')

As always, preparation for an activity provides an insight into the nature of that activity. So what sort of training does a lexicographer need? Alain Rey suggests that the lexicographer needs theoretical knowledge that includes (but is more than) linguistics:

For would-be lexicographers, learning linguistics boils down to choices. Each topic in linguistics has more or less importance according to the types of dictionaries involved, the intention of the authors, and above all the target: learners, native or non-native speakers, children or grown-ups etc. Lexicography has often been called a branch of applied linguistics, which I take to be an oversimplified view, since much knowledge other than linguistics is involved. What is really needed is 'applied linguistics for lexicography'. It has to be defined and promoted as a didactic domain, along with applied rhetorics, applied ethnology, applied literary studies, etc. ... for the benefit of lexicography. Such a domain would centre on semantics (not only lexical) and morphology, but it would not leave out syntax, phonetics and/or phonemics. It would be close to sociolinguistics and anthropology, and would include part of terminology, LSP and documentary content analysis.

(Rey 1984: 95)

What is interesting to us is, first, that identification with (followed by rejection from) applied linguistics and then, second, the appeal to a quite narrow view of linguistics. What emerges is that Rey's view of applied linguistics for would-be lexicographers is in the tradition of linguistics applied: learn up on semantics, syntax morphology, phonetics and phonemics (or phonology).

We shall be looking at the training of applied linguists in Chapter 6. As I explain there, it is my view that there is a common core of knowledge and skill that all applied linguists need and thereafter they may specialise in one or more areas of interest. That seems to me what Rey is basically saying, that there is a central aspect of lexicography which is applied linguistics, a normative intervention on language in use. As such it is not primarily of interest to theoretical linguistics, which is not, as we have seen, concerned with language in use. The problem with Rey's formulation is that he emphasises a linguistic content without recognising that that content must be shaped for the needs of the applied linguist, who in this case is the lexicographer in embryo. His 'applied linguistics for lexicography' therefore becomes applied linguistics which lexicographers need. As do language testers, language teachers, language planners, speech therapists and so on. They will all need the further specialist input peculiar to their own vocation, just as lexicographers do.

Rey does have an insight into the importance of a carefully designed applied linguistics which is not linguistics applied:

In my own experience of more than twenty-five years of dictionary editing, many good or excellent theoreticians and scholars in linguistics proved unable to cope with such specific tasks as:
- analysing the sub-classes of occurrences of a word or lexical unit in a given corpus that would provide a lexicographically satisfactory structure;
1. writing good definitions
2. choosing the right examples from a corpus

I was often puzzled by such problems and discovered slowly that good linguists may well ignore everything relevant to producing a text about words, idioms and phrases that was supposed to be used by, and useful to, somebody besides their fellow linguists.

(ibid: 95)

Rey continues with the necessary professional skills and these need not delay us here. What is relevant is his insistence on the need of the lexicographer for an expanded conception of linguistics, involving 'epistemology ... technology, anthropology, the history of culture, the theory of literature (etc.) as the occasion might require' (ibid: 97).

Such an expanded view of the linguistics necessary to the lexicographer matches our own view of applied linguistics, whether we call it an expanded linguistics or not. Our argument here is that after a course at the graduate level in applied linguistics the successful student has covered all the applied linguistics needed for the profession of lexicography. Of course the personal skills and the professional skills that Rey refers to are extra.

Lexicographers compile dictionaries. But what is a dictionary? The word is used so widely that it may seem that the only agreed definition that encompasses all uses of the term is that it refers to a set of presentations about words. There are many definitions; one that has achieved some respect is that of C. C. Berg: 'a dictionary is a systematically arranged list of socialized linguistic forms compiled from the speech habits of a given speech-community and commented on by the author in such a way that the qualified reader understands the meaning of each separate form, and is informed of the relevant facts concerning the functions of that form in its community' (Berg quoted in Green 1996: 22).

Further definitions examine the characteristics which make a reference book a dictionary. J. Rey-Debove offers the following criteria:

- a list of separate graphic statements
- a book designed for consultation
- a book with two structures (word-list and contents)
- a book in which items are classed by form or content
- a repository of information that is linguistic in nature
- a repository of information that is explicitly didactic
- a source of information about signs
- a place where the word-list corresponds to a pre-determined set and is structured if not exhaustive

Such technical definitions make clear just how complex is the task of the lexicographer and what sorts of knowledge and skills are necessary. But such a complex list necessarily has many holes, in that many collections that not only are labelled dictionaries but are referred to by that apellation do not conform in all characteristics. And what the list does not include is the crucial problem of selection. As we have seen, this is the necessary challenge to the curriculum designer and mutatis mutandi to the language tester (Davies et al. 1999). It is always the case that in any intervention on language which aims to capture its characteristics for whatever purpose (teaching, testing, listing its vocabulary) a selection must be made since the whole of the language can never be captured. (Indeed what does 'the whole of the language' mean? Given the dynamic of change there is never at any point in time when the whole of the language is available to be captured, except in the case of a language that is long dead.)

Selection of items for a dictionary brings into sharp focus the problem and eventually the impossibility of distinguishing the descriptive and the prescriptive. As we have just seen, all description inevitably involves some measure of prescription. No English dictionary claims to do more than sample the 4 million words of English: the second edition of the *Oxford English Dictionary* and Webster's third edition each contains less than 500,000 words. 'For the most part what to leave out will not be in contention. There are, for example, more than 6 million registered chemical compounds: the great majority of these will not be selected. But there are seriously contentious areas such as the obscenities, those taboo words for sexual and excretory activities, and their inclusion arouses anger and must now be treated with care or relegated to specialist dictionaries of slang even though such reticence is a fairly modern phenomenon' (Green 1996: 24).

Their targets may change over time (thus the conservative outrage at the changes in the third edition of Webster have been replaced by current ultra-liberal demands, notably of the politically correct variety in relation to terms of racist and gender abuse, insisting that that terms such as 'nigger' and 'Jew' should be excluded. For the applied linguist there is need to balance the reality of actual language use and at the same time to be sensitive to the attitudes towards that use since attitudes are part of that context of use. As Green writes:

> [T]he lexicographer is in an invidious position. Damned if he (or she) does and damned if he (or she) doesn't. The role of the dictionary-maker is to reflect the language, which in turn is a reflection of the culture in which it exists. If the culture in part is racist, sexist and in other ways politically incorrect, then so too in part must the dictionaries be. The best they can offer is some parenthetical declaration that a given word or phrase, in a given definition or usage, is so. Otherwise, if they start censoring out such material, of what real worth can they be considered.
>
> (1996: 379–80)

Selection in a different sense can be an indication of the extent of separation of a language variety from its origins. Thus the first dictionary of American English appeared in 1828 (Noah Webster) and the first of Australian English in 1981. There are dictionaries of New Zealand, Canadian, South-African English, Caribbean English, Singaporean English, Indian English but not of German English, Mexican English and so on. At least if there are, then they are essentially lists of local terms. It appears that a dictionary is a symbol of separation. Which explains why there is no German or Mexican since their separation is otherwise declared.

7   LANGUAGE TREATMENT (*TRAITEMENT DE LANGUES*/ARTIFICIAL LANGUAGES)

'If you are to go to the trouble of learning a language you need to feel that you will get a return for your toil this very year. A man may plant an orchard and wait six years for his apples; but six months is long enough to wait for verbs and prepositions to bear fruit.'

(I. A. Richards 1943: 155)

Utopianism, that millennial belief in the perfectibility of human language so that communication is facilitated, logic encouraged and language learning made readily (and easily) accessible to all is an old story. When there is a natural language which has become the language of wider discourse through imperial success (Latin until the seventeenth century, English in the twentieth century), the appeal of the problem-free invention or modification diminishes. But in the seventeenth century when Latin went into decline in the West, the search for an improved international language increased.

Artificial languages have two major advantages over natural languages: they are not the property of any state who claim priority of possession since it is their mother tongue; and they can be constructed on a logical basis. If an artificial language is composed entirely of invented elements (and therefore known as an *a priori* artificial language), it is more likely that it will fulfil the logical criterion (since it can be designed as if it were some kind of mathematics); if it is based in part on elements of grammar and vocabulary from one or more natural languages, it is known as an *a posteriori* artificial language. The *a posteriori* variety may be less strong on logic (and therefore not meet the second criterion of an artificial language) but its part dependency on natural languages gives it the right feel for learning and perhaps for development. Many artificial languages have combined features that are both *a priori* and *a posteriori*.

The most successful artificial languages are Volapuk, Esperanto and Interlingua. Schleyer's Volapuk combined *a priori* and *a posteriori* elements: the vocabulary was largely taken from European languages, mainly English, modified so as to make it easier to learn by 'old people, children and Chinese': thus 'red' became 'led' and 'rose' 'lol'.

Here is the beginning of the Lord's Prayer in Volapuk:

O Fat obas, kel binol in suls,
paisaludomoz nem ola.

In spite of the modifications, Volapuk (the name modified from the English for 'world' and 'speech') proved too difficult to learn and was overtaken by Esperanto, also created in the 1870s. Esperanto was more deliberately *a posteriori*, based on the Romance languages, with smaller roles for other European languages. Esperanto has been very successful, with some 10 million speakers world wide. Zamenhof, the inventor of Esperanto, in very near all cases used existing Romance vocabulary and yet made the rules sufficiently flexible that the language could incorporate new words to meet new needs. As such, Esperantists do have some justification when they call it a living language. Whether they are also justified in their view that Esperanto provides the solution to the world's communication needs is questionable. Their claim is based on the following factors:

1. Esperanto has been shown to be capable of written and spoken development in a number of fields, in science and literature.
2. The language can be quickly learnt, no doubt because it cleverly combines features of a natural language with the logic of a constructed one.
3. It is internationally acceptable. The merit of this argument is less obvious and it seems likely that Esperanto remains less acceptable to speakers of non-European languages. There is a view that Esperanto is slowly changing its base as non-European speakers learn it and introduce their own vocabulary. But there is an irony there: if Esperanto does change in ways such as this, it could render it less easy to learn in the future by Romance speakers.
4. It has survived for 100 years and gained considerable support. But again, that support is not in any sense mass support. Those who have learnt the language and use it tend to be those who are interested in Esperanto rather than in international communication.

Interlingua takes the Esperanto idea a stage further in that it contains very little *a priori* elements. The alternative name for Interlingua, *Latino sine flexione* (Latin without inflexions), makes clear that the language is Romance in grammar (without gender and without inflexions), and Romance and/or English in vocabulary.

Gode, who developed Interlingua in the 1950s, was never interested in the replacement by Interlingua of any natural language. Rather, he saw it as a useful addition. He intended it to be used for science and technology and above all for translations, abstracts and summaries, for largely passive use. Once again, as with Esperanto, the ambition to make international communication easier is unreal precisely because the language favours those who themselves have a Romance background and at the same time does not offer the abundant advantages (not only for passive reading of science and technology abstracts) that learning a natural 'international' language (such as English) must offer.

Volapuk, Esperanto and Interlingua are all artificial languages in that they all make use of some *a priori* elements and they combine several natural languages rather than being based on one only. Modified languages differ from artificial ones in that they have no *a priori* elements and they are indeed based on one natural language. The best example is Basic English (C. K. Ogden 1937). Like Interlingua, the purpose of Basic English was to promote mainly technical communication: hence its name B(ritish) A(merican) S(cientific) I(nternational) C(ommunication). It consists of 850 English words, 'selected to cover everyday needs ... the working principle is that all words not on this list can be replaced by words that are ... The simplification of the vocabulary is achieved at the expense of a more complex grammar and a greater reliance on idiomatic construction' (Crystal 1995: 356).

Basic English was found to be easy to learn to read but difficult to write in with any facility, perhaps because it was fundamentally a means of vocabulary selection and control, leaving the learner (especially the non-English-speaking learner) to grapple with the complexities of circumlocution. It has been remarked that Ogden simplified the vocabulary at the expense of the grammar. Furthermore its claim to contain only 850 words was flawed in that those 850 were head words, which meant that there were in fact very many more which were based on those head words.

Applied linguistics has shown little interest in artificial and modified languages, unless we are to claim that Zamenhof, Gode, Ogden and the other inventors were themselves applied linguists. In the sense that they have made use of linguistic principles for an extra-linguistic purpose, in this case wider communication, they certainly have a claim to being applied linguists. But it would seem that their approach to applied linguistics is from the linguistic end, that they are being linguists applied rather than applied linguists. And it is indeed the case that the artificial languages, notably Esperanto, have attracted support from linguists on the grounds that they can meet certain of the criteria we have already discussed and furthermore actually look natural. Modified languages, on the other hand, seem more likely to appeal to non-linguists, rather than to linguists, who take exception to all forms of simplification. Hence their appeal to politicians such as Churchill and Roosevelt, both of course first-language speakers of English.

But the applied linguist has shown little or no interest. Why is that? Large maintains:

> The very number of artificial languages invented indicates a deeply-felt need, at least among the linguistically inclined, to impose order and rationality on the haphazard instruments which have evolved for human communication. Points of syntax are disputed endlessly, yet there is very little debate about the way in which the international auxiliary or the world language would actually be chosen and implemented. Perhaps this is not very surprising: it is a shame to sully the intellectual discussion of language with the grubby facts of political reality. If supporters of an international language are to win credibility, however, reality, no matter how unpleasant, must be confronted.

(Large 1983: 157–8)

And since the focus of the applied linguist is on language in context, he/she is likely to regard artificial languages with a jaundiced eye. In Chapter 4 (section 4) we made the basic argument that for the applied linguist, language problems involve more than language, listing the factors that must be taken into account.

Confronted by this list of factors that must be taken into account we can wonder that artificial languages were ever considered viable. We have quoted Large on the political aspect but an equally strong case against artificial languages can be made on the other grounds, for example educational (providing the necessary resources for teaching and learning), sociolinguistic (natural languages provide a major source of identity for their speakers: it is difficult to see how this can transfer to an artificial language, which has as one of its purposes the denial of local identity), psychological (how motivated will people be to learn a language that, at least at present, has very little to offer, not many speakers, no films, no pop songs, few books and so on), cultural (natural languages are culture bearing but how can an artificial language fulfil this function until it too becomes a natural language and then prone to all the problems that artificial languages seek to avoid).

Crystal (1987) is not optimistic about take up for artificial languages, even on semantic grounds where he points to the lack of semantic matching across languages: 'Speakers of different languages may translate their mother-tongue words into an artificial language, but this does not necessarily mean that they understand each another any better. The figurative, idiomatic and connotative uses of words will differ: for example, American and Soviet attitudes to a word like capitalism will not alter simply because both sides agree to use the same artificial language label' (Crystal 1987: 355).

As we shall see in Chapter 7, the applied linguist has been accused of being seduced by power, of furthering the spread of dominant languages and not giving sufficient support to the declining languages of minority groups. That may or may not be the case: for many applied linguists it seems perfectly possible to support language spread as a means of furthering wider communication as much among the minorities as elsewhere and at the same time to offer support and expertise to the speakers of declining languages in their attempts to survive. But above all the applied linguist is likely to take a realistic view of the situation; and in the case of language treatment, if the factors we have suggested he/she must take into account are relevant, then it is likely that projects to develop artificial languages and modified languages such as Basic English will be regarded as both flawed and irrelevant to the solution of language problems.

8 CONCLUSION

In the last three chapters we have exemplified the work of applied linguistics, first (in Chapter 3) as distinct from that of linguistics; second (in Chapter 4) in the fields of language teaching and learning; and third (in Chapter 5) in other areas of language use. We turn in Chapters 6 and 7 to more general considerations. In Chapter 6 we discuss the professionalising of applied linguistics, while in Chapter 7 we query how far current philosophical developments in the humanities and social sciences have affected applied linguistics and in particular how influential the various 'critical' stances (e.g. critical applied linguistics, critical discourse analysis) are. We end Chapter 7 and the book with a state-of-the-art review, in which we take stock of applied linguistics at the end of the twentieth century and estimate what the future holds for the discipline.

Chapter 6

The professionalising of applied linguists

'Let me recite what history teaches, history teaches.'
(Gertrude Stein, 'If I Told Him (A Completed Portrait of Picasso)'.)

1 INTRODUCTION

Now that we have exemplified the work and methods of applied linguistics, ranging widely across the kinds of language problems addressed by the discipline, we turn in the final two chapters to two fundamental questions, that of the status of the profession and that of the philosophical foundation of the subject. First, then, in this chapter we discuss the extent to which applied linguistics can be regarded as a distinct profession, its growth from early beginnings after the Second World War, its institutional organisation, its provision of training and education for new members and its concern with professional ethics.

2 THE GROWTH OF APPLIED LINGUISTICS

2.1 The flight to the professions

Applied linguistics has not escaped the so-called flight to the professions that has been on the increase since the 1960s. In academia it has been seized on by those disciplines for which there are direct vocational opportunities outside the academy. Like other applied disciplines such as social work and business studies, applied linguistics has been largely taken up by those who are already working in the field. For that reason the entry has been at the postgraduate level and also for that reason those seeking qualifications in applied linguistics are not typically seeking a career change so much as career enhancement, perhaps by moving into a more developmental or research or management area but still broadly within applied linguistics.

The beginnings of applied linguistics in the UK can be traced back to the 1950s.

2.2 Applied linguistics in Edinburgh

In an unpublished paper (1974) Pit Corder noted that:

The British Council had, ever since the war, together with the Foreign Office, been much concerned with the quality and organisation of the teaching of English as a second language in overseas countries. It had become gradually apparent to them that there was a level of knowledge and expertise in the development of teaching programmes and materials and in the preparation of English teachers for which no adequate training programmes existed in British universities. Clearly, a component in this knowledge and expertise was linguistic. Linguistics was known to be well-established in Edinburgh at the post-graduate level. Consequently, approaches were made by the British Council and the Foreign Office to the Principal of the University to explore the possibility of the University providing facilities for advanced training and research into the teaching of English as a second language.

After discussion of possible names for the new unit, such as:

1. Centre for the Advanced Theory and Practice of Teaching English as a Second Language, and
2. Centre for Advanced Research and Instruction on the Teaching of English as a Foreign Language

it was decided to use the name: 'School of Applied Linguistics' with the subtitle 'Research and Training in the Teaching of English as a Second Language'.

The first Director of the new School, Ian Catford (1959), later commented:

For some years now, the term 'Applied Linguistics' has been gaining currency. The Michigan periodical *Language Learning* has carried the sub-title 'A Journal of Applied Linguistics' since its inception in 1948. In 1954 one of the Georgetown Monographs on Languages and Linguistics appeared with the title 'Applied Linguistics in Language Teaching', and the term has appeared in a number of other publications. More significantly, perhaps, 'Applied Linguistics' was the title of a Section of the 8th International Congress of Linguists at Oslo in 1957. In this context of the growing acceptance of the term 'Applied Linguistics' it is not surprising that it should have received academic recognition with the opening, in October 1957, of the School of Applied Linguistics in the University of Edinburgh.

Three other universities in the UK (Bangor, Leeds and London, University College) joined Edinburgh in the early 1960s in developing applied linguistics (not always with the same title), as did Reading and Essex later. For the most part, the primary object was to provide experienced overseas teachers, particularly those who were actively concerned with the control of English-teaching policy and the training of teachers, with an intensive training in the disciplines which were thought to be relevant to language teaching, and in methods of research in this field. Delivering that training meant regularly renewing the input (the source) while remaining faithful to the needs of language teaching, the output or target in this field.

With the passage of time since 1957 there have been changes in applied-linguistics programmes. First, there has been a re-evaluation of what is meant by 'training' and a growing understanding that training is meaningless unless it is broader, more conceptual, an education rather than a training. Second, there have been important changes in the disciplines which are thought to be relevant to language teaching, for example more linguistics and less phonetics; psychology has become psycholinguistics and sociolinguistics has become a major component. During the same period more recent cross-disciplines have emerged, subjects such as second-language acquisition, discourse analysis and language proficiency testing.

2.3 Source and target

The central debate in applied linguistics has always been about the tension between the source (linguistics alone or a consortium of disciplines bearing on language studies) and the target (teaching English to speakers of other languages (TESOL) or a wider concern with language in the world). What Edinburgh succeeded in doing was to maintain a steady gaze at both ends, both the source as consortium and the object as TESOL. A lack of balance at one end can mean that the source becomes too narrow. Emphasising the source at the expense of the target is likely to divert applied linguistics towards greater control by linguistics.

Equally, overemphasis on the target can mean a possessive concern with the here-and-now, with attempting to solve the problems of the local situation and with a momentum towards practical solutions and away from theoretical underpinnings. Overemphasis on the target is likely to take applied linguistics into mainstream academic education.

2.4 The importance of speculation

Balancing source and target is very much in the tradition of the eighteenth-century Enlightenment, which was of such importance in the development of academic, vocational and technical education. The ideas of analysis, of toleration, of openness to ideas free of the restraints of religious conformity, and of improvement, all these optimistic and humanist projects are found in the excitements of the Enlightenment. It was after all the Age of Revolutions, and yet people retained a sense of responsibility.

Broadie writes of 'a concept of the interrelation between the three disciplines of ethics, economics and engineering. Solutions to engineering problems have immediate economic consequences which themselves have to be judged in terms of ethical criteria. The three form a system of thought, a unity of disciplines' (1997: 19).

And within the ranks of the Enlightenment there raged the age-old battle between realists and nominalists (or perhaps more accurately conceptualists). For David Hume 'nature is in large measure a product of our own imaginative activity. We make the world we live in' (Broadie 1997: 19), while Thomas Reid espoused a kind of naive realism, what came to be called the Philosophy of Common Sense: sensations were not mere ideas or subjective impressions but carried with them the belief in corresponding qualities as belonging to external objects. Reid insisted that such beliefs belong to the common sense and reason of mankind and in matters of common sense the learned and the unlearned, the philosopher and the day-labourer are upon a level. Echoes here perhaps of today's ethnomethodology and perhaps too of the extreme relativism of some postmodernists, which we consider in some detail in Chapter 7.

Also very much in the Enlightenment tradition was the importance given to speculation, which is now often contrasted with empiricism. From the *OED* sense of 'contemplation, consideration or profound study of some subject' and 'conclusion reached by abstract or hypothetical reasoning' speculation has come to be used in somewhat disparaging ways, often preceded by 'mere', 'bare' or 'pure', implying conjecture or surmise. This of course quite apart from its more operatic senses of 'action or practice of buying and selling goods, lands, stocks and shares etc in order to profit by the rise or fall in the market value as distinct from regular trading or investment; engagement in any business enterprise or transaction of a venturesome or risky nature, but offering the chance of great or unusual gain'. Alas! try as they may no applied-linguistic speculator has, as far as I am aware, yet reached great or unusual gain!

It turns out that speculation and empiricism should not in fact be in conflict. What contradicts empiricism is rationalism. While 'empiricism' attracts the comment: 'reason cannot of its own provide us with knowledge of reality without reference to sense experience and the use of our sense organs' (Angeles 1981: 75), rationalism has this one: 'reality is knowable … independently of observation, experience and the use of empirical methods; reason is the principal organ of knowledge and science is basically a rationally conceived deductive system only indirectly concerned with sense experience' (ibid: 236).

It would be convenient to agree that speculation combines the two senses of (random) conjecture and of reasoning attaching to some explanatory theory, while empiricism means the use of experimental methods to validate a theory. However, what seems to have happened is that empirical has appropriated to itself the package of the scientific methods, theory *plus* controlled enquiry, while speculation has increasingly been marginalised to the armchair, the haphazard and the guess.

Happily, speculation is not just a snapper-up of unconsidered trifles. In the same definition of speculative philosophy, we read: 'in the non-pejorative sense: philosophy which constructs a synthesis of knowledge from many fields (the sciences, the arts, religion, ethics, social sciences) and theorizes (reflects) about such things as its significance to humankind, and about what it indicates about reality as a whole' (Angeles 1981: 272). We should remember this noble description next time applied linguistics is labelled 'mere' speculation!

2.5 Conclusions

Since the 1950s applied linguistics has spread widely. There are now some thirty-five national affiliates of AILA, and applied linguistics is taught as an academic discipline throughout the world. As Brumfit remarks it is now very varied, ranging from an engagement with the isms of critical analysis and postmodernisms (gender, development, multiculturalism, poverty and racism), to a general deconstruction of existing paternalist universalisms, to the focusing on one linguistic theory and, its opposite, to the emphasis on contrastive analysis and a concern with teaching methodology.

The professionalising of applied linguistics in this period has inevitably raised the issue of coherence. Should we expect graduates in applied linguistics from different universities to have followed the same courses? The answer is surely no for content but yes for concept. The three basic concepts are: language use, language learning and investigating (or researching) the using and the learning. These concepts are where coherence lies.

Successful development of the profession of applied linguistics is closely linked to its insistence on maintaining a balance between source and target. Given the absence in applied linguistics of sanctions (nobody can be prevented from claiming to be an applied linguist, however unqualified and unprincipled), applied linguists offer one another the support and the scrutiny of an 'ethical milieu' (Homan 1991). The tension between theory and practice in applied linguistics, between complexifying and simplifying has always existed. Tensions, of course, suggest that balance is to be found somewhere between. The attraction of applied linguistics is precisely that it is a theorising activity, moving from practice to theory, janus-like, offering a framework for explanation and a blueprint for action.

3 THE PROFESSION OF APPLIED LINGUISTICS

3. 1 A general need

A new profession develops to meet a general need. At first the trainers will be members of existing professions, but gradually ad-hoc training will be set up; this will move on to part- and then full-time training courses, at first of short duration and then year-long initiations and finally three- or four-year apprenticeships that we know as Ph.D. programmes. And in due course the professional institutions that these neophytes set up will come to take responsibility for the approval of new training programmes, while the responsibility for teaching the new applied-linguistics students becomes the responsibility of those who have now emerged from the newly set up degree programmes.

3.2 Institutional applied linguistics

The main international body in the field is AILA, the International Association of Applied Linguistics.

The first academic journals of international standing to devote themselves explicitly to applied linguistics appear to have been in North America, the journal *Language Learning* (1948), and in Europe the *International Review of Applied Linguistics* (*IRAL* 1963). Other internationally recognised journals have since appeared, notably the *TESOL Quarterly* (1966), the official academic publication of the US-based association of Teachers of English to Speakers of Other Languages, and *System* (1973), and, most recently, but probably most authoritatively, *Applied Linguistics* itself (1980), under joint British and North-American editorship, sponsored by the British and American Associations for Applied Linguistics (BAAL and AAAL), and published in cooperation with the International Association of Applied Linguistics (AILA). Since 1981 *Annnual Review of Applied Linguistics* has appeared, published by Cambridge University Press. The major abstracting journal in the field is *Language Teaching*, published quarterly by Cambridge University Press, and carrying a substantial 'state of the art' review in each issue (Johnson and Johnson 1998: 10).

We should add:

Australian Review of Applied Linguistics (1980)
International Journal of Applied Linguistics (1991)
Issues in Applied Linguistics (1990)

There are, in addition, important journals in sub-areas of applied linguistics, for example:

Discourse and Society (1990)
English for Specific Purposes (1980)
English Language Teaching Journal (1946)
Journal of Multilingual and Multicultural Development (1980)
Language and Education (1986)
Language and Literature (1992)
Language Teaching (1968)
Language Testing (1984)
Language Testing Update (1985)
Language, Culture and Communication (1988)
Second Language Research (1985)
Studies in Second Language acquisition (1978)
World Englishes (1982)

3.3 Defining a profession

The definition of a profession appears to be straightforward. In Webster's Third Dictionary (1994), the definition of profession is:

a calling requiring specialised knowledge and often long and intensive preparation, including instruction in skills and methods as well as in the scientific, historical and scholarly principles underlying such skills and methods, maintaining by force of organisation or concerted opinion high standards of achievement and conduct, and committing its members to continued study and to a kind of work which has for its prime purpose the rendering of a public service.

What has happened this century is a flight into professionalism, a result of the rising proportion of occupations that have required a high standard of education.

Many of these occupations have aspired to professional status. In the first half of this century the number of males in professional employment in the UK increased five-fold (from 1 to 5 per cent). The criteria for professional status can be short-listed (by Wilensky 1964, for example) or long-listed (Musgrave 1965). On the basis of the short-list (full-time, a training system, a professional association, a code of ethics), applied linguistics makes the cut. The issue is less clear on the long-list: knowledge base, conditions of service, public recognition, all yes; control of entry, controlling professional association, code of professional conduct, all are queries.

3.4 Need for reflection

We can distinguish perhaps between a profession and a trade union in terms of knowledge and what the teacher-education literature calls theory. Accounts all emphasise the need for the professional of reflection, of being aware. Educationists such as Wallace (1991, 1998), Woodward (1991) emphasise the need to operation-alise this awareness through action research, whereby all teaching is a means of reflecting on theory, fusing the one into the other. This is not a new idea: Michael Young's *Innovation and Research in Education* (1965) argued for making education a continuing experiment. In applied linguistics much of the teaching at Master's level can be thought of as innovative, as a form of action research, encouraging reflection.

Where does the reflection, the ability to reflect, come from? Is it innate, to be over-easily labelled as a matter of personality and therefore not our responsibility, or can it be taught? In my view it is teachable. The bringing together of the how to reflect and the what to reflect on is, I suggest, exactly what applied linguistics is about. It is after all a commonplace among those who teach applied linguistics that new students (with or without language-teaching experience) begin their courses by not seeing why applied linguistics asks the questions it does ask and end their courses by asking those very questions themselves through their projects, and their disser-tations and their seminars.

3.5 Strong and weak professions

'Strong' professions (for example medicine, law) establish their own regulatory bodies which control entry. 'Weak' professions (such as applied linguistics) lack such sanctions. Hence the importance of the 'ethical milieu'. But weak professions can establish a professional association (with regularised membership, an office, officers, publications and so on); to become 'strong' professions they also need to reach agree-ment on recognised qualifications licensing members to practise as professionals, control (through licensing) on entry to the profession and therefore on standards and behaviour. This control is difficult to achieve and probably requires legal support. Unlike medicine or law (or indeed psychology) there is no restriction on who can practise as an applied linguist. However, in the absence of external sanctions informal control can be exercised through the 'ethical milieu'. Through formalised training programmes leading to degrees and certificates, through internal discussion, conferences such as the triennial AILA Congress and annual meetings of the national associations, through regular publications of *Applied Linguistics* and the other general and specialised journals in the field, through agreement, as far as possible, on what is required to become a professional applied linguist.

Weak professions may compensate themselves for their lack of sanctions by condemning the power exercised by traditional professions. This is the point made by Marshall, who maintains there is an ideological aspect to professionalism:

> Recent sociological work has tended to view professionalisation as the establishment of effective interest group control over clients, with socially constructed problems as a means of exercising 'power' in society. This approach treats professional ethics as an ideology, rather than an orientation necessarily adhered to or meaningful in practice. Entry and knowledge controls function as a form of status exclusion from privileged and remunerative employment. In this respect, professional organisations make an interesting comparison with trade unions, for although formal professional ethics preclude collective bargaining and industrial conflict, in practice many associations have found themselves becoming more and more unionate, whilst many unions practise quasi-professional job-entry control.
>
> (1994: 419)

4   ETHICS IN APPLIED LINGUISTICS

4.1   Current concern

In this last section of the chapter I refer to the recent upsurge in interest in professional ethics and consider its impact on the profession of applied linguistics.

Ethics, the study of how we are to live, of right and wrong, also known as moral philosophy, has been called 'the emperor of the social sciences' (Scriven 1991: 134). But it is only in the 1990s that the emperor has been reclothed. Coady and Bloch refer to the current 'obsession with ethics … not the ethics of private individuals so much as the ethical behaviour of groups, whether these groups are professions, businesses, government or non-government organisations' (1996: 1).

There is another reason for this current 'obsession' with ethics, which is its neglect in the first part of the twentieth century. That period, writes Singer (1986), 'was aberrant … due to the influence of logical positivism, with its implication that ethical statements were nothing more than the evincing of emotions' (Singer 1995: 42–3).

Linguistic philosophy, concerned as it was with meaning rather than knowledge, queried the whole basis of ethics, maintaining that ethical statements were essentially circular. 'Ethics, as I conceive it, is the logical study of the language of morals' (Hare 1952: v).

The critical turn in the last decades has made the quest for meaning equally problematic and in a paradoxical way has prompted the search for fragments of knowledge as bulwarks against the emptiness that postmodernism threatens.

Docherty discusses the 'basis of an ethical demand in the postmodern', admitting that 'there is no escape from the necessity of judging in any specific case. Yet' he agonises 'we have no grounds upon which to base our judging' (1993: 26).

Hence, no doubt, the currrent search for ethical guidance as to what may be expected in group behaviour. This search is reflexive in that it seeks to provide some small certainty for the group and at the same time it helps to define an identity for the group.

Rawls refers to two (equal) principles of justice:

[F]irst each person engaged in an institution or affected by it has an equal right to the most extensive liberty compatible with a like liberty for all; and second, inequalities as defined by the institutional structure or fostered by it are arbitrary unless it is reasonable to expect that they will work out to everyone's advantage and provided that the positions and offices to which they attach or from which they may be gained are open to all.

(1967: 221)

And so one of the chief roles for ethics is to balance these two principles, the individual and the social. This requires thought and imagination as much as law-making, offering: 'a way of conceptualising difference which renders it compatible with equality, but also, and crucially, does not simply increase social differentiation' (Mendus 1992: 414).

The danger, of course, is that in our attempts to be fair we end up by destroying completely the social, making all morality individual and therefore never ever achieving fairness anyway. Indeed, Osborne, lamenting the influence on philosophy of post-structuralism and feminism, suggests that we are left only with 'personal ethics or the search for small forms of valid knowledge' (1992: 181).

This is a counsel of despair, but Jackson (1996) shows a way of avoiding such a solipsist trap. Discussing codes of practice she points out that morality is never absolute. For example, codes of health and safety require appropriate protection of employees. At the same time, in all such cases there is a clause (either implicit or explicit) which limits employers' responsibility to 'within reason'. Otherwise, their duty would be impossible to fulfil.

Without the recognition of the 'within reason' limitation, we are likely to exaggerate the demands of morality and to assume wrongly that you cannot get on in business or carry out your profession unless you are prepared to cast aside or compromise principles. This is not so. Morality as typically encoded in codes of practice constrains action within reason.

4.2 Professional morality in applied linguistics

Ethics has a clear role in institutional settings where there is concern to declare and to limit individual rights and responsibilities. This applies particularly to professions. House offers this definition: 'Ethics are the rules or standards of right conduct or practice, especially the standards of a profession' (1990: 91).

These rules are often encoded in a Code of Practice or Code of Ethics. The British Association for Applied Linguistics, which celebrated its thirtieth anniversary in 1997, issued a document for discussion in 1994 entitled 'Draft Recommendations on Good Practice in Applied Linguistics'. Good practice in applied linguistics, the document makes clear, is based on the acknowledgement of responsibilities to a variety of stakeholders, including the subject of applied linguistics itself:

> Most of this document is organised around the different work relationships that applied linguists engage in, and within these, it offers a checklist of important issues, cross-referencing to other guidelines where these may be of value. This document isn't designed as a set of criteria for professional accreditation in applied linguistics, and it doesn't provide any recipes for professional decision-making. In a changing climate of teaching and research, its suggestions are intended to help applied linguists to maintain high standards and to respond flexibly to new opportunities, acting in the spirit of good equal opportunities practice and showing due respect to all participants, to the values of truth, fairness and open democracy, and to the integrity of applied linguistics as a body of knowledge and a mode of inquiry.
>
> (BAAL 1994: 2)

The stakeholders are those with whom applied linguists have work relationships. They include colleagues, students, the public, researchers, informants and sponsors. The recommendations are quite admirable and, in want of anything more enforceable, necessary. But they do have something of the unrealistic about them. Thus:

> Contracts with sponsors raise issues that are too numerous and too complex to be treated adequately in the present document. These include: the composition of steering committees; lines of communication; the ownership of data and findings; publication rights; contract termination. Applied linguists need to be careful about the terms on which they accept contracts for investigation, as well as being very clear about the amount of autonomy which they will be able to exercise ... Before signing a contract, applied linguists would be well-advised to seek expert advice, and to refer to the detailed suggestions in, for example, CVCP 1992, Sponsored University Research; Recommendations and guidance on contract issues.
>
> (ibid: 13)

The harsh reality is that in these days of contract research, of over-production and resource shrinkage, it is difficult in many cases to turn down a contract for a project on the grounds of principle alone, on the abstraction of ethics which, however admirable, is unenforceable in the profession as a whole. But we should not give up. 'You must go on. I can't go on, I'll go on' Beckett (1959: 418) wrote. The fact of probable non observance of a code of conduct is not grounds for its abandoning. These are early days for applied linguistics, the professional esprit de corps takes time to build and in the meantime the sense of the ethical milieu slowly develops.

Koehn (1994) considers that what characterises a profession is that it serves clients rather than makes a customer-type contract. The profession's moral authority is established by its unconditional concern for the client's good, by its willingness to act when needed, by its willingness to sustain its service, by its certified competence, by its preparedness to demonstrate its accountability, by its discretion on behalf of its clients and by its self-monitoring. Professions make a public statement that dedicates their agents to a position of public trust, and it is notable that it is the agent (the member of the profession) who is bound not the client. In a contract, on the other hand, the obligation lies equally on both parties. What the professional offers is service or duty, to be professional, to act professionally rather than to be successful, since success cannot be guaranteed.

The relativisation of all knowledge(s) within postmodernism inevitably bears heavily on education. Those areas of education in which language is both means and end, whether in the teaching of the first or the second/foreign language, have become notable sites for struggle, since what is seen to be at stake is socialisation into a culture as well as the shaping of modes of cognitive development. It is not surprising therefore that in applied linguistics there is both the yearning for an ethics and at the same time a mistrust of what may be regarded as the imposition of a universal ethics.

4.3 Limits on ethics

Group ethics must aim at balance: not too much (the 'within reason' limitation) but not too little. What is at issue here is the danger of an incestuous concern with the protection of members of the profession by avoiding and covering over complaints and offences to avoid litigation. Educational linguistics does not in general have the life and death risks that medicine does, but all professional activity involving language provides for potential complaints and legal action because of the intrusive nature of the activity and its normative role.

Safeguards for professional practitioners, in applied linguistics as much as in medicine, are necessary but it is important that the safeguards are also applicable to stakeholders other than the professionals themselves. Otherwise they become not safeguards but fortresses.

Coady and Bloch note that the current obsession with group ethics has produced a proliferation of written statements setting out what the group intends. 'One reaction of these groups to the challenges of government and to the cynicism of clients and taxpayers is to proclaim their ethical standards through establishing or reestablishing codes of ethics' (1996: 1). It may be that our concern with codes represents a kind of false consciousness with regard to professionalism, a kind of flag of convenience to justify the public and professional claims of an activity in relation to society at large. Hence the doubts about the value of codes. It may therefore be more important to look at less formal statements about an activity, such as the training and the socialising of apprentices. Atkinson writes of practical job training in clinical medicine as 'doctrinal conversion' and of 'passing through the mirror'. And he comments that 'most studies of professional socialisation have tended to concentrate on how the novice comes to take on the appropriate perspectives and understandings, behaviour and values which characterise their newly-gained occupational culture' (Atkinson 1981: 19–20).

4.4 Judging project ethics

I return now to the five examples of applied linguistics I discussed in the first part of Chapter 2 and consider then from the standpoint of applied-linguistics ethics. We also consider them from the point of view of critical applied linguistics (CAL), asking ourselves to what extent CAL is a politically correct substitute for ethics.

What might be the role of professional ethics in the five exemplar projects we described in the first part of Chapter 2? They were language-programme evaluation in South India; a second-language literacy study; pedagogical grammar; workplace communication; and critical pedagogy. I now examine those projects in terms of their ethical responsibilities to the various stakeholders discussed in the BAAL (1994) document. I do not, of course, intend to be critical of the applied linguists involved in these projects and will not be investigating whether or not they addressed the ethical issues raised here. The point I make is that there are ethical issues to be addressed; it is professionally important that they be addressed.

4.4.1 Language-programme evaluation in South India

The BAAL document contains this advice: 'When working away from one's own locality, it is important to consider the interests of local scholars and researchers. In locations away from the UK, matters such as the disparity of resources or access to publications may need to be handled with sensitivity. The status of "visiting expert" can also be problematic, although seeking the active involvement of local applied linguists may help to avoid this' (BAAL 1994: 4–5). Questions would need to be asked about the ethical neutrality of the South India project, with respect to the possible bias of the visiting experts, both the British and the Indian; and about the involvement of the programme sponsor (the British Overseas Development Administration through the British Council) in the evaluation.

4.4.2 Second-language literacy study

This project was part of a much larger investigation into second-language literacy which researched the issue both historically and empirically. It became clear during the project that there was uncertainty among the team members as to their ethical and professional obligations, in relation to both quantity of work to be done, in terms of the share of the funding available and in terms of their final publication responsibilities. The BAAL document draws attention to this matter:

> [W]hen working in collaborative or team research with other researchers, research assistants, clerical staff or students, applied linguists should make everyone's ethical and professional obligations clear. Care should be taken to clarify the roles,

rights and obligations of team members in relation to: the division of labour and responsibilities; access and rights in data and fieldnotes; access to travel and conference expenses; publications; co-authorship in publication.

(ibid: 4)

Probing of the ethical aspects also reveals that the authors of the critical survey may not have not considered the more basic question of why this project had been funded in the first place and to what extent an interventionist approach to second-language literacy represents an unwelcome intrusion.

4.4.3 Pedagogical grammar

The BAAL document contains this passage: 'It is important to take account of equal opportunities issues, to be alert to issues arising from inequalities of power between teachers and students, and to ensure that students are treated on the basis of their abilities and potential, regardless of their gender, "race", religion, sexual orientation, physical disability, family circumstances or other irrelevant factors' (ibid: 5).

This pedagogical grammar project could be regarded as unfairly advantaging English native speakers since the grammatical distinctions made call on native-speaker intuitions. The question is whether native speakers can be regarded as unfairly privileged (Davies 1991a).

4.4.4 Workplace communication

The report on the project explains that it is based on an analysis of 'recordings of genuine examples of ... conversations and meetings ... to find out how each side interprets what has happened in the conversation' (Gumperz et al. 1979: 9). The ethical question to the forefront in this type of project has to be concerned with the roles and rights of the informants used by the researchers, those whose discourse was recorded and then analysed for use in the Crosstalk materials. The document advises: 'Applied linguists should respect the rights, interests, sensitivities, and privacy of their informants. It is important to try to anticipate any harmful effects or disruptions to informants' lives and environment, and to avoid any stress, undue intrusion and real or perceived exploitation. Researchers have a responsibility to be sensitive to cultural, religious, gender, age and other differences' (BAAL 1994: 9). Questions would need to be asked about the care taken to ensure that the informants used in this project were properly, that is ethically treated.

4.4.5 Critical pedagogy

The BAAL document states under the section dealing with responsibilities to the public:

Awareness of the impact of one's work: in setting up research, consideration should be given to conflicting interests. In principle, greater access to well-founded information should serve rather than threaten the interests of society. But it is necessary to consider the effects of research on all groups within society, including those that are not directly involved. Information can be misconstrued or misused. Applied linguists should try to anticipate likely misinterpretations, and the damage they might cause, and counteract them when they occur.

(ibid: 7)

In his advocacy of 'critical pedagogy' the researcher in this project makes the following comment: 'Broadly speaking, then, critical pedagogy aims to change both schooling and society, to the mutual benefit of both' (Pennycook 1994a: 297). Questions would need to be asked here regarding the outcome of such research towards students, given that attention appears to have moved away from language and culture, and their interaction, towards politics: 'critical pedagogy takes schools as cultural and political arenas where different cultural, ideological and social forms are constantly in struggle' (ibid: 297).

4.5 A CAL view: ethics again?

Critical applied linguistics (CAL) brings into applied linguistics a postmodern view of knowledge and of the ways in which it is socially constructed (see Chapter 7). CAL rejects all grand theories of language in use such as the inevitability of English as a world language, proffering 'scepticism towards all metanarratives' (Lyotard 1984). It outs traditional applied linguistics as an enterprise which is hegemonic and has never been neutral (Rampton 1997: 20).

Such critiques have of course long been expressed by traditional applied linguists, most vividly by those who position themselves ideologically as neo-Marxists. But, at its most sophisticated, CAL, while accepting the role that larger social and economic and political systems play in power relations, argues that their impact on everyday experience cannot so easily be predicted (Pennycook 1994b).

We now re-examine the first four of these projects from the point of view of critical applied linguistics. The fifth, as a product of CAL, is not discussed here. What might be the approach of CAL to the four exemplar projects we have described in this chapter?

4.5.1 Language-programme evaluation in South India

A CAL analysis of this project might begin with questions related to the extent of the involvement of all stakeholders in the evaluation, noting, for example, that students were not involved and that in all cases the final arbiters were two external judges, both of whom had all the credentials of neo-colonial attitudes. Next, the four college activities would be considered, and it would be pointed out that the compulsory link to a British funding body, reinforced by the involvement of British institutions (including the British Council and British, or British-controlled, publishers) removed all aspects of choice from local players. And finally the need for English language, which these projects were supposedly satisfying, would itself be shown to be questionable, in that it was a constructed need, or could so be interpreted; that there were other options (e.g. English not tied to a British–English model and to UK resources, Tamil, Hindi) that the acceptance of the funding structure did not permit.

Perhaps the severest criticism would be reserved for the two evaluators. In addition to the doubts mentioned above about their allegiances, it would also be noted that they took no responsibility for querying the guidelines of their evaluation brief and as such themselves contributed to the continuation of the power structure within which these Indian colleges, their students and staff, were locked into a client role. In short the CAL position would be that since the fundamental neo-colonial relationship was ethically wrong, no tinkering with the surface features would produce any results of interest or value.

4.5.2 Second-language literacy study

To an extent CAL takes an individualist approach to the solution of language problems. With regard to the bilingual literacy project CAL would therefore maintain that judgements based on group performance are uninteresting and that there can be no exception to the principles of individual rights and individual access. As such, there would be strong support for the provision of first-language literacy as a means of ensuring cognitive growth and as a bridge to the acquisition of literacy in the second language. The doubts expressed by the project's applied linguists would therefore be dismissed as once again hegemonic, reflecting a patronising view as to the role and superior efficacy of a language such as English.

As can be seen, in the cases of the examples of the language-programme evaluation and the second-language literacy study, CAL would offer what might be regarded as an idealistic ethical view, taking no account either of the availability of resources or of the social facts of for example the position in the world (in India, or in Australia) of English. And so in spite of its claims to be socially concerned, CAL appears to be individually oriented. This puts a question mark against its role within applied linguistics as it has been practised, since that practice has always been socially aware, context sensitive, attempting to bring together what is known about language and local realities. CAL looks much more like the abstraction we expect in theoretical linguistics. But of course the bottom line of CAL is that it does raise the fundamental question within applied linguistics, which is whether its traditional practice has in fact been misguided.

4.5.3 Pedagogical grammar

The practice of providing in a pedagogical grammar 'tightly controlled practice in writing sentences' would be derided by CAL as making discourse (or grammar) part of language rather than looking 'at how meanings are a product of social and cultural relationships and then (turns) to see how these may be realised in language' (Pennycook 1994b: 116).

Unless, therefore, Mitchell's (1990) use of the sentences:

1. Mary is as tall as her father.
2. Mary and her father are identical in height.

is deliberately intended to make the familiar unfamiliar by locating 'the context of language use, the speakers and their intentions in a wider social, cultural, and political context', then the CAL conclusion would be that pedagogical grammar is simply giving instruction in how sentences can be put together.

Is this fair? Mitchell's appeal to logical, semantic and pragmatic meanings as well as lexicogrammatical resources suggests that in his view pedagogical grammars are offering explanations as to why things are said, not just how things are said. Whether he is correct or not, there is of course a further somewhat obvious point to make against so strong a CAL position and this is that the sole purpose of pedagogical grammars can be claimed to be to set out the how: the why is quite deliberately left for other areas of language teaching.

4.5.4 Workplace communication

The CAL requirement to make 'the familiar unfamiliar by locating the context of language use, the speakers and their intentions in a wider social, cultural, and political context' would at first blush suggest that the work described under work-place communication meets the CAL criteria. Gumperz et al. is based on an analysis of 'recordings of genuine examples of ... conversations and meetings ... to find out how each side interprets what has happened in the conversation' (1979: 9).

This does seem to meet the CAL requirement. The film and its accompanying material are intended to facilitate advice and teaching in workplace communication skills. They are based on real conversations and interviews, such as the college librarian interview, and take account of feedback from both sides of their interpretations and of what they thought went wrong in terms of inferencing.

It appears that this approach may meet the kind of awareness that Pennycook is looking for. Indeed, perhaps because workplace communication has always been heavily influenced by critical discourse analysis, of all four examples discussed this one is the nearest as it stands to the aims of CAL.

Can we ignore the assumed stipulation that the interview quoted must be held in English, on the grounds that the candidate is likely to be fully fluent in his variety of English? But this is precisely the point: his variety of English! What is lacking – and what CAL might point to – is that in terms of the wider social, cultural and political context, not only are such Asian migrants disadvantaged, but no account is taken of differential communicative competences. What is needed surely is that the Interview Board contain at least one member who is a speaker of the Asian English spoken by the candidate.

And yet, even here, on its own home ground, doesn't CAL go a little far? As we saw with the second-language literacy study, CAL appears to make claims on the basis of individual requirements. How possible is flexibility for an interview panel which needs consistency across candidates, not all of whom are likely to speak the candidate's variety of English? Furthermore, the post under interview presumably needs someone who can fully control the varieties of English in use in the college library. It is unlikely that in the context of a London borough, the composition of the student body would contain only speakers of the candidate's variety of Asian English. It therefore seems not unfair that the interview panel should, even indirectly, make judgements about the candidate's control over their variety of English which they, not unreasonably, take for granted?

5 CONCLUSION

In this chapter we have examined the institutionalising of applied linguistics as a distinct profession. We move, in Chapter 7, to a consideration of the postmodern and critical influences on applied linguistics.

Applied linguistics: no 'bookish theoric'

'... the bookish theoric,
... mere prattle, without practice,
Is all his soldiership.'

(William Shakespeare, *Othello*: I, i, 24–7.)

1 INTRODUCTION

In Chapter 7 I query how far current philosophical developments in the humanities and social sciences have affected applied linguistics and in particular how influential the various 'critical' stances (for example, critical applied linguistics and critical discourse analysis) are. Chapter 7 ends with a state-of-the-art review in which we take stock of applied linguistics and estimate what the future holds for the discipline.

2 WHAT IS POSTMODERNISM?

The term postmodernism refers to the contemporary sense of scepticism felt by scholars in the humanities and social sciences with regard to progress, in the validity of knowledge and science and generally in universal explanations and the optimism of the Enlightenment: 'we begin to see a shift in emphasis away from what we could call scientific knowledge towards what should properly be considered as a form of narrative knowledge' (Docherty 1993: 25).

Those professing ideas associated with postmodernism speak of rejecting the grand meta narratives of modernity, such as liberalism, Marxism, democracy and the Industrial Revolution, and a championing of the local, the relative and the contingent. It rejects the totalising idea of reason on the grounds that there is no unique reason, only reasons (Lyotard 1984). This emphasis on cultural relativity has established itself in the soft rather than in the hard sciences, above all in literary and cultural studies, which in some academic settings have merged into an over-arching study of contemporary cultural manifestations, especially film and media. In continental Europe (largely France, Germany and Italy) the influence has also reached into philosophy, in part because the 'intellectual' there has always enjoyed greater stature than in the UK (Matthews 1996: 206). Furthermore, the concentration in the UK on linguistic philosophy in the mid-twentieth century was unique to English-speaking countries, leaving continental philosophy to pursue its post-Hegelian interests in the larger questions of knowledge and purpose.

This reflexive concern with the meaning and methodology of the study that one is engaged in, a kind of decentring or reflective awareness (Donaldson 1978), the so-called 'critical turn' in the social sciences and the humanities, has inevitably affected applied linguistics. The increasing influence there of critical applied linguistics, itself a manifestation of the postmodern surge in the 1970s and 1980s may now be on the wane, but its origins and its meaning demand our close attention.

Postmodernism encompasses post-structuralism, itself a reaction against the paradigm shift of structuralism which brought the Enlightenment up to date for the mid-twentieth century. Structuralism rejected the emphasis on the subjective of 'modern' grand theories such as existentialism and psychoanalysis in favour of the objective patterning in social life that derives from the work of Saussure and Levi-Strauss. This patterning was found in fields such as: 'anthropology, linguistics and philosophy, [which] needed to focus on the super-individual structures of language, ritual and kinship which make the individual what he or she is. Simply put, it is not the self that creates culture, but culture that creates the self' (Cahoone 1996: 5).

Linguistics, both general and applied was influenced by this scientific claim of structuralism, as seen in Bloomfield's appeal to linguists to 'wait on science' and in institutional titles such as Reading University's Department of Linguistic Sciences; and the landmark volume of Halliday et al. (1964).

In its turn structuralism was rejected by post-structuralism which castigated the scientific aspirations of structuralism as pretensions. The problem with post-structuralism's rejection was that of the baby and the bath water. It was one thing to reject what was seen to be the pretensions of a scientific linguistics intent on finding out 'the truth'; it was a very different matter to move on from that to abandon the methods of rational enquiry that linguistics and other social disciplines had developed, on the ostensible grounds that if there was no truth to be found then there really was no appropriate methodology for pursuing the study. This is both a counsel of despair and at the same time an unfortunate linking of the pessimism that is endemic to postmodernism to the age-old clash between nominalism and realism (see below).

Docherty, who is no opponent of postmodernism, points to the basic premise of all scholarly observation and critical study: that the outcome will permit generalisation. If there is no appropriate methodology to carry out the observation and the critical study then how is it possible to judge any event or act: 'how can one legitimise an "event" of judging? With respect to what can one validate what must effectively be a singular act?' (1993: 25). To this Docherty has no answer except to say that an answer must be found: 'it is here that the real political burden and trajectory of the postmodern is to be found: the search for a just politics, or the search for just a politics' (ibid: 26–7).

In his article, 'Towards a postmodern pedagogy' (1991/96), Giroux offers nine suggestive principles for a critical pedagogy. In these principles we have a connection between postmodernism and the critical turn. The thrust of these principles is to emphasise the need to challenge existing norms, to value difference, and to regard teachers as transformative individuals; they are 'cultural workers engaged in the production of ideologies and social practices' (Cahoone: 1996: 695).

This helpfully takes us on to the postmodern turn as it has affected applied linguistics in the version that has come to be known as critical applied linguistics (CAL). Docherty notes:

> [T]here is hardly a single field of intellectual endeavour which has not been touched by the 'spectre' of 'the postmodern'. It leaves its traces in every cultural discipline from architecture to zoology, taking in on the way biology, forestry, geography, history, law, literature and the arts in general, medicine, politics, philosophy, sexuality, and so on.
>
> (1993: 1)

Unsurprisingly, therefore, applied linguistics in its CAL version has also felt the spectre of the postmodern. It has felt the spectre particularly in the importance it ascribes to experience, as attested by Giroux's acknowledgement of bell hooks' views on the primacy of experience. This takes us back to earlier in this book (Chapter 2) where, referring to the Religious Society of Friends (Quakers), we discussed the experiential approach that has to a large extent characterised applied linguistics in its UK applied-linguistics empiricist version. In other words, it encourages us to view the CAL version of applied linguistics as unlimited reflection on experience, unchecked and unvalidated by its own professional community.

3 CHANGE IN APPLIED LINGUISTICS PRACTICE

Applied linguistics as practised in the 1960s is recorded in the widely praised volume by S. P. Corder (*Introducing Applied Linguistics*, 1973). We can consider the view of applied linguistics set out in that volume as essentially modernist (or structuralist). Changes have inevitably taken place since the Corder book appeared and therefore the question we address is whether those changes can in any sense be regarded as post-structuralist or postmodernist. We might speculate that it would be surprising if that were not the case, since the involvement of applied linguistics in both the humanities and the social sciences has exposed it to the zeitgeist.

Corder divides his book into three parts:

1. Language and Language Learning
2. Linguistics and Language Teaching
3. The Techniques of Applied Linguistics

As we have seen, he writes: 'I am enough of a purist to believe that "applied linguistics" presupposes "linguistics"; that one cannot apply what one does not possess' (Corder 1973: 7).

Corder's orientation in applied linguistics is, as we saw in Chapter 1, that of linguistics applied. It is not surprising therefore that half the book (Parts 1 and 2) deals with language from a linguistic point of view. The subsections here are:

Part 1
Views of language
Functions of language
The variability of language
Language as a symbolic system

Part 2
Linguistics and language teaching
Psycholinguistics and language teaching
Applied linguistics and language teaching
The description of languages: a primary application of linguistic theory

While Part 1 provides a linguistic view of language, Part 2 offers a linguistic approach to language teaching. Part 3 then examines the practice of applied linguistics, now that the linguistic scene has been set, making it possible to apply what one knows rather than what one does not.

In comparing Corder's view of applied linguistics with what has happened since his book appeared, it is on his Part 3, where he is concerned with the practice of applied linguistics, that our comparison should focus. While leaving a discussion of the theorising (in particular the approach of so-called critical applied linguistics) to the last part of this chapter, we recognise that such a distinction between theory and practice is difficult to support. For those who profess a critical applied-linguistic approach to the subject, what they do is as much practice as it is theory. Nevertheless, to facilitate discussion, we will maintain the fiction that practice and theory are separate.

Corder's Part 3: 'The Techniques of Applied Linguistics' contains the following subsections:

Comparison of varieties
Contrastive linguistic studies
The study of learners' language: error analysis
The structure of the syllabus
Pedagogic grammars
Evaluation, validation and tests

The first three of these he tells us concern selection; it would appear that the next two deal with grading or sequencing and the last one is a free-standing discussion of monitoring the outcomes of the other five chapters. To an extent, therefore, this division by Corder represents an older model, that of language-teaching method-ology (Mackey 1965) or methodics, the division of language-teaching studies into three parts: selection, gradation and presentation. Here we miss out on the last part which Corder presumably regards as not properly part of applied linguistics, more the concern of language-teacher education.

Varieties, contrastive analysis, error analysis, syllabus development, pedagogical grammars and testing: that was the practice of applied linguistics in the 1960s. When we compare the 1960s and the 1990s there are two differences. The first is the expected one that these areas have developed over time: the comparison of varieties has branched into world Englishes, stylistics, discourse analysis, gendered language and so on. Contrastive linguistic studies and the study of learners' language (error analysis) have moved on apace, at first contrastive studies being revitalised by the study of learners' language to become the current study of second-language acquisition, itself also heavily influenced by developments in linguistic grammars. Syllabus studies have become curriculum studies, widening their brief and thereby taking far more of the context in which language teaching takes place into account. Pedagogical grammars might well now be called a pedagogical approach to grammar, while evaluation, validation and tests may well be termed assessment or even perhaps classroom-based assessment.

The second difference concerns what was glaringly missing in the list of chapters in the Corder book. It contained no single chapter with sociolinguistics in its title. This omission seems grave in view of the take-over of applied linguistics by the social turn since 1975. The same is not true of linguistics in its Chomskyan canon, where the quest is still very much in the realist tradition for the truth of language in itself or in the head, with no appeal to context. There are many linguists who do not share this view of linguistics and who consider that a linguistics without the social dimension is a contradiction. But in applied linguistics the social aspect dominates, and it does do for two reasons. The first reason is that in the partial move from linguistics applied to applied linguistics it has been accepted that the social is essential to all understanding of language in use, that in the specific case of language teaching all formal language learning must take account of the context in which that learning takes place and furthermore that the context determines and affects that learning, hence the imposing on to linguistic competence of the superseding communicative competence.

The second reason (and this is not wholly unrelated to the influence of the social) is that there is noticeable now a loss of confidence in the techniques offered by Corder and widely used in the 1960s and 1970s (and indeed 1980s) as general statements of how to proceed. Discourse studies is a good example of that loss of confidence since what it does with exemplary success is to discuss how to analyse and read *a text* rather than how to analyse and read *texts*. Where have we heard this before? Isn't it reminiscent of Lyotard: there is no one unique reason, there are only reasons?

What this suggests is that Corder, and that era of applied linguistics, were indeed 'modern' and 'structuralist', and that in its subsequent practice applied linguistics has become less concerned with over-all solutions. As with the development of communicative competence in part, this has been influenced by the lack of success in using applied linguistics to improve language teaching in any direct way. What it also shows is that applied linguistics is really concerned with approaches and questions and not with solutions. As it actually has always been. What has changed is that this has perhaps become more explicitly marked in the practice.

4 THE NEW CRITIQUE OF APPLIED LINGUISTICS

4.1 Changes

Changes in applied-linguistics practice there have been, but in our view these can be accounted for by appealing to a move from the linguistics-applied to the applied-linguistics model. This has meant bringing the social aspect of language in use into a central position and to an extent downgrading the linguistic and the psycho-linguistic. But there has also been a major change in the rhetoric used to discuss applied linguistics and this has spilled over, as we saw earlier, into practice.

4.2 Emergence of a theory

Corder took an essentially modernist view, that applied linguistics needed theory to explain the practical (and of course the empirical). He himself appeared content early on with an explanatory theory based in linguistics but his own development led him to seek a theory of practice. A theory has indeed emerged since Corder's retirement in the early 1980s, a theory deriving from post-structuralism and postmodernism, the theory calling itself variously 'theory', 'critical theory', 'critical discourse analysis' and 'critical applied linguistics'. We have referred to this theory in Chapters 2 and 6 above. Here we offer a critique of that theory, making clear that in our view it is an inadequate theory to explain and support applied-linguistics practice.

4.3 Rise of relativism

We have maintained that opposition to the realist pursuit of the unique truth does not of necessity end up in the kind of unthinking and impotent relativism that we find, for example in Peim (1993) in his consideration of the value of critical theory to the teacher of English as a mother tongue: .

> The implications of post-structuralist, sociological and sociolinguistic theory throw into doubt all the language practice of (the discipline) English, including all those practices associated with creativity, with self-expression, as well as those that emphasize social aspects of language, like correctness or appropriateness, for example ... The realization of a general field of language and textuality systematically excluded from English represents greatly extended possibilities ... I'm proposing here ... that this more inclusive field be addressed, a field of language and textuality, in which questions of power and ideology, for example, could not be ignored ... To reconstruct English in this way means addressing ... issues of race, class and gender, issues in relation to culture and democracy, concerning among other things, language differences and power, what it means to be literate.
>
> (Peim 1993: 8–9)

It is tempting to wonder how it is that the iconoclasm that has led postmodernism to overthrow all grand theories seems to lead to the setting up of alternatives in their place: race, class, gender, culture, democracy and, above all, power. But what is even more puzzling about Peim's project is what it actually means for language teachers: are they to abandon all skill training? Are all lessons to be concerned with discussions of power? Or are we dealing with the criteria for selection of texts for learners so that they necessarily focus on these 'grand issues'?

A more helpful advocate of the relative position can be found in Block (1996). Block argues, in a characteristic postmodern way against grand theory, in his case the single theory of second-language acquisition research, advocated, he maintains, by Long (1990), Beretta and Crookes (1993). But he is not opposed to the role of a theoretical approach: 'why do we think in applied linguistics that we have to act "scientific" where "scientific" is understood as what is done in physical sciences? We study language acquisition, a phenomenon which is extremely sensitive to changes of context and, this being the case, I propose ... that we evaluate theories in relation to context and purpose' (Bloch 1996: 77).

Critiques of the colonial and the imperial such as we find in the post-colonial views of Kachru (1985) and the post-imperial of Phillipson (1992) can be identified as both modernist and postmodernist. They are postmodernist because they stand up for the rights of the marginalised, whom they wish to empower: to that extent they decry the hegemonising juggernauts of the colonial and the imperial with relation to their totalising influence on English.

And yet they are also modern in that they both offer a single explanation for the phenomenon, in the case of the post-colonial effect on English, the explanation of world Englishes, itself a development of the wider theory of varieties. In the case of the post-imperial, English is charged with the crime of (English) linguistic imperialism, of devaluing and then destroying local languages and so by definition local cultures; we can account for this hypothesis in terms of the one grand theory of linguicism which brooks no argument (Skutnabb-Kangas and Phillipson 1997). Such an approach to theorising applied linguistics resembles a rather simplistic Marxism (see below). It provides an explanation but there is no obvious way in which it can be upheld; it cannot obviously be subjected to the classical Popperian method of disproof, and as such makes the mistake not of failing to explain but of over-explaining, of being for a theory too powerful, so that it explains everything every-where. For such a claim to stand up we need a higher standard of proof, such as is found in the natural sciences.

4.4 Critical discourse analysis

The critique of applied linguistics most often associated with Marxism is that by Fairclough (1989), who has written extensively on critical discourse analysis (CDA). 'Critical' we can now see has to do with theorising and so by 'critical' here is meant using discourse analysis techniques to provide a political critique of the social context – from a Marxist viewpoint. Feminist writings about applied linguistics take a similar approach but from a feminist position.

Fairclough defines what he calls critical language study thus:

Critical is used in the special sense of aiming to show up connections which may be hidden from people – such as the connections between language, power and ideology ... critical language study analyses social interactions in a way which focuses upon their linguistic elements, and which sets out to show up their generally hidden determinants in the system of social relationships, as well as hidden effects they may have upon that system.

(Fairclough 1989: 5)

He is candid about his own starting-point and about his own political purpose:

I write as a socialist with a genuinely low opinion of the social relationships in my society and a commitment to the emancipation of the people who are oppressed by them. This does not, I hope, mean that I am writing political propaganda. The scientific investigation of social matters is perfectly compatible with committed and 'opinionated' investigators (there are no others!) and being committed does not excuse you from arguing rationally or producing evidence for your statements.

(ibid: 5)

Stubbs (1997) is sharply critical of what he regards as the excess of politics and the lack of linguistics in approaches such as Fairclough's:

A repeated criticism [of CDA] is that the textual interpretations of critical linguists are politically rather than linguistically motivated, and that analysts find what they expect to find, whether absences or presences. Sharrock and Anderson (1981) are ironic with reference to critical linguists such as Kress and Fowler: 'One of the stock techniques employed by Kress and his colleagues is to look in the wrong place for something, then complain that they can't find it, and suggest that it is being concealed from them (p. 291).'

(Stubbs 1997: 102)

Stubbs also points out that the approach of CDA has a long pedigree and but was developed by, among others, literary critics such as I. A. Richards (1929), Leavis (1938) and more recently Fish (1980), by phenomenologists such as Schutz (1970) and so on.

4.5 Widdowson's critique

It is possible that the theory espoused by Fairclough, whether modernist or post-modernist, is too powerful, in the sense we have already encountered, of being non-falsifiable. This is basically the criticism made by Widdowson in his critique of critical applied linguistics, more specifically critical discourse analysis (1998: 136–51).

In his critique Widdowson comments on three key texts all published in the 1990s. These are Caldas-Coulthard and Coulthard (1996), Fairclough (1995) and Hodge and Kress (1993). These texts all speak to the need to develop a socially responsible theory of language, committed to social justice. (Widdowson is aware of the difficulty that so praiseworthy a cause presents to those seeking to evaluate it: they render themselves easy targets as enemies of goodness, truth, justice and so on.) He points out that theory, however embryonic, is therefore crucial to the validity of the social justice project. 'It is rightly recognized in all of these books that without such theoretical support, the particular analyses (no matter how ingenious and well-intentioned) reduce to random comment of an impressionistic kind' (Widdowson 1998: 137). Yet in spite of the recognition of the need for an explanatory theory which is open to falsification, 'Fairclough and his critical colleagues', as Widdowson sees it, 'expose how language is exploited in the covert insinuation of ideological influence' to their satisfaction 'by the careful selection and partial interpretation of whatever linguistic features suit their own ideological position and disregarding the rest' (Widdowson: 146).

Widdowson's attack adds force to our own conclusion that what critical discourse analysis (and indeed critical applied linguistics) represents is an offshoot of post-modernism, masquerading as modernity. After all, as we have already noted, the boundaries between the two movements are vague and ill-defined. Widdowson takes Roger Fowler (1981) to task for his cavalier attitude towards theory; for Fowler theory is 'only instrumental, a tool-kit for expedient use, a descriptive device' (Widdowson: 150) in the critical pursuit.

How, then, is 'critical' being used in critical discourse analysis, critical applied linguistics and so on? Hammersley explains the use as follows:

> [I]t implies an abandonment of any constraint on the evaluation of the discourse and contexts that are studied. A central feature of both linguistics and much social science in the twentieth century has been a rejection of normative approaches in favour of an exclusive concern with factual inquiry ... What the term 'critical' generally refers to ... is forms of research which assume: that we can only understand society as a totality and that in producing knowledge of society critical research reveals what is obscured by ideology, such ideology being pervasive and playing an essential role in preserving the status quo.
>
> (1996: 4–5)

It is not difficult to understand the appeal of such a model which unites theory and practice and at the same time is ameliorative in purpose, to an applied discipline such as applied linguistics.

4.6 Critical applied linguistics

But there are further treatments of 'critical' which range more widely in applied linguistics. I shall consider here views expressed by Pennycook (1994a, 1994b) and Rampton (1997). First Pennycook, who approaches discourse analysis from a Foucauldian position, argues that the traditional applied-linguistic approach (which Widdowson would represent) and the critical discourse analysis approach of Fairclough are incommensurable. As both are with the approach he advocates, which:

offers a number of possibilities for engaging critically with language and meaning without falling into some of the materialist or deterministic pitfalls that critical discourse analysis can present. Like critical discourse analysis, it locates the context of language use, the speakers and their intention in a wider social, cultural and political context than the view common to discourse analysis in applied linguistics. This, I believe, is a crucial step in opposing the discourse of pragmatism in applied linguistics and in acknowledging the political in second language education.

(Pennycook 1994b: 133)

Such an approach, which turns on its head both the applied linguistics and the critical discourse analysis view of the relation between language and discourse by positing that discourses produce rather than reflect social reality, Pennycook locates within postmodernism. He explicitly advocates this admittedly relativist stance for applied linguistics on the grounds that it opens the way to a more effective involvement with the major stakeholders.

Writing of the teaching of English as an International Language (EIL) he claims that the approach he advocates can deal with issues seriously rather than following critical discourse analysis, which deals with 'serious issues' (such as crime, abortion and so on). And dealing with issues seriously enables him to make the link both with language being learnt and with the lives of his students (Pennycook 1994a: 132–3).

Pennycook's solution is clearly not directly ameliorative; but neither is it one of despair, unlike the extreme forms of postmodernism. His hope is that 'while we cannot know ourselves or the world around us in any objective fashion, we nevertheless need to ask how it is we come to think as we do' (ibid: 134).

However, Pennycook is unhappy about the hegemonic effect of applied linguistics on language teaching and in his book (1994b) he makes a case for what he terms 'critical pedagogy', which we have already discussed in Chapters 2 and 6:

To teach critically implies a particular understanding not only of education in general but also of the critical educator … In order to pursue critical pedagogies of English, then, we need a reconceptualisation of the role for teachers and applied linguists that does away with the theory-practice divide and views teacher/applied linguists as politically engaged critical educators.

(1994b: 303)

Not so very far from Fairclough after all, it would appear. And it is all very well to make common cause with the need to bring theory and practice together but what exactly does that mean for teaching (or indeed any other application) in the practice of institutions? It is almost as though the whole of applied linguistics was about theory making in some kind of vacuum where there is only virtual learning and teaching and where what the applied linguist does is to engage in debates, each one different from the next, with no point of commonality, all incommensurable, and lacking even the inadequate tool-kit of critical discourse analysis.

The influence of CAL is pervasive and can be unhelpful. In the following extract from a book review (Djité 1996) what becomes clear is that CAL leads the author under review to a kind of impotent inertia, critiquing the present and at a loss about the future. That is the danger inherent in modish CAL:

> The epilogue to the book [Rubagumya 1994] takes the issue of 'critical language awareness' even further, into the realm of the prevailing ideology in language policy and language planning in Africa. In spite of the paradoxical language attitudes of African populations towards the languages of the former colonisers, the author questions the 'common sense', 'pragmatism' and 'wisdom' of the decision of independent African nations to retain these languages. He argues that, if English, French and, to a lesser extent, Portuguese are useful to a lucky few (the elite), they are neither relevant nor useful to the majority who are thus locked out of the democratic process, because they cannot fully participate in the political and economic life of their own country. He comes to the conclusion that the continued defence and promotion of this language policy in Africa can only benefit the political elite who, by so doing, aim to retain their political an economic power over the masses, and the former colonisers who want to maintain their influence over African countries through their language and technology. However, the author is not advocating a rejection of these international languages; rather, he would like to see their place and role re-assessed critically in order to empower the African people.
>
> (Djité 1996: 77)

This is confusing. Is the reviewer agreeing or disagreeing with the author? And what exactly is the author advocating for an African language policy? Are African languages to replace the former colonial ones? Apparently not. Then the language situation should remain as it is but people be made critical of it? Is that likely to improve their proficiency or indeed encourage them to become more literate, more proficient language users? The remedy seems muddled, though it certainly is critical.

4.7 Rampton's 'open field'

Finally in this discussion of the critical and the postmodern, I turn to Rampton (1997). Rampton points to the still-present fault line between the linguistics-applied and the applied-linguistics views of applied linguistics and argues that the attempt to develop an applied-linguistics model (citing both Widdowson and Brumfit) has failed because it simply has not accounted adequately for the work in second-language acquisition research and English-language teaching that has been done under its aegis. If applied linguistics is not to slip back into a comfortable accommodation with the linguistics-applied model (here he mentions Corder) then it needs to be repositioned. Citing the work of Hymes and Bernstein, Rampton argues for a model so different that it would seem to abandon completely any coherence to which applied linguistics might lay claim:

> If in the past in applied linguistics there has been a tendency to attribute special privileges to the generalist, casting him or her as either the central character, sage

or master of ceremonies, this now seems less relevant. Understood as an open field of interest in language, in which those inhabiting or passing through simply show a common commitment to the potential value of dialogue with people who are different, there is no knowing where, between whom or on what the most productive discussions will emerge.

(1997: 14)

It is hard not to see such a scenario as dismissive totally of the attempt since the 1950s to develop a coherent applied linguistics. The fact that the coherence is shaky and that the definitions are uncertain does not mean that the attempt should be abandoned. Rampton is in essence denying the value of a profession which seeks to address institutional problems of language in use. They are, he seems to be saying, open to all. Well indeed, of course they are; but the right of others to address them does not mean that we have to give up on the coherence of applied linguistics.

Brumfit is more resolute. Writing in the Rampton-edited issue of *The International Journal of Applied Linguistics*, which we have already quoted from, he argues:

[A] discipline that is solely the place of meeting of people who could equally well be psychologists, linguistics, cultural theorists – or indeed teachers, therapists or translators – will fragment into separate groupings for each of these practical activities and each of those disciplines, and will fail to address the complexity of language. What holds applied linguistics together is the concern to theorise and analyse social roles and institutions which address language problems, and thus the problems which non-researchers, sometimes unwittingly, confront ... A working definition of applied linguistics will then be: the theoretical and empirical investigation of real-world problems in which language is a central issue.

(1997b: 91–3)

Rampton's recipe for applied linguistics takes us to the extreme of postmodernism, even if unintentionally, since what he proposes suggests that there is no vocation of applied linguist, just individuals working in some loose sense of collaboration. This would seem to fly in the face of all the efforts we have described in Chapter 6 towards the professionalising of applied linguistics and also, as Brumfit points out, to counter the normal condition of any science which is to exist in a permanent state of tension with overlapping disciplines. It is not clear that Rampton does himself take up a postmodern stance, but his advice to applied linguistics could certainly be construed in that way, in the sense that it denies the existence of applied linguists. All is practice: there is no theory except in the Lyotard sense of theories or, as he maintained, no unique reason, just reasons.

If Rampton take us to the edge of postmodernism in his proposals, then what Brumfit (1997b) does is to return us to a very Enlightenment view of applied linguistics. This view insists that there is a coherence to applied linguistics – its blurrings at the edges are no different from those of any other discipline. And while properly dismissing the chaos to which Peim (1993) invites us, he also avoids the attractive relativism to which Block (1996) beckons.

4.8 A theorising approach

Modernist approaches (such as CDA) and postmodernist critiques (such as CAL) of applied linguistics are, as we have seen, seductive. They provide a useful debate on the nature of the discipline, they need to be taken into account. But they must not be allowed to take over, cuckoo-like. Because their interest at the end of the day is not primarily in what Brumfit calls 'real-world problems in which language is a central issue'. And since this is what applied linguistics is about, it is difficult to consider critical approaches as other than marginal to the applied-linguistics enterprise.

In his critique of critical discourse analysis, Widdowson makes the following comment: 'It would appear that what the theory presented here really amounts to is the reaffirmation of the familiar Whorfian notion of linguistic determinism, but applied not only to cognition in respect of the language code, but in respect to its use in communication as well' (Widdowson 1998: 139).

Whorfianism, the notion of linguistic determinism (or linguistic relativity), asserts that thinking and language are so closely connected that our view of the world is determined by the structure of our first language or mother tongue.

Is Widdowson correct about the influence of Whorfianism in CDA? Surely the proponents of critical discourse analysis and of the Foucauldian approach of critical applied linguistics cannot be quite so naive as to fall for the functional fallacy? And yet, perhaps that is the case. Certainly there is a trace of strong Whorfianism running through the certainties of both CDA and CAL which seems to take for granted that language is a direct reflection of meaning. Such a restricted view reflects a meagre view of the resources available to language.

But perhaps at bottom this is a philosophical disagreement between those traditional views of reality, realism and nominalism, realism meaning that universals exist in reality independently of our consciousness and nominalism the opposite.

For the nominalist there is no one-to-one relationship between language and concept: language is a code for referring to meaning but is not of itself that meaning. That must mean that only the very weakest Whorfian position is tenable; it must also mean that the critical approach to discourse analysis or to applied linguistics is vitiated by its own attachment to a realist (and Whorfian) view of language, cognition and meaning. Postmodernist approaches simply take the realist position to its extreme: there is indeed no truth (reason) to be discovered, only truths (reasons). But there is still the fixation on truth. The nominalist, the empiricist and the applied linguist are not concerned with truth but with a theorising explanation. They place themselves in a compromise position between the grand theory of the modernist and the relativity of the postmodernist. Theory, yes but not grand theory. Explanation for the time being – not truth for all time. The search for a theory of applied linguistics is surely misconceived, rather like the hunting of the snark in Lewis Carroll's poem. Applied linguistics does not need a unitary theory; what it requires is an openness to influences and theories from elsewhere, so that professional applied linguists can adopt a theorising approach to language problems.

5 CONCLUSION

The need for a world-wide expansion in English at the end of the Second World War and the resources found for that expansion permitted the rise of an independent applied linguistics. It was probably fortunate that the 'primary object' of teacher education in English as a Foreign Language (see Chapter 6) was dominant for much of that time since it made for the coherent development in applied linguistics as a theorising discipline. Over the forty or so years of its existence applied linguistics has grown and spread. The question I address is whether that growth must lead to fragmentation and shatter all coherence in the discipline.

There are three possible directions for fragmentation: theory, ideology and practice. The first is towards a powerful theory, as we see in current second-language acquisition (SLA) research, attracted at present by the explanatory power of Universal Grammar. That is the micro view but there is a macro view also, which would draw all applied linguistics towards linguistics, the view that applied linguistics is 'really' linguistics applied.

The second fragmentation is that applied linguistics is taken over by the ideology of one or other political variety, the CDA practised by Fairclough, or the more radical, if also more nebulous CAL promoted by Pennycook. There are other ideological possibilities which point away from a political or postmodern outcome: one such alternative would be the linguistics of Harris's language-in-use project.

Finally, there is the practice emphasis which would shift applied linguistics to a future largely within teacher education. Such an outcome has precedents, not only in its attention to the primary object of language-teacher education discussed in Chapter 6 but also in the concerns of those applied linguists whose careers have been spent working in applied linguistics within Faculties of Education.

In addition, there is a fourth scenario, the 'open field of interest in language' put forward by Rampton and discussed above. Such a proposal could, as we saw, lead to a situation in which language problems would be approached by a diverse group who would lack the common experience, understanding and shared language of applied linguistics. They would be unable to frame the relevant questions and propose ways forward. Rampton's solution of an open field does not seem attractive. Is there an alternative?

I think there is. Rampton's analysis of the present state of applied linguistics may make sense but his solution does not. Perfect coherence in applied linguistics is no more to be expected, or, indeed, desired, than in any other academic area. The three sources of fragmentation we have mentioned, the pull towards linguistics applied, the lure of ideology and the concern for practice, these are all signs of a flourishing and creative and concerned profession. What applied linguists need to do is to encourage these developments, rejoicing in them as signs of vitality, while making sure that the primary emphasis on constant re-engagement with the experience of language in use continues. This requires asking the right questions about institutional language problems and then generalising to other contexts where similar problems can be shown after analysis to exist. Such an approach, which theorises practice, will be explanatory and at the same time provide a set of options for action.

Glossary[1]

a posteriori: an artificial language based on elements from one or more natural language.

a priori: an artifical language composed entirely of invented elements.

aboriginal: one indigenous to a country, whose ancestors have lived there during recorded history.

accent: features of pronunciation that identify where a person is from, regionally or socially. Technically distinct from dialect since a standard dialect may be pronounced with a regional accent.

acceptance: acknowledgement by an educated native speaker of a language that a sentence or other linguistic unit conforms to the norms of the language.

achievement test: instrument designed to measure what a person has learned within a given period of time of a known syllabus or course of instruction.

aphasia: loss of speech or of understanding of language, owing to brain damage.

appropriacy: acknowledgement by an educated native speaker of a language that a sentence or other linguistic unit is suitable or possible in a given social situation.

aptitude: innate language learning ability.

artificial language: a language which has been invented to serve some particular purpose.

authentic reading materials: genuine texts rather than those invented solely for language teaching purposes.

background speakers: home-users of a language that is not the official medium of the speech community.

1. The author is indebted to a number of reference works for the definitions in this glossary, in particular to the following:

Crystal, David (1997), *A Dictionary of Linguistics and Phonetics*, 4th edn, Oxford: Blackwell.

Davies, Alan, Annie Brown, Cathie Elder, Kathryn Hill, Tom Lumley and Tim McNamara (1999), *Dictionary of Language Testing*, Cambridge: Cambridge University Press.

Johnson, Keith and Helen Johnson (eds) (1998), *Encyclopedic Dictionary of Applied Linguistics*, Oxford: Blackwell.

Richards, Jack C., John Platt and Heidi Platt (1992), *Longman Dictionary of Language Teaching and Applied Linguistics*, London: Longman.

Basic English: a modified natural language (rather than an artificial language) promoted by C. K. Ogden in the early 1930s (BASIC being an acronym for British American Scientific International Commercial).

Berlitz: the name associated with many language schools world-wide employing a particular method of language teaching in which the target language only is used in class and all the teachers are native speakers.

British Council: a government-funded but independent organisation concerned to foster interest in British culture, including both English language and literature.

case grammar: an approach to grammatical analysis devised by Charles Fillmore in the late 1960s within the generative grammar framework but emphasising certain semantic relationships.

CDA: critical discourse analysis analyses how linguistic choices in texts are used to maintain and create social inequalities.

census: official numbering of a population and its characteristics, carried out in many countries every ten years.

cleft palate: a birth malformation in which a gap exists in the middle or on either side of the roof of the mouth, causing problems in speech production.

clinical linguistics: either the application of linguistics to a medical setting involving language disorders or the practice of professionals such as speech therapists working in those areas.

codification: producing systematic statements of the rules and conventions of a language variety. The variety usually chosen for codification is the standard dialect and the act of codifying increases its acceptance as the standard.

communicative competence: knowledge of how to use a language appropriately as well as the ability actually to do so.

competence: the unconscious or implicit knowledge of language that the native speaker has, and which is the object of linguistics to systematise in rules.

construct: a theory of linguistic knowledge or ability that may be operationalised in a language test.

context of situation: a term deriving from the work of the anthropologist Bronislaw Malinowski referring to the relationship between external world features such as place and participants and a language utterance.

contrastive linguistics: a method of exploring structural similarities and differences between languages, important in historical linguistics and formerly influential in language teaching.

corpus linguistics: a use of the computer to collect a large sample of language both spoken and written for purposes of description.

correctness: the strongly held notion that there are right and wrong language usages.

critical applied linguistics: a judgemental approach by some applied linguists to 'normal' applied linguistics on the grounds that it is not concerned with the transformation of society.

critical discourse: an approach to language use as the manifestation of political ideology.

critical pedagogy: an approach to teaching similar to that of critical applied linguistics.

critical period: the claim that there is a stage in human development during which natural language acquisition is possible, usually placed before puberty. Also known as the sensitive period.

cultural relativity: the view that the values and concepts of a culture are unique to that culture.

curriculum: the total teaching programme of a school or educational system. Sometimes used synonymously with syllabus.

DAL: Department of Applied Linguistics, University of Edinburgh.

declension: a traditional term for a class of nouns, adjectives or pronouns; the usual contemporary linguistic term is word-class.

deficit grammar: the grammar of those whose language development is said to be incomplete. An unfavourable view today with regard to differences among social groups but relevant to the kinds of loss dealt with in clinical linguistics.

descriptive linguistics: the approach which sets out to describe the facts of language usage as they are at a particular period of time.

diachronic: the dimension of linguistic investigation which studies the historical development of languages.

dialect: a regional or social variety of a language, frequently used to refer to any variety which is not the standard,

diglossia: a situation in which two distinct varieties of a language are used in a speech community for quite distinct purposes, for example Classical and Standard Egyptian Arabic in Egypt.

direct method: an approach to language teaching emphasising the spoken language.

direct question: a question which may be answered without inferencing.

discourse: connected texts larger than a sentence.

discriminatory language: racist, sexist etc. language which is hurtful to disempowered groups in society.

Durkheim: Emile Durkheim (1858–1917), French sociologist, one of the founders of modern sociology.

dysarthria: speech abnormalities caused by neuromuscular disorders.

dyslexia: partial inability to read, characterised by associative learning difficulty.

ebonics: a term used for the variety of English spoken by Afro-Americans, also known as Black (American) English.

ECAL 1–4: the *Edinburgh Course in Applied Linguistics*, volumes 1–4.

Educational linguistics: applied linguistics focusing on educational problems.

EFL: English as a Foreign Language.

elaborated code: the term used by Basil Bernstein to refer to the variety of language used in schools and, by implication, by the middle classes.

elaboration: that stage in language standardisation when the aspiring dialect is in the process of (deliberate) development, largely in terminology.

English comparative: a term used for the adjective or adverb used in comparison, for example 'nicer than', 'more lively than'.

Enlightenment: the wide-ranging European intellectual development in the eighteenth century, scientific, technical, philosophical etc.

epicene: a noun or pronoun which can relate to either sex without changing its form.

epistemic relativism: the assumption that propositions are not interpreted in the same way by different groups.

epistemology: the theory or science of the methods or grounds of knowledge.

error: a term used in second-language teaching to refer to a non-trivial deviation from the target language.

error analysis: a procedure typically used in conjunction with contrastive analysis to determine the extent of transfer from the first to the target language.

ESP: English for Specific Purposes.

Esperanto: the most successful artificial auxiliary language, invented by Ludwig Zamenhoff in the late nineteenth century.

ethical milieu: the sense of right conduct shared by members of a profession.

ethics: the science of human duty, often synonymous with morality.

ethnography: study of the forms and functions of communicative behaviour, both verbal and non-verbal, in particular social settings.

ethnomethodology: the use of transcripts of conversations to develop descriptions of the interlocutors' knowledge, especially of the social situation in which they interact. The sociological partner to discourse analysis.

experimentally: by experience, by means of experiment.

factorial: referring to a method of analysis used to reduce a large number of variables to a smaller number known as 'factors'.

false negative: a person classified as failing a test who would have gone on to succeed in the area for which the test is a predictor.

false positive: a person classified as passing a test who would have gone on to fail in the area for which the test is a predictor.

field professional: a specialist in the professional area which has its own specialist language usages, for example a vet.

first-language acquisition: the normal development in a child of his or her first language.

Firth: J. R. Firth (1890–1960), first Professor of Linguistics in the United Kingdom (at the University of London), an important influence on the development of systemic linguistics.

Fish: Stanley Fish (1938–   ), American stylistician.

forensic linguistics: the use of linguistic techniques to investigate crimes in which language forms part of the evidence.

Foucault: Michel Foucault (1926–1984), French philosopher.

function: the use of a language form either in other parts of the system (a noun used as subject) or more generally in situations.

functional linguistics: a linguistic theory taking account of verbal interaction and therefore less abstract than generative linguistics.

genre: type of spoken or written discourse or text recognised as distinct by members of a speech community (for example lecture, shopping list, advertisement).

grading: the staging or arranging of teaching material according to some predetermined order, for example of difficulty.

grammatical model: a method of explaining a linguistic theory.

Halliday: Michael A. K. Halliday (1925–   ), foremost contemporary theoretician of Firthian systemic linguistics.

hegemony: a term used by Antonio Gramsci (1891–1937) for the rule of a social or economic system which is exerted by persuading the disempowered to accept the system of beliefs, values etc. of the ruling class.

HRT: high-rise tone, associated with a shift in English intonation patterns, observed recently among young people in New Zealand and Australia.

IALS: Institute for Applied Language Studies, University of Edinburgh.

idealisation: the degree to which linguists ignore the variability of their raw data.

immersion programmes: a form of bilingual education in which children who speak only one language enter school where a second language is the medium of instruction for all pupils. Originating in Canada (French immersion for English-speaking children) there are now several versions of immersion programmes, depending on the age at which learners begin and the extent of the immersion.

inclusive language: the attempt to revise public documents so as to make them refer to members of both sexes.

informants: those whose knowledge (often as native speakers) is being accessed.

instrumental policy: the political and administrative policy associated with ends rather than means.

interlanguage: the various stages of the learner's second-language development.

Interlingua: like Esperanto, an *a posteriori* artificial language; it was developed by Giuseppe Peano in the early twentieth century.

Labov-type markers: distinguishing social class etc. features, for example the glottal stop, prominent in the sociolinguistic methodology developed from the 1960s onwards by the American linguist, William Labov.

language assessment: measuring or evaluating language ability.

language awareness: the ambition to develop explicit linguistic understanding in the secondary school.

language death: the point at which there are no living speakers of a language.

language decay: the early stages of language death when speakers stop using the dying language for certain functions, for example work.

language planning: the systematic approach to developing language as a national or regional resource.

language-programme evaluation: the process of judging a language programme.

language shift: the process by which a community gives up a language completely in favour of another one.

language treatment: the developing of a language for particular purposes, for example for modernisation, also known as language engineering.

Leavis: F. R. Leavis (1895–1978), British literary critic.

lexicogrammatical: the interconnection of vocabulary and grammar in systemic linguistics.

linguicism: the destruction of a minority language by a more powerful one.

linguistic determinism: *see* Whorf.

linguistic ecology: the study of the interaction of language with its environment.

LOTEs: languages other than English (Australian).

LSP: languages for specific purposes.

Malinowski: Bronislaw Malinowski (1884–1942), London-based anthropologist, inventor of 'participant observation' and originator of the notion of the context of situation.

medium of instruction: the language used for teaching subjects other than the language itself.

meta narratives: large-scale all-embracing explanatory theories associated with the Enlightenment 'project', for example psychoanalysis, Marxism.

methodics: an attempt to develop a science of language-teaching methodology.

modernism: the whole era of grand meta narratives, that is the Enlightenment 'project'.

module: a component of a course, degree or diploma.

morphology: the grammar of the word.

mother tongue: the language first learned (L1), the language of which one is a native speaker.

MSc: Master of Science, first postgraduate degree.

multilingual: one who is proficient in several languages.

multiple literacies: literacies in different modalities, for example in books, television, advertising.

native speaker: *see* mother tongue.

nativist: the belief that normal development proceeds without external influence or intervention.

neuroanatomy: the anatomy of the nervous system.

neuropediatrics: the clinical study of children's nervous system.

neuropsychology: relating to the psychology of the nervous system.

nominalism: the view which regards universals or abstract concepts as mere names without corresponding realities.

non-U: usages which are marks of social inferiority.

norms: standards governing the choice of language code, what to say and when to say it.

notions: semantico-grammatical categories common across languages, for example duration.

overview questions: questions which require the use of inferencing.

pedagogical grammar: a grammatical description of a language which is intended for teaching purposes

personal chair: (in the United Kingdom) a professorship awarded to a university scholar by his or her own institution on the basis of international reputation.

phenomenology: the philosophical study of abstract essences and their connections: the inspiration for ethnomethodology.

phonic method: the method of teaching reading by sounding out each letter.

Plain English Movement: an organisation dedicated to making the public use of English simpler.

politically correct: a label attached to language use which is consciously non-discriminatory.

Popper: Karl Popper (1902–1994), London-based philosopher, best known for his principle of scientific falsifiability.

positivism: a movement associated with August Comte in the mid-nineteenth century, a development of the Enlightenment 'project', and linked to empiricism.

post-colonial: cultural developments following and influenced by the Western powers' colonial period in Africa, Asia and the Americas.

post-imperial: *see* post-colonial.

postmodernism: an extended version of post-structuralism.

post-structuralism: cultural movement, largely in the humanities, doubting the Enlightenment 'project' and large explanatory meta narratives.

pragmatics: the study of language from the point of view of its users and of the choices they make.

prescriptivism: an approach to language which lays down rules of correctness.

primary factor: the first and largest variable in a factor analysis, the dominating underlying ability.

proficiency: ability to use a language.

proficiency test: instrument used to assess proficiency.

profile scores: a method of providing an assessment of proficiency in different areas.

proscriptive: the negative side of prescriptivism.

psycholinguistics: the study of the relation between linguistics and psychological processes.

raising: in phonetics and phonology a process affecting tongue height.

realism: the philosophy that studies truth independent of the human mind and therefore asserts that universals exist in the external world even when they are not perceived.

register: a variety of language defined according to its social use.

reliability: consistency, often referring to test results,

restricted code: the term used by Basil Bernstein to refer to the language used in closed settings, for example a prison, a code which is interpretable only in context and therefore not understandable in public settings.

rhetoric: the study of effective and persuasive speaking and writing.

Richards: I. A. Richards (1893–1979), British literary critic and student of language.

Romance: the term for languages deriving from Latin, for example Italian and French.

SAL: School of Applied Linguistics, University of Edinburgh.

school bilingual programme: a curriculum that permits students to study in more than one language.

Schutz: Alfred Schutz (1899–1959), Austrian and American social philosopher, major influence on ethnomethodology.

second language: any language which is learnt formally or informally after the first, often synonymous with foreign language.

semantics: the branch of linguistics concerned with the study of meaning.

sensitive period: *see* critical period.

sequencing: ordering a set of language teaching materials so that they follow some logical order.

simplified reading materials: teaching materials such as books, papers, in which the grammar and vocabulary have been deliberately made easier for the reader, much used in second-language teaching.

SLA: second-language acquisition.

sociolinguistics: the study of the relation between linguistics and social processes.

speech pathology: the study of abnormalities in the development and use of language in children and adults.

speech therapy: the profession concerned with remedying speech pathologies.

stakeholder: anyone who might be affected by an intervention such as a language test.

standard language: the dialect selected and codified for official purposes, including education.

stylistics: the study of varieties of language (for example register), including literary varieties.

syllabus: the school curriculum for one subject, but *see* curriculum.

symbolic policy: an official policy that is concerned with promoting favourable attitudes rather than language use.

symptomatology: the study of symptoms.

synchronic: the study of a language at one point in time.

treatment: deliberate language development or invention, usually known by its French name, *traitement*. Similar to language engineering.

turn: collective term for trends in twentieth century thought, all of which appeal to language as the furthest point philosophy can reach.

U: the language usages of the socially powerful.

UCH: unitary competence hypothesis, the view that there is one general factor underlying language ability.

ultimate attainment: the level of proficiency characteristic of the educated native speaker.

unit credit scheme: a language-learning system proposed by the Council of Europe in connection with the Threshold Levels.

universal grammar: the view that the aim of linguistics is to specify the unique form of human grammar.

Utopianism: an unrealistic ambition to achieve an ideal social world.

validity: the truth value of a test, the quality that establishes whether it is measuring what it claims to measure.

variety: a neutral term for a language code, used for dialect, register etc.

vernacular: a language variety which is local rather than official or international.

Volapuk: the creation of Johann M. Schleyer in 1879, an artificial language combining features of both *a posteriori* and a *priori* languages.

washback: the influence of a language test on teaching and learning.

whole-word method: a method for teaching children to read by recognising whole words.

Whorf: Benjamin Lee Whorf (1897–1946), American linguist, associated with linguistic determinism or relativism, the idea that the language we speak dictates how we think.

workplace communication: the use of language in work settings, important in a migrant situation where employment depends on language proficiency.

Exercises

EXERCISE 1 (ON CHAPTER 1)

J. Trim, 'Applied linguistics in society', in P. Grunwell (ed.), *Applied Linguistics in Society*, London: CILTR, 1988, p. 6.

The following text is taken from a keynote address given by John Trim, then Chair of the British Association of Applied Linguistics (BAAL), at the 1987 Annual Meeting, which celebrated the twentieth anniversary of the Association's founding.

Trim recalls the events leading up to the founding of BAAL, including the earlier founding of the International Association of Applied Linguistics (usually known by its French title, Association Internationale de Linguistique Appliquée). In this excerpt, Trim remarks on the increasing need for applied-linguistic interventions and the lack of interest in such work by the dominant school of linguistics. The point is similar to that made by Dell Hymes (1971) in his discussion of communicative competence.

> Unfortunately, Chomskyan linguistics ... appears to have contributed little or nothing to the development of applied linguistics, that is to say, to our empirical understanding of the workings of language in the individual and society, and the application of that knowledge, in an interdisciplinary framework, to the treatment of problems of language acquisition, learning and use. Indeed, Chomsky foresaw clearly that this would be the case. The distinction of 'competence' and 'performance', initially helpful in creating space for an autonomous linguistics could be – and has been used to insulate linguistics from empirical accountability. As the earlier excitement of psychologists over its apparent implications for child language acquisition has faded, it seems probable that mainstream linguistics has never been so academically encapsulated, with so little interest in its social consequences and having so little to contribute to the understanding and solution of the many urgent language problems with which society and the individuals which compose it find themselves faced, at a time when communication, still predominantly through the medium of natural language, is becoming more complex, more problematic, more central to organised society. It is surely a cause for deep regret and deep concern if professional academic linguists are so absorbed by

problems of government and binding in syntax that communication engineers, information technologists, logopaedists and aphasiologists, language planners, translators and interpreters, educationists concerned with normal child language development and the language aspects of learning across the curriculum as well as all those concerned with the increasing internationalisation of life, from the management of multinational corporations, the conduct of international and supranational organisations and authorities to the impact on individual lives of personal mobility and the need for access to information, must all fend for themselves and develop, ad hoc, their particular linguistic expertise.

Questions

1. The applied linguist, it is suggested, is interested more in performance than in competence. What is meant by this distinction and why is it important for applied linguistics?
2. List six of the areas that Trim considers require intervention by the applied linguist.
3. Give reasons for agreeing or disagreeing with the writer when he states that 'communication ... is becoming more complex, more problematic, more central to organised society'.

EXERCISE 2A (ON CHAPTER 2)

R. Harris, 'Communication and Language', Oxford: OUP, 1978, in N. Love (ed.), *Selected Writings of Roy Harris*, London: Routledge, 1990, pp. 139–40

In the following text, the author, Roy Harris, considers how the nineteenth-century experimental chemist, Joseph Priestley (who was also an amateur linguist), would view current attitudes towards applied-linguistic issues. Harris notes that for Priestley language could not be removed from other aspects of human life. Priestley, so Harris imagines, would be bewildered by linguists' lack of interest in the social role of language. Priestley saw language as given to man by God, just as the human body is, and as the doctor watches over the body and endeavours to keep it healthy, so the grammarian watches over the health of the language, generally taking care of it.

> [Priestley] would be surprised to see what a great gap had opened up between theoretical linguistics, on the one hand, and practical linguistics on the other. He would find, for example, that many a modern phonologist would be extremely unsympathetic to the idea that phonologists have anything to learn from experimental investigation into the facts of phonetics. Similarly, he would find that remarkably few modern theories of grammar show any great inclination to discover for themselves to what extent the grammatical rules they posit are borne out by observable speech behaviour.
>
> What would strike him about much of modern linguistic theory would be its remoteness from practicalities, the very abstractness – one might almost say

unreality – of its more prominent controversies, the degree of social irrelevance which it had achieved, and, in many ways, seemed only too pleased to have achieved. He might ask why linguistic matters of immediate importance to modern society were often rejected by linguistic theorists as being outside the area of their main concern. He might ask why, for example, it was still necessary in 1975 for the Bullock Report to state that 'all subject teachers need to be aware of the linguistic processes by which their pupils acquire information and understanding'. He might ask why, in an age of newspapers, radio and television, so little is known about the linguistics of the mass media (about how, for instance, a news bulletin should be structured in order to achieve maximum communicational effectiveness.) He would be struck by the fact that whereas we claim to have a theoretical linguistics, we have no linguistics of the living-room, or of the court room or of the class room, or of any other form of socially institutionalised linguistic exchange. He might ask why the theoretical linguistics of a civilisation which depends increasingly on language can apparently tell us so little about how the processes of linguistic communication are shaping the very form and content of that civilisation.

He might even go on to ask himself why the linguistic theorist does not apparently feel any social obligation to concern himself with such matters, but is content to pass the questions on to educationalists, sociologists, psychologists or whoever else happens to be standing by. For he surely would not fail to see how the very terms 'applied linguistics', 'sociolinguistics', 'psycholinguistics', and so on reflect the theoretical linguist's view of the subordinate status of those fields, and of his own central importance.

In short, something that would strike Joseph Priestley most forcibly, I suggest, is the extent to which modern theoretical linguistics had somehow managed to lose sight of the fact that language has to do, in the first and last resort, with communication between human beings, or managed at least to treat this central fact as if it were somehow a concern of subsidiary or peripheral importance.

Questions

1. The writer clearly thinks that Priestley would be puzzled by the view expressed in the sentence quoted from the Bullock Report (*A Language for Life* 1975, a government report on the teaching of English in schools in England and Wales). Exactly what point is the writer making here about teachers and language? Give your reasons for agreeing or disagreeing with the writer's position.

2. The writer considers that linguistics should take an interest in language problems. In your view is this consideration made from 'a linguistics applied' or from an 'applied linguistics' point of view. Give your reasons for the view you take.

3. What form might a study of the 'linguistics of the living-room, or of the court room or of the class room' take? What would be the value of such a study?

4. Give three examples of 'socially institutionalised linguistic exchange' in which you have participated during the past week.

EXERCISE 2B (ON CHAPTER 2)

R. B. Kaplan, 'On the scope of linguistics, applied and non-', in R. B. Kaplan (ed.), *On the Scope of Applied Linguistics*, Rowley, Mass.: Newbury House, 1980, pp. 63–6.

The following text is taken from a 1980 collection of articles by different authors who present their views on the scope of applied linguistics. Robert Kaplan, who edits the collection, makes clear in this article his commitment to a mature and confident applied linguistics which is no longer subservient to linguistics. He considers that applied linguists have identified themselves too closely with language teaching and that it is now time for them to turn to the many areas of human activity that need their attention. To do this, Kaplan argues, they must develop a theory of applied linguistics.

I would contend that there is virtually no human activity in which the applied linguist cannot play a role. The analysis of literature, in which cultural traditions are stored over time, may be an appropriate area for the applied linguist to apply certain aspects of linguistics, leaving arguments over aesthetics to more traditional literary scholars. Indeed, the uses of language for the storage and retrieval of all sorts of information, including cultural and aesthetic information, whether the storage occurs in oral forms, traditional books, or computerized systems, is a proper sphere for the activities of applied linguists.

What I have been trying to argue is that applied linguists are the most humanistic among the breed of linguists who are most directly concerned with the solution of human problems stemming from various uses of language. Linguists, on the other hand, are specialists who solve language problems related to some of the sub-systems of the body of language. Because their study is scientific, they are limited to those sub-systems which can be made static and which can be isolated from the complex range of variables that affect human behavior. What they find is of the greatest use to applied linguists; and the problems that applied linguists discover in their attempts to deal with human problems ought to be the central concern of theoretical linguists. That has not, unfortunately, been the case; on the contrary, applied linguists have convulsed themselves trying to apply to something every new notion of the theoretical linguist, whether that notion has been demonstrated valid or useful, or not ...

This paper is not a clarion call to the service of humanity. I do not mean to suggest that the world will go to hell in a handbasket if applied linguists do not get cracking. I do mean to suggest that the peculiar circumstances of the time ... the enormous impetus in the developing world for equality of opportunity and improvement in the general standard of living through the instant attainment of modernity and technology, and the peculiar place of the languages of wider communication in these global circumstances, have created a situation in which the services of the applied linguist are perhaps more necessary than they have been in the past. Those services are not yet more welcome, but I think the need will soon create the welcome. If applied linguists have become identified with language teaching, it is an identification they must work to overcome; if applied linguists are not seen as contributing members of society, it may be the result of their own lethargy and their acceptance of the identification with language teaching. If there is a polarity between applied and theoretical linguistics, it may result from a myopia on both sides. Thus, if applied linguists choose to assert the independence of their discipline, the time seems to be appropriate, but the assertion of that independence depends upon the willingness to do applied linguistics rather than merely to apply linguistics. The speculations raised in this paper as examples of possible spheres of activity for applied linguistics may be lunatic speculations; if they are, someone ought to demonstrate their lunacy. Even if they are, surely there are areas of activity both less lunatic and less abstract that applied linguists can busy themselves with. It seems to me unnecessary to expend more time in defining the scope of applied linguistics; rather, it seems to me time to develop a theory of applied linguistics which will permit the development of algorithms which in turn will permit applied linguists to deal systematically (rather than willy-nilly) with the kinds of human problems that obviously do concern them, a theory which will make it unnecessary to perpetuate the kind of intentional fallacy ... which attempts to place applied linguistics at the center of the known universe. That is a clarion call.

Questions

1. The writer contends that 'there is virtually no human activity in which the applied linguist cannot play a role'. How far do you agree? How does the writer reconcile this statement with his later comment that 'applied linguists have become identified with language teaching'?
2. The writer advocates the development of a theory of applied linguistics. To what extent do you think a theory of applied linguistics is (a) desirable and (b) possible?
3. 'The speculations raised in this paper as examples of possible spheres of activity for applied linguistics may be lunatic speculations.' Are they lunatic speculations? Make a case for or against regarding them as lunatic speculations.

EXERCISE 3 (ON CHAPTER 3)

Here are four excerpts (Glossolalia, Welsh, Spoken American English and Manx). The origin of each text is given below. In each case try to determine whether the motivation for the work described can be regarded as linguistics applied or as applied linguistics.

Glossolalia: extract from H. N. Malony and A. A. Lovekin (1985), *Glossolalia: Behavioral Science Perspectives on Speaking in Tongues*, Oxford: Oxford University Press, p. 33.
Welsh: extract from M. Ball (1993), *The Celtic Languages*, London: Routledge, pp. 295–6.

Spoken American English: extract from K. Aijmer and B. Altenberg (1991), *English Corpus Linguistics: Studies in Honour of Jan Svartvik*, London and New York: Longman, p. 65.

Manx: extract from M. Ball (1993), *The Celtic Languages*, London and New York: Routledge, pp. 659–70.

(a) Glossolalia

For example, in analyzing the glossolalic speech of one of Wolfram's (1966) subjects, Samarin reaches the following conclusion:

> Thus even a cursory examination of the sample text reveals that *siyanayasi* occurs only at the end of a macrosegment [a sentence] and is very often preceded by *kita* … In other words, glossic syllables are not simply spewed out in a haphazard sort of way …
>
> (1968, p. 60)

Among the answers Samarin (1972) received when he asked, 'Why do you think glossolalia is a language?' were the following: 'It sounds too much like a language not to be.' … 'I don't feel the type to just rattle on making sounds.' … 'because I seem to learn it' (*passim* pp. 105–107).

More thoughtful answers included references to the same words appearing over and over, short words (like conjunctions or prepositions) connecting phrases, different endings and prefixes being used, the rise and fall of voice tone, pauses for breath, rhythm cadence, and the seeming grouping of phrases into groups (Samarin, 1972c, pp. 106–107).

However, the word structure of a given utterance is not all that apparent nor is the dissecting of the material into phrases and sentences an easy task. For example, a prayer by Rev. d'Esprit (Samarin's prime subject studied over several days) began like this: 'kupoy shandre filé sundrukuma …' Yet, Samarin (1972c) concluded:

> [Rev. d'Esprit] was undoubtedly influenced by the rhythm of the utterance, making each 'word' come out with a final accented syllable. But there was no good reason for not beginning as follows: 'Ku poyshandré fi lésundru.' Other linguistically trained persons have looked at this text, and none of them arrives at exactly the same results that are presented here.
>
> (p. 81)

(b) Welsh

Sporadic attempts have been made from time to time to narrow the gap between the pronunciation of Literary Welsh and Colloquial Welsh. A late nineteenth-century grammarian sought to persuade Welsh people to read, for example, written *gwelant* as [gwelan], written *pethau* as [peøa] and written *carrai* as [kare] (Jones 1893). He argued that since major languages such as English and French were not pronounced as they were written there was no valid reason why Literary Welsh should be. More recent (but equally unsuccessful) ventures in this direction are those by Jones (1964: 53–6), and by the Welsh school examining authority in a booklet distributed to schools (Welsh Joint Education Committee 1967). These more recent attempts have been motivated largely by the perception of an increasing gap between the literary and non-literary registers, a gap which is thought, somewhat naively, to be a major contributory factor in the failure of second-language teaching programmes in schools, and in the widespread incompetence among Welsh speakers in reading and writing their native language.

Through the nineteenth century the orthography was a field of conflict as one committee or individual after another attempted to standardize practices. Standardization was not finally achieved until a committee of the Board of Celtic Studies published a spelling manual (University of Wales Press 1928).

(c) Spoken American English

It is obvious to all concerned that there is a conspicuous gap in these materials: a comparably large computerized corpus of spoken American English as used by adults. Such a corpus would provide a rich source of data for all those interested in the nature of spoken American English and, more generally, of spoken language, whether their interests are descriptive, theoretical or pedagogical. For example, it has been suggested that the grammar of spoken language is still little understood (Halliday 1987); the Corpus of Spoken American English (CSAE) will provide materials for extensive studies of all aspects of spoken English grammar and lexicon. It will at the same time have an obvious value for studies of differences between speech and writing, and thus can contribute to an understanding of how the educational system can facilitate the child's transition from accomplished speaker to accomplished writer. It will be of obvious value to sociologists and linguists studying the structure of conversational interactions. It will constitute a basic source of information for those engaged in teaching English as a second language, who will be able to draw on it in either a research or a classroom setting for examples of linguistic and interactional patterns that are characteristic of conversation. And, because the transcription into standard English orthography will be linked with sound, linguists and speech researchers will gain a useful tool for studying the relation of auditory phenomena to linguistic elements, which will ultimately contribute to the goal of enabling computers to recognize speech. In a larger time frame, this corpus will provide an invaluable source of information on the English language as it was spoken colloquially in America towards the end of the twentieth century.

(d) Manx

There has always been in Manx schools a recognition that, despite the use of the 'English code' from the 1872 Act [...] in the Manx education system, there was a strong flavour of Manxness about the whole arrangement. Most of the pupils bore Manx names: (forenames) Juan, Finlo, Orry, Kiree, Joney, etc: (surnames) Cowle,

Clague, Corlett, Kelly, Mylchreest, Quine, etc. – the list goes on. They spoke an Anglo-Manx dialect, lived in places bearing Manx names, and their teachers used the occasional greeting of *moghrey mai* (m r 'mai] 'good morning' or *fastyr mie* [fast 'mai] 'good afternoon/evening'. Efforts to have Manx taught in Island schools, which failed in the early years of the century, did not begin to bear fruit until 1974 when a new Director of Education, Mr Alun Davies, a native Welsh speaker, was appointed. He was sympathetic to the idea, provided that there were people capable of teaching Manx. The situation then was that there were a number of individuals, usually YCG members, competent in Manx, but not trained teachers, and a few trained teachers (about a dozen at the outside) both competent in Manx and able to teach it. The latter were mainly concentrated in the thirty-two primary schools and were given the opportunity of introducing Manx into the classroom when and where they saw fit. In the five secondary schools at that time there was no teacher on the staff able in Manx. To remedy this the Director of Education sanctioned the use of 'laymen/laywomen' to teach Manx once a week during lunchtime break as a 'club' activity. The first of such clubs was set up in the Easter term of 1976 at Ballakermeen High School, Douglas. I was one of the teachers on that occasion.

In 1982 a GCE 'O' Level examination in Manx was instituted, preparation for which took place at evening classes initially for adults at the College of Further Education (now the Isle of Man College). The idea was that teachers with an 'O' Level qualification would be in a position to teach Manx formally in the schools. One or two secondary-school teachers took up this option. However, a lack of 'takers' for the examination caused it to be suspended four years later. Its replacement by a GCSE examination, with more emphasis on the spoken language, is now in preparation as part of the present (1992) scheme.

EXERCISE 4 (ON CHAPTER 4)

The following extract makes a connection between language and cultural values. To what extent are they connected? If you were involved with the selection of the new bishop would you be in favour of a Gaelic speaker or not. What would be your reasons?

4.1 Gaelic-speaking Bishop?

A row has broken out among parish priests in the Roman Catholic diocese of Argyll and the Isles over whether the successor to the disgraced bishop, Roderick Wright, should be required to speak Gaelic.

The diocese, which has been without a bishop for more than two years since Mr Wright resigned and fled to England with a married woman, is split down language lines.

Many of the island priests believe the new bishop must be able to speak the language of the Gaels, but other parish priests are fundamentally opposed to making fluency in the language a requirement for the post.

Monsignor Roderick Macdonald of Glencoe is one of those who has spoken out against the move. He said yesterday: 'Gaelic just does not come into it at all.

'I know what some of the island priests are saying, but they are always saying that. Whenever Cardinal Winning says something, they suggest that it would have been better if he had said it in Gaelic.

'Of course all the islanders speak English, some of them don't speak Gaelic.'

However, not everyone in the diocese is in agreement.

Father Joe Toal of Benbecula was adamant that the new bishop will speak Gaelic. He said: 'It was inappropriate for Right Rev Mgr Macdonald to express such an opinion as strongly as he did. It was a real kick in the teeth for island Catholics, people who pray and think in Gaelic every day of their lives.'

The campaign for a Gaelic-speaking bishop is connected to the renaissance of Gaelic in other areas.

Fr Toal said that the Church must not be left behind. He said: 'The way I and many others see it, Gaelic is becoming more and more important in the public life of Scotland. The language has a special place in the media, education and the arts. The Church needs a strong voice in the Gaelic world, someone who will give leadership and is capable of putting the Church's message across convincingly.'

[...]

The press officer for the Roman Catholic Church in Scotland, Father Tom Connelly, said he believed a 'healing' message was more important than a 'Gaelic' one.

A former editor of the Scottish Catholic Observer, Hugh Farmer, said he thought the row was a local difficulty. He said: 'The best bishop of Argyll and the Isles there ever was spoke not a word of Gaelic and he did more for the Gaelic traditions and culture before him or since. Bishop Stephen McGill is retired now, but he was there between 1960 and 1968.'

He added: 'It is not a Gaelic-speaking bishop they need, it's a good holy pastor: Gaelic is not an issue.'

(Extract from A. O'Henley and A. Gray, 'Priests split on need for new bishop with Gaelic', *The Scotsman*, 9 March 1999, p. 4.)

EXERCISE 5 (ON CHAPTER 5)

The following passage refers to work on police communication. The author makes clear in the last paragraph quoted that he regards this as part of applied linguistics. How would you suggest applied linguistics rise to the challenge 'to contribute to increasing understanding of the linguistic aspects of communication'?

5.1 Police radio procedures

Report after report into modern disasters tells the same story. Many are at least partly caused, and almost all are exacerbated, by poor communication procedures, such as misleading wording by the initiator, or failure by the recipient to check understanding. One writer refers to 'the deadly problem of communication under stress', and comments that 'too many lives have been lost as a result of confusion over words'.[1]

Fortunately, most faulty communication practice does not result in disasters, although the potential is always present. The cost in inefficiency, nonetheless, is incalculable, even at the most apparently trivial level. I was a member of a team which conducted extensive research into police radio procedures in the United Kingdom in the early 1990s. In one typical region, officers were making on average one communicative exchange every two minutes over a forty-eight hour period. More than 12% of these exchanges required two or more transmissions simply to establish the identity of the calling officer (which should be the first utterance in the exchange: 'This is Alpha Delta 1-0 calling control'). Air-time, which had an actual monetary value to the force, was being squandered because of an elementary failure in procedures. An example occurs in the following exchange, which was typical of many in our data. None of the three officers (A, B, D) calling control (C) has given any identification, although C appears to recognize one of them (204). The first three transmissions are simultaneous:

A   Somebody making off through the graveyard ...
B   Yeah, we've got a van coming in with a few – ...
D   ... [name] please
C   Yeah, several callers there er caller saying [name]
B   Yes, control, we've got three coming in
C   Yes, 2-0-4, can you confirm three in custody?
D   Yes
C   2-0-4 can you confirm three in custody?
D   Yes, yes

After nine transmissions, nothing has been achieved. Such confusion probably causes nothing worse than annoyance and inefficiency, but routine communication can at any time, without warning, have to deal with an emergency, with predictable results: 'in the crash of Air Florida into the Potomac River ... more than ten communication channels were used chaotically'.[2]

The challenge for applied linguists is to contribute to increasing understanding of the linguistic aspects of communication. Most of the limited amount of research and development in the area of operational communication is linguistically naive, with the result that procedures and guidelines are, at best, vague or, at worst, positively misleading.

(Extract from M. Garner, 'Tell them to mind their language', *Australian Language Matters* (Oct/Nov/Dec 1998), p. 13.)

1. Silverstein, Martin E., *Disasters: Your Right to Survive*, Washington DC 1992, p. 7.
2. Silverstein, p. 123.

EXERCISE 6 (ON CHAPTER 6)

Here are two proposed principles which might be included in a Code of Ethics for applied linguists. Write eight further principles so as to cover all ethical responsibilities of applied linguists.

1. Applied linguists should not allow the misuse of their professional knowledge and skills.
2. Applied linguists should continue to develop their professional knowledge and share this knowledge with colleagues and other relevant professionals.

EXERCISE 7 (ON CHAPTER 7)

List the skills and areas of knowledge that the professional applied linguist brings to a language problem. To what extent does such professional expertise justify the claim in this book that a coherent discipline of applied linguistics now exists?

References

Aijmer, K. and B. Altenberg (1991), *English Corpus Linguistics: Studies in Honour of Jan Svartvik*, London: Longman.

AILA Statutes (1964), *Statutes*, Nancy: Association Internationale de Linguistique Appliquée.

Alderson, J. Charles and Alexander H. Urquhart (1985), 'The effect of students' academic discipline on their performance on ESP reading tests', *Language Testing*, 2(2): 192–204.

Alderson, J. Charles, Caroline Clapham and Diane Wall (1995), *Language Test Construction and Evaluation*, Cambridge: Cambridge University Press.

Allen, J. Patrick B. and S. Pit Corder (eds) (1973–5), *The Edinburgh Course in Applied Linguistics*, vols 1–3. Vol. 1 (1973), *Readings for Applied Linguistics*; vol. 2 (1974), *Techniques in Applied Linguistics*; vol. 3 (1975), *Papers in Applied Linguistics*, London: Oxford University Press.

Allen, J. Patrick B. and Alan Davies (eds) (1977), *The Edinburgh Course in Applied Linguistics*, vol. 4, *Testing and Experiment in Applied Linguistics*, London: Oxford University Press.

Angeles, Peter A. (1981), *Dictionary of Philosophy*, New York: Barnes and Noble.

Annamalai, E. (1994), 'India: language situation', in Ronald E. Asher (ed.), *The Encyclopedia of Language and Linguistics*, vol. 3, Oxford: Pergamon Press, pp. 1651–3.

Annamalai, E. (1998), 'Language planning in India', Paper given in Department of Linguistics, University of Melbourne, August 1998, unpublished.

Anthony, Tony, D. Bogle, Tom T. S. Ingram and M. McIsaac (1971), *The Edinburgh Articulation Test*, London: Longman.

Asher, Ronald E. (ed.) (1994), *The Encyclopedia of Language and Linguistics*, vols 1–11, Oxford: Pergamon Press.

Atkinson, Paul (1981), *The Clinical Experience*, Farnborough: Gower.

BAAL (1994) *Draft Recommendations on Good Practice in Applied Linguistics*, Lancaster, British Association for Applied Linguistics.

Bailey, Richard W. (ed.) (1987), *Dictionaries of English: Prospects for the Record of our Language*, Cambridge: Cambridge University Press.

Baldauf, Richard and Robert B. Kaplan (1998), *Language Planning: From Practice to Theory*, Clevedon: Multilingual Matters.

Ball, Martin (1993), *The Celtic Languages*, London: Routledge.

Baron, Dennis (1981), 'The epicene pronoun: the word that failed', *American Speech* 56: 83–97.

Beckett, Samuel (1959), *Molloy, Malone Dies, The Unnamable*, London: Calder Publications.

Beech, John R., Leonora Harding, with Diana Hilton-Jones (eds) (1993), *Assessment in Speech and Language Therapy*, London: Routledge.

Beretta, Alan (1990), 'Theory construction in SLA: complementarity and opposition', *Studies in Second Language Acquisition*, 13(4): 493–511.

Beretta, Alan and Graham Crookes (1993), 'Cognitive and social determinants of discovery in SLA', *Applied Linguistics*, 14 (3): 250–75.

Bernstein, Basil (1971), *Class, Codes and Control 1*, London: Routledge and Kegan Paul.

Bialystok, Ellen (1997), 'The structure of age: in search of barriers to second language acquisition', *Second Language Research*, 13(2): 116–37.

BIP (Penny Mckay, Alan Davies, Brian Devlin, Jean Clayton, Rhonda Oliver, Susan Zammit) (1997), *The Bilingual Interface Report: the relationship between first language development and second language acquisition as students begin learning English in the context of schooling*, Canberra: Commonwealth of Australia.

Birdsong, David (1992), 'Ultimate attainment in second language acquisition', *Language*, 68: 706–55.

Block, David (1996), 'Not so fast: some thoughts on theory culling, relativism, accepted findings and the heart and soul of SLA', *Applied Linguistics*, 17(1): 63–83.

Bloomfield, Leonard (1933), *Language*, London: Allen and Unwin.

Bloomfield, Morton (1975), 'Introduction', in Einar Haugen and Morton Bloomfield (eds), *Language as a Human Problem*, Guildford: Lutterworth Press, pp. xi–xix.

Brice Heath, Shirley (1983), *Ways with Words: Language, Life and Work in Communities and Classrooms*, Cambridge: Cambridge University Press.

Bright, William (ed.) (1992), *International Encyclopedia of Linguistics*, vol. 1, New York: Oxford University Press.

Broadie, Alexander (ed.) (1997), *The Scottish Enlightenment: An Anthology*, Edinburgh: Canongate.

Broadie, Alexander (1997), 'Introduction: what was the Scottish enlightenment?' in Alexander Broadie (ed.), *The Scottish Enlightenment: An Anthology*, Edinburgh: Canongate, pp. 3–31.

Broca, Paul (1865), 'Sur le siège de la faculté de language articulé', *Bulletin de la Société d'Anthropologie*, 4: 200–8.

Broderick, George (1993), 'Revived Manx', in Martin J. Ball (ed.), *The Celtic Languages*, London: Routledge, 654–63

Brown, H. D. (1987), *Principles of Language Learning and Teaching*, Englewood Cliffs New Jersey: Prentice-Hill.

Brumfit, Christopher (ed.) (1983), *Language Teaching Projects for the Third World*, ELT Documents 116, Oxford: Pergamon Press in association with the British Council.

Brumfit, Christopher (1997a), 'Theoretical practice: applied linguistics as pure and practical science', *AILA Review*, No. 12: 18–30.

Brumfit, Christopher (1997b), 'How applied linguistics is the same as any other science', *International Journal of Applied Linguistics*, 7(1): 86–94.

Buckle, Richard (ed.) (1978), *Debrett's U and Non-U Revisited*, London: Debrett's Peerage Ltd.

Bugarski, Ranko (1987), 'Applied linguistics as linguistics applied', in Olga Miseka Tomic and Roger W. Shuy (eds), *The Relation of Theoretical and Applied Linguistics*, New York: Plenum Press, pp. 3–19.

Byng, S. and Max Coltheart (1986), 'Aphasia theory research requirements', in E. Hjelmquist and L. Nilsson (eds), *Communication and Handicap*, Amsterdam: Elsevier.

Cahoone, Lawrence (ed.) (1996), *From Modernism to Postmodernism: An Anthology*, Malden, Mass.: Blackwell.

Cahoone, Lawrence (1996), 'Introduction', in Lawrence Cahoone (ed.), *From Modernism to Postmodernism: An Anthology*, Malden, Mass.: Blackwell, pp. 1–23.

Caldas-Coulthard, C. R. and Malcolm Coulthard (eds) (1996), *The Theory and Practice of Critical Discourse Analysis*, London: Routledge.

Cameron, Deborah (1985/1992), *Feminism and Linguistic Theory*, London: Macmillan.

Canale, Michael and Merrill Swain (1980), 'Theoretical bases of communicative approaches to second language teaching and testing', *Applied Linguistics*, 1(1): 1–47.

Carter, Ronald (1993). *Introducing Applied Linguistics: An ABC Guide*, London: Penguin.

Catford, John (Ian) C. (1959), 'Applied Linguistics at Edinburgh', Edinburgh School of

Applied Linguistics (unpublished).

Catford, John (Ian) C. (1998), '*Language Learning* and applied linguistics: a historical sketch', *Language Learning*, 48(4) December: 465–96.

Chambers, J. K. and M. F. Hardwick (1986), 'Comparative sociolinguistics of a sound change in Canadian English', *English World-Wide*, 7: 23–46.

Chomsky, Noam (1957), *Syntactic Structures*, The Hague: Mouton.

Christophersen, Paul (1973), *Second-Language Learning: Myth and Reality*, Harmondsworth: Penguin.

Clapham, Caroline, Charles J. Alderson and Diane Wall (1997), *Introduction to Language Testing and Evaluation*, Cambridge: Cambridge University Press.

Clark, John L. (1987), *Curriculum Renewal in School Foreign Language Learning*, Oxford: Oxford University Press.

Coady, Margaret and Sidney Bloch (1996), 'Introduction', in Margaret Coady and Sidney Bloch (eds), *Codes of Ethics and the Professions*, Melbourne: University of Melbourne Press, pp. 1–10.

Coady, Margaret and Sidney Bloch (eds) (1996), *Codes of Ethics and the Professions*, Melbourne: University of Melbourne Press.

Cook, Guy (1998), 'Linguistics and language teaching', in Keith Johnson and Helen Johnson (eds), *The Encyclopedic Dictionary of Applied Linguistics*, Oxford: Blackwell, pp. 198–207.

Cook, Guy and Barbara Seidlhofer (eds) (1995), *Principle and Practice in Applied Linguistics: Studies in Honour of H. G. Widdowson*, Oxford: Oxford University Press.

Cooper, Robert L. (ed.) (1982), *Language Spread: Studies in Diffusion and Social Change*, Bloomington: Indiana: Indiana University Press.

Corder, S. Pit (1973), *Introducing Applied Linguistics*, Harmondsworth: Penguin.

Corder, S. Pit (1974) 'Teaching Linguistics, Edinburgh', Edinburgh: Department of Linguistics, unpublished.

Corder, S. Pit (1981), *Error Analysis and Interlanguage*, Oxford: Oxford University Press.

Criper, Clive and Alan Davies (1988), *ELTS Validation Project Report*, London: British Council.

Crystal, David (1987), *The Cambridge Encyclopedia of Language*, Cambridge: Cambridge University Press.

Crystal, David (1992), *An Encyclopedic Dictionary of Language and Linguistics*, Oxford: Blackwell.

Crystal, David (1995), *The Cambridge Encyclopedia of the English Language*, Cambridge: Cambridge University Press.

Crystal, David, Paul Fletcher and Michael Garman (1976), *The Grammatical Analysis of Language Disability*, London: Arnold.

Culler, Jonathan (1981), *The Pursuit of Signs: Semiotics, Literature, Deconstruction*, London: Routledge.

Culler, Jonathan (1982), *On Deconstruction: Theory and Criticism after Structuralism*, Ithaca: Cornell University Press.

Cumming, Alister (1993), 'Editor's Preface', *Language Learning* 43(1): 1–2.

Cummins, James (1984), *Bilingualism and Special Education: Issues on Assessment and Pedagogy*, Clevedon: Multilingual Matters.

Davies, Alan (1965), *Proficiency in English as a Second Language*, Ph.D. thesis, University of Birmingham, unpublished.

Davies, Alan (1967), 'The English proficiency of overseas students', *British Journal of Educational Psychology*, 37(2): 107–22.

Davies, Alan (1987), 'When professional advice and political constraints conflict: the case of Nepal', *Focus on English*, Madras: British Council.

Davies, Alan (1990), *Principles of Language Testing*, Oxford: Blackwell.

Davies, Alan (1991a), *The Native Speaker in Applied Linguistics*, Edinburgh: Edinburgh University Press.

Davies, Alan (1991b), 'An evaluation model for English language teaching projects in South India: the policy of change', *Australian Review of Applied Linguistics*, 114(2): 73–86.

Davies, Alan (1991c), 'British Applied Linguistics: the contribution of S. Pit Corder', in Robert Phillipson, Eric Kellerman, Larry Selinker, Michael Sharwood-Smith and Merrill Swain (eds), *Foreign/Second Language Pedagogy Research (A Commemorative Volume for Claus Faerch)*, Clevedon: Multilingual Matters, pp. 52–60.

Davies, Alan (1996), 'Ironising the myth of linguicism', *Journal of Multilingual and Multicultural Development*, 17(6): 485–96.

Davies, Alan (1997a), 'Review' of Michael Clyne, A. Jenkins, I. Y. Chan, R. Tsokalidou and T. Wallner (1995), *Developing Second Language from Primary School* (1995), in *Australian Language Matters*, 5(1): 18–19.

Davies, Alan (1997b), 'Demands of being professional in language testing', *Language Testing* 14(3): 328–39.

Davies, Alan, Annie Brown, Cathie Elder, Kathryn Hill, Tom Lumley and Tim McNamara (1999), *Dictionary of Language Testing*, Cambridge: University of Cambridge Local Examinations Syndicate and Cambridge University Press.

Djité, Paulin G. (1996), 'Review' of Casmir M. Rubagumya (ed.) (1994), *Teaching and Researching Language in African Classrooms*, Clevedon: Multilingual Matters, in *Journal of Multilingual and Multicultural Development*, 17(1): 75–8.

Docherty, Thomas (ed.) (1993), *Postmodernism: A Reader*, Hemel Hempstead: Harvester Wheatsheaf.

Docherty, Thomas (ed.) (1993), 'Postmodernism: An Introduction', in Thomas Docherty (ed.), *Postmodernism: A Reader*, Hemel Hempstead: Harvester Wheatsheaf, pp. 1–32.

Donaldson, Margaret (1978), *Children's Minds*, London: Fontana/Collins.

Doody, Margaret (1980), 'How shall we sing the Lord's song upon an alien soil? The new episcopalian liturgy', in Leonard Michaels and Christopher Ricks (eds), *The State of the Language*, Berkeley: University of California Press, pp. 108–24.

Dorian, Nancy (1981), *Language Death: The Life Cycle of a Scottish Gaelic Dialect*, Philadelphia: University of Philadelphia Press.

Eades, Diana (ed.) (1995), *Language in Evidence: Issues Confronting Aboriginal and Multicultural Australia*, Sydney: University of New South Wales Press Ltd.

Elder, Catherine (1997), 'What does test bias have to do with fairness?', *Language Testing*, 14(3): 261–77.

Ellis, Rod (1990), 'A response to Gregg', *Applied Linguistics*, 11(4): 384–91.

Enkvist, Nils Erik and Gun Leppiniemi (1990), 'Anticipation and disappointment: an experiment in protocolled reading of Auden's "Gare du Midi"', in Les Hickey (ed.), *The Pragmatics of Style*, London: Routledge, pp. 191–207.

EOU (1998), *What Did I Say? Using Non Discriminatory Language*, The University of Melbourne, Parkville Victoria 3052, Australia: The Equal Opportunity Unit.

Eysenck, Michael W. (ed.) (1990), *The Blackwell Dictionary of Cognitive Psychology*, Oxford: Blackwell.

Fairclough, Norman (1989), *Language and Power*, London: Longman.

Fairclough, Norman (1995), *Critical Discourse Analysis*, London: Longman.

Ferguson, Charles (1959), 'Diglossia', *Word*, 15: 125–40.

Fillmore, Charles J. (1997), 'A linguist looks at the ebonics debate', *Linguist List*, vols 8–49.

Fillmore, Charles J., Daniel Kempler and William S-Y Wang (eds) (1979), *Individual Differences in Language Ability and Language Behavior*, New York: Academic Press.

Fish, Stanley E. (1980), *Is There A Text In This Class? The Authority of Interpretive Communities*, Cambridge Mass.: Harvard University Press.

Fowler, Roger (1981), *Literature as Social Discourse: the Practice of Linguistic Criticism*, London: Batsford.

Freeman, Donald C. (ed.) (1970), *Linguistics and Literary Style*, New York: Holt Rinehart and Winston Inc.

Freeman, Donald C. (ed.) (1981), *Essays in Modern Stylistics*, London: Methuen.

Frisby, J. P. (1990), 'Perception, computational theory of', in M. W. Eysenck (ed.), *The Blackwell Dictionary of Cognitive Psychology*, Oxford: Blackwell.

Garner, Mark (1998), 'Tell them to mind their language', *Australian Language Matters*, Oct–Dec.

Gellner, Ernest (1983), *Nations and Nationalism*, Oxford: Blackwell.

Gibbons, John (1995), 'What got lost? The place of electronic recording and interpreters in police interviews', in Diana Eades (ed.), *Language in Evidence*, Sydney: University of New South Wales Press, pp. 175–86.

Giroux, Henry A. (1991/1996), 'Towards a postmodern pedagogy', in Lawrence Cahoone (ed.), *From Modernism to Postmodernism: An Anthology*, pp. 687–97.

Gould, Julius and William L. Kolb (ed.) (1964), *A Dictionary of the Social Sciences*, London: Tavistock.

Graves, Robert and Alan Hodge (1943), *The Reader over your Shoulder*, London: Jonathan Cape.

Green, Jonathon (1996), *Chasing the Sun: Dictionary-Makers and the Dictionaries they Make*, London: Pimlico/Random House.

Gregg, Kevin R. (1990), 'The variable competence model of second language acquisition and why it isn't', *Applied Linguistics*, 11(4): 364–83.

Grunwell, Pamela and Alan James (eds) (1989), *The Functional Evaluation of Language Disorders*, London: Croom Helm.

Gumperz, John, Tom Jupp and Celia Roberts (1979), *Crosstalk*, Ealing: National Centre for Industrial Language Training.

Halliday, Michael A. K., Angus McIntosh and Peter D. Strevens (1964), *The Linguistic Sciences and Language Teaching*, London: Longman.

Hammersley, J. (1996), 'On the foundations of critical discourse analysis', Centre for Language in Education Occasional Papers, Southampton Centre for Language in Education.

Hare, R. M. (1952), *The Language of Morals*, Oxford: Clarendon Press.

Harris, Roy (1978), *Communication and Language*, Oxford: Oxford University Press (also excerpted in Nigel Love (ed.), *Selected Writings of Roy Harris*, London: Routledge, pp. 136–50).

Haugen, Einar (1966), 'Dialect, language and nation', *American Anthropologist*, 68(4): 41–61. (Also published in John B. Pride and Janet Homes (eds), *Sociolinguistics* (1972), Harmondsworth: Penguin, pp. 97–111.) All references to the 1972 edition.

Hawkins, Peter (1989), 'Discourse aphasia', in Pamela Grunwell and Alan James (eds), *The Functional Evaluation of Language Disorders*, London: Croom Helm, pp. 183–99.

Hays, D. G. (1971), 'Applied computational linguistics', in George E. Perren and John L. M. Trim (eds), *Applications of Linguistics*, Cambridge: Cambridge University Press, pp. 65–84.

Hickey, Leo (ed.) (1990), *The Pragmatics of Style*, London: Routledge.

Hill, Kathryn, Alan Davies, Jennie Oldfield and Nadine Watson (1997), 'Questioning an early start: the transition from primary to secondary foreign language learning', *Melbourne Papers in Language Testing*, 6(2): 1–20.

Hjelmquist, E. and L. Nilsson (eds) (1986), *Communication and Handicap*, Amsterdam: Elsevier.

Hodge, Robert and Gunther Kress (1993), *Language as Ideology*, 2nd edn, London: Routledge.

Holmes, Janet (1991), 'Language and gender', *Language Teaching*, 24(4): 207–20.

Holmes, Janet (1992), *An Introduction to Sociolinguistics*, London: Longman.

Homan, Roger (1991), *The Ethics of Social Research*, London: Longman.

House, E. R. (1990), 'Ethics of evaluation studies', in H. J. Walburg and G. D. Haerte (eds), *The International Encyclopedia of Educational Evaluation*, Oxford: Pergamon, pp. 91–4.

Howard, Ronald and Gillian Brown (1997a), 'Introduction', in Ronald Howard and Gillian Brown (eds), *Teacher Education for LSP*, Clevedon: Multilingual Matters.

Howard, Ronald and Gillian Brown (eds) (1997), *Teacher Education for LSP*, Clevedon: Multilingual Matters.

Howatt, Anthony P. R. (1984), *A History of English Language Teaching*, Oxford: Oxford University Press.

Hymes, Dell H. (1971), *On Communicative Competence*, Philadelphia: University of Pennsylvania Press.

Ilson, Robert (ed.) (1986), *Lexicography: An Emerging International Profession*, Manchester: Manchester University Press.

Ingram, David (1980), 'Applied linguistics: a search for insight', in Robert B. Kaplan (ed.), *On the Scope of Applied Linguistics*, Rowley, Mass.: Newbury House, pp. 37–56.

Jackson, J. (1996), *An Introduction to Business Ethics*, Oxford: Basil Blackwell.

Jakobson, Roman (1960), 'Concluding statement: linguistics and poetics', in Thomas A Sebeok (ed.), *Style in Language*, Cambridge, Mass.: Technology Press, pp. 350–73.

Jakobson, Roman (1987), *Language in Literature*, Cambridge, Mass.: Harvard University Press.

Jensen, Marie-Therese (1991), 'Linguistic evidence accepted in the case of a non-native speaker of English', in Diana Eades (ed.), *Language in Evidence*, Sydney: University of New South Wales Press, pp. 127–46.

Johnson, Keith and Helen Johnson (eds) (1998), *The Encyclopedic Dictionary of Applied Linguistics*, Oxford: Blackwell.

Joseph, John E. and Talbot J. Taylor (1990a), 'Introduction: ideology, science and language', in John E. Joseph and Talbot J. Taylor (eds), *Ideologies of Language*, London: Routledge, pp. 1–6.

Joseph, John E. and Talbot J. Taylor (eds) (1990b), *Ideologies of Language*, London: Routledge.

Kachru, Braj B. (1981), 'Language policy in South Asia', *Annual Review of Applied Linguistics*, Rowley, Mass.: Newbury House, pp. 60–82.

Kachru, Braj B. (1985), 'Standards, codification and sociolinguistic realism: the English language in the outer circle', in Randolph Quirk and Henry G. Widdowson (eds), *English in the World: Teaching and Learning the Language and Literatures*, Cambridge: Cambridge University Press in association with the British Council, pp. 11–30.

Kaplan, Alice (1993), *French Lessons: A Memoir*, Chicago: University of Chicago Press.

Kaplan, Robert B. (1980a), 'On the scope of linguistics, applied and non-', in Robert B. Kaplan (ed.), *On the Scope of Applied Linguistics*, Rowley, Mass.: Newbury House, pp. 57–66.

Kaplan, Robert B. (ed.) (1980b), *On the Scope of Applied Linguistics*, Rowley, Mass.: Newbury House.

Kaplan, Robert B. and Henry G. Widdowson (1992), 'Applied linguistics', in William Bright (ed.), *International Encyclopedia of Linguistics*, vol. 1, New York: Oxford University Press, pp. 76–80.

Kennedy, Chris (ed.) (1989), *Language Planning and English Language Teaching*, New York: Prentice Hall.

Kerr, Jean (1993), 'Assessment of acquired language problems', in John R. Beech, Leonora Harding, with Diana Hilton-Jones (eds), *Assessment in Speech and Language Therapy*, London: Routledge, pp. 99–127.

Koehn, D. (1994), *The Ground of Professional Ethics*, London: Routledge.

Kuper, Adam (1973/1993), *Anthropology and Anthropologists: The Modern British School*, London: Routledge.

Labov, William (1966), *The Social Stratification of English in New York City*, Washington D.C.: Center for Applied Linguistics.

Labov, William (1994), *Principles of Linguistic Change: Internal Factors*, Oxford: Blackwell.

Language Learning (1967), 'Editorial Note', 17: 1–2.

Large, J. Andrew (1983), *The Foreign-Language Barrier: Problems in Scientific Communication*, London: André Deutsch.

Laufer, Batia and Paul Nation (1995), 'Vocabulary size and use: lexical richness in L2 written production', *Applied Linguistics*, 16(3): 307–22.

Laver, John, Sheila Wirz, J. Mackenzie and Steve Hillier (1981), 'A perceptual protocol for the analysis of vocal profiles', Edinburgh University Linguistics Department: *Work in Progress*, 14.

Leavis, Frank R. (1938), *New Bearings in English Poetry: A Study of the Contemporary Situation*, London: Chatto and Windus.

Lo Bianco, Joe (1987), *National Policy on Languages*, Canberra: Australian Government Publishing Service.

Long, Michael (1990), 'The least a second language acquisition theory needs to explain', *TESOL Quarterly*, 24 (4): 649–66.

Love, Nigel (1990), *Selected Writings of Roy Harris*, London: Routledge.

Lyotard, Jean-François (1984), *La Condition postmoderne*, Paris: Minuit (1979), trans. G. Bennington and Brian Massumi, *The Postmodern Condition: A Report on Knowledge*, Manchester: Manchester University Press.

Mackey, William F. (1965), *Language Teaching Analysis*, London: Longman.

Mackey, William F. (1966), 'Applied linguistics: its meaning and use', *English Language Teaching*, XX(1): 197–206.

Macquarie Dictionary of Australian English (1981), Sydney: Macquarie University.

Marshall, Gordon (1994), *The Concise Oxford Dictionary of Sociology*, Oxford: Oxford University Press.

Malony, H. Newton and A. Adams Lovekin (1985), *Glossolalia: Behavioral Science Perspectives on Speaking in Tongues*, New York: Oxford University Press.

Matthews, Eric (1996), *Twentieth Century French Philosophy*, Oxford: Oxford University Press.

Mead, Margaret (1964), 'Applied anthropology', in Julius Gould and William.T. Kolb (eds), *A Dictionary of the Social Sciences*, London: Tavistock, p. 32.

Mendus, S. (1992), 'Losing the faith: feminism and democracy', in R. M. Stewart (ed.) (1996), *Readings in Social and Political Philosophy*, Oxford: Oxford University Press, pp. 409–17.

Milroy, Leslie (1987), *Language and Social Networks*, Oxford: Basil Blackwell.

Mitchell, W. Keith (1990), 'On comparisons in a notional grammar', *Applied Linguistics*, 11(1): 52–72.

Musgrave, Peter W. (1965), *The Sociology of Education*, London: Methuen.

Nickalls, John L. (ed.) (1975), *Journal of George Fox*, London: Religious Society of Friends.

Nunan, David (1990), 'Action research in the language classroom', in Jack C. Richards and David Nunan (eds), *Second Language Teacher Education*, Cambridge: Cambridge University Press, pp. 62–81.

Ogden, C. K. (1937), *Basic English: A General Introduction with Rules and Grammar*, 6th edn, London: Kegan Paul, Trench, Trubner.

O'Henley, A. and A. Gray (1999), 'Priests split on need for new bishop with Gaelic', *The Scotsman*, 9 March.

Oller, John W. Jr (ed.) (1983), *Issues in Language Testing Research*, Rowley, Mass.: Newbury House.

Oller, John W. Jr (1998), 'Language testing and cognitive learning', Plenary address, Language Testing Research Colloquium, Monterey, Cal. unpublished.

Olson, David R. (1994), *The World on Paper*, Cambridge: Cambridge University Press.

Osborne, R. (1992), *Philosophy for Beginners*, New York: Writers and Readers Publishing Inc.

Peim, Nicholas (1993), *Critical Theory and the English Teacher*, London: Routledge.

Penfield, W. G. and L. Roberts (1959), *Speech and Brain Mechanisms*, Princeton: Princeton

University Press.

Pennycook, Alistair (1994a), *The Cultural Politics of English as an International Language*, London: Longman.

Pennycook, Alastair (1994b), 'Incommensurable discourses', *Applied Linguistics*, 15(2): 115–38.

Perren, George E. and John L. M Trim (eds) (1971), *Applications of Linguistics*, Cambridge: Cambridge University Press.

Peters, Pam (1995), *The Cambridge Australian English Style Guide*, Melbourne: Cambridge University Press.

Phillipson, Robert (1992), *Linguistic Imperialism*, Oxford: Oxford University Press.

Phillipson, Robert, Eric Kellerman, Larry Selinker, Michael Sharwood-Smith and Merrill Swain (eds) (1991), *Foreign/Second Language Pedagogy Research (A Commemorative Volume for Claus Faerch)*, Clevedon: Multilingual Matters.

Prabhu, N. S. (1987), *Second Language Pedagogy*, Oxford: Oxford University Press.

Pride, John and Janet Holmes (eds) (1972), *Sociolinguistics*, Harmondsworth: Penguin.

Quirk, Randolph (1961), *The Use of English*, London: Longman.

Rampton, Ben (1995a), *Crossing: Language and Ethnicity among Adolescents*, London: Longman.

Rampton, Ben (1995b), 'Politics and change in research in applied linguistics', *Applied Linguistics*, 16(2): 233–56.

Rampton, Ben (1997), 'Retuning in applied linguistics', *International Journal of Applied Linguistics*, 7(1): 3–25.

Rawls, J. (1967), 'Distributive justice', in Peter Laslett and W. G. Runciman (eds), *Philosophy, Politics and Society* (3rd series), Oxford: Basil Blackwell, pp. 219–34.

Rey, Alain (1986), 'Training lexicographers: some problems', in Robert Ilson (eds), *Lexicography: An Emerging International Profession,* Manchester: Manchester University Press, pp. 93–100.

Rey-Debove, J. (1971), *Etude linguistique et semiotique des dictionaires français contemporains* (quoted in Jonathon Green (1996) above).

Richards, I. A. (1929), *Practical Criticism: A Study of Literary Judgement*, London: Kegan Paul, Trench, Trubner and Co. Ltd.

Richards, Jack, John Platt and Heidi Platt (1985/1992), *Longman Dictionary of Language Teaching and Applied Linguistics*, Harlow: Longman.

Richards, Jack C. and David Nunan (eds) (1990), *Second Language Teacher Education*, Cambridge: Cambridge University Press.

Richards, Jack C. and Ted S. Rodgers (1986), *Approaches and Methods in Language Teaching*, Cambridge: Cambridge University Press.

Richards, I. A. (1943), *Basic English and its Uses*, London: Kegan Paul.

Roberts, Celia, Evelyn Davies and Tom Jupp (1997), *Language and Discrimination: A Study of Communication in Multi-Ethnic Workplaces*, London: Longman.

Robins, R. H. (1971/1980), *General Linguistics: An Introductory Survey*, London: Longman.

Ross, Alan S. C. (1954), 'Linguistic class-indicators in present-day English', *Neuphilologische Mitteilungen*, 55.

Ross, Alan S. C. (1978), 'Language: U and non-U. Double-U, E. and non-E', in Richard Buckle (ed.), *Debrett's U and Non-U Revisited*, London: Debrett's Peerage Ltd, pp. 28–48.

Ross, John R. (1979), 'Where's English?', in Charles J. Fillmore, Daniel Kempler and William S-Y Wang, *Individual Differences in Language Ability*, New York: Academic Press, pp. 127–63.

Rubagumya, Casmir M. (ed.) (1994), *Teaching and Researching Language in African Classrooms*, Clevedon: Multilingual Matters.

Ryan, Ann and Alison Wray (eds) (1997), *Evolving Models of Language*, Clevedon: BAAL in assoc. with Multilingual Matters Ltd.

Samarin, W. J. (1972), *Tongues of Men and Angels: The Religious Language of Pentecostalism*,

New York: Macmillan.

Sampson, Geoffrey (1980), *Schools of Linguistics*, London: Hutchinson.

Sarup, Madan (1993), *An Introductory Guide to Post-Structuralism and Postmodernism*, Hemel Hempstead: Harvester Wheatsheaf.

Schutz, Alfred (1970), *On Phenomenology and Social Relations: Selected Writings*, ed. by Helmut R. Wagner, Chicago: University of Chicago Press.

Scriven M. (1991), *Evaluation Thesaurus*, 4th edn, Newbury Park: Sage.

Searle, John R. (1995), *The Construction of Social Reality*, Harmondsworth: Penguin.

Selinker, Larry (1972), 'Interlanguage', *International Review of Applied Linguistics*, 10: 209–31.

Selinker, Larry (1992), *Rediscovering Interlanguage*, London: Longman.

Sharrock, W. W. and D. C. Anderson (1981), 'Language, thought and reality, again', *Sociology*, 15: 287–93.

Singer, Peter (1995), 'Applied ethics', in Ted Honderich (ed.), *The Oxford Companion to Philosophy*, Oxford: Oxford University Press, pp. 42–3.

Skutnabb-Kangas, Tove, Robert Phillipson and Mart Rannut (eds) (1994), *Linguistic Human Rights: Overcoming Linguistic Discrimination*. Contributions to the Sociology of Language 67, Berlin: Mouton de Gruyter.

Spolsky, Bernard (1978), *Educational Linguistics*, Rowley, Mass.: Newbury House.

Spolsky, Bernard (1980), 'The scope of educational linguistics', in Robert B. Kaplan (ed.), *On the Scope of Applied Linguistics*, Rowley, Mass.: Newbury House, pp. 67–73.

Stein, Gertrude (1988), 'If I told him (A completed portrait of Picasso)', in *The Caedmon Treasury of Modern Poets Reading Their Own Poetry* (CPN 2006), New York: Caedmon.

Stenhouse, Lawrence (1975), *An Introduction to Curriculum Research and Development*, London: Heinemann Educational.

Stern, H. H. (1983), *Fundamental Concepts of Language Teaching*, Oxford: Oxford University Press.

Stewart, R. M. (ed.) (1996), *Readings in Social and Political Philosophy*, Oxford: Oxford University Press, 1996.

Stewart, William A. (1968), 'A sociolinguistic typology for describing national multilingualism', in Joshua A. Fishman (ed.), *Readings in the Sociology of Language*, The Hague: Mouton, pp. 531–45.

Strevens, Peter D. (1975), 'Second language learning', in Einar Haugen and Morton Bloomfield (eds), *Language as a Human Problem*, Guildford: Lutterworth Press, pp. 151–62.

Strevens, Peter D. (1980), 'Who are applied linguists and what do they do? A British point of view, upon the establishment of the American Association of Applied Linguistics', in Robert B. Kaplan (ed.), *On the Scope of Applied Linguistics*, Rowley, Mass.: Newbury House, pp. 28–36.

Strevens, Peter D. (1992a), 'Applied linguistics: an overview', in William Grabe and Robert Kaplan (eds), *Introduction to Applied Linguistics*, Reading, Mass.: Addison-Wesley, pp. 13–31.

Strevens, Peter D. (1992b), 'Applied linguistics: history of the field', in William Bright (ed.), *International Encyclopedia of Linguistics*, vol. 1, New York: Oxford University Press, pp. 80–4.

Stubbs, Michael (1986), *Educational Linguistics*, Oxford: Blackwell.

Stubbs, Michael (1997), 'Critical comments on Critical Discourse Analysis (CDA)', in Ann Ryan and Alison Wray (eds), *Evolving Models of Language*, Clevedon: BAAL in assoc. with Multilingual Matters Ltd, pp. 100–116.

Swain, Merrill and Sharon Lapkin (1982), *Evaluating Bilingual Education: A Canadian Case Study*, Clevedon: Multilingual Matters.

Tarone, Elaine E. (1990), 'On variation in interlanguage: a response to Gregg', *Applied Linguistics*, 11(4): 392–400.

Taylor, Talbot J. (1990), 'Normativity and linguistic form', in Talbot J. Taylor and H. G. Davis (eds), *Redefining Linguistics*, London: Routledge, pp. 118–48.

Taylor, Talbot J. and H. G. Davis (eds) (1990), *Redefining Linguistics*, London: Routledge.

Tomic, Olga M. and Roger W. Shuy (eds) (1987), *The Relation of Theoretical and Applied Linguistics*, New York: Plenum Press.

Trim, John L. M. (1988a), 'Applied linguistics in society', in Pamela Grunwell (ed.), *Applied Linguistics in Society*, London: CILTR, pp. 3–15.

Trim, John L. M. (1988b), *Consolidated Report of the Programme of International Workshops for Trainers of Teachers of Modern Languages 1984–1987*, Strasburg: Council of Europe.

Trudgill, Peter (1983), *On Dialect: Social and Geographical Perspectives*, Oxford: Blackwell.

Van Els, Theo, Theo Bongaerts, Guus Extra, Charles van Os and Anne-Mieke Janssen-van Dieten (1977) (references to English translation, 1984), *Applied Linguistics and the Learning and Teaching of Foreign Languages*, London: Edward Arnold.

Wallace, Michael J. (1991), *Training Foreign Language Teachers: A Reflective Approach*, Cambridge: Cambridge University Press.

Wallace, Michael J. (1998), *Action Research for Language Teachers*, Cambridge: Cambridge University Press.

Warburg, Jeremy (1966), *Verbal Values*, London: Edward Arnold.

Watkins, T. Arwyn (1993), 'Welsh', in Martin J. Ball (ed.), *The Celtic Languages*, London: Routledge, 289–348.

Webster, Noah (1994), *Ninth New Collegiate Dictionary of the English Language*, New York: Black Dog and Leventhal.

Weir, Cyril and Jon Roberts (1994), *Evaluation in ELT*, Oxford: Blackwell.

Wells, Herbert G. (1940), *The Common Sense of War and of Peace*, London.

Wernicke, Carl (1874), *Der aphasische symptomen complex. Eine psychologische Studie auf anatomischer Basis*, Breslau: Cohn und Weigert.

Widdowson, Henry G. (1975), *Stylistics and the Teaching of Literature*, London: Longman.

Widdowson, Henry G. (1980), 'Applied linguistics: the pursuit of relevance', in Robert B. Kaplan (ed.), *On the Scope of Applied Linguistics*, Rowley, Mass.: Newbury House, pp. 74–87.

Widdowson, Henry G. (1995), 'Discourse analysis: a critical view', *Language and Literature*, 4(3): 157–72.

Widdowson, Henry G. (1996), *Linguistics*, Oxford: Oxford University Press.

Widdowson, Henry G. (1998), 'Review article: the theory and practice of critical discourse analysis', *Applied Linguistics*, 19 (1): 136–51.

Wilensky, H. L. (1964), 'The professionalization of everyone?', *American Journal of Sociology*, 70(2): 137–58.

Wilkins, David (1994), 'Applied linguistics', in Ronald E. Asher (ed.), *The Encyclopedia of Language and Linguistics*, vol. 1, Oxford: Pergamon Press, pp. 162–72.

Wirz, Sheila L. (1993), 'Introduction: historical considerations in assessment', in John R. Beech and Leonora Harding with Diana Hilton-Jones (eds), *Assessment in Speech and Language Therapy*, London: Routledge, pp. 1–15.

Wolf, G. and Nigel Love (eds) (1998), *Linguistics Inside Out: Roy Harris and his Critics*, Amsterdam and Philadelphia: Benjamins.

Wolfram, Walt A. (1966), *The Sociolinguistics of Glossolalia*. Master's Thesis. Hartford Seminary.

Woodward, T. (1991), *Models and Metaphors in Language Teacher Training*, Cambridge: Cambridge University Press.

Young, Michael (1965), *Innovation and Research in Education*, London: Routledge and Kegan Paul.

Index